Beowulf
&
Grendel

Also by John Grigsby:

Warriors of the Wasteland

The Truth Behind
England's Oldest Myth

Beowulf
&
Grendel

JOHN GRIGSBY

WATKINS PUBLISHING
LONDON

First published in the UK in 2005
Reprinted 2006

Watkins Publishing, Sixth Floor, Castle House,
75–76 Wells Street, London W1T 3QH

Distributed in the USA and Canada by Sterling Publishing Co., Inc.
387 Park Avenue South, New York, NY 10016

3 5 7 9 10 8 6 4 2

Designed and typeset by Paul Saunders

Printed and bound in Great Britain

British Library Cataloguing-in-Publication Data Available

Library of Congress Cataloging-in-Publication Data Available

ISBN 13: 978-1-84293-153-0
ISBN 10: 1-84293-153-9

www.watkinspublishing.com

CONTENTS

List of Illustrations	vii
List of Plates	vii
Acknowledgements	viii
Prologue: Where Now the Horse and Rider?	I
Introduction: The Keenest for Fame	7

Part I OLD ENGLAND — 17

CHAPTER 1	Clans of the Sea Coasts	19
CHAPTER 2	Former Days	26
CHAPTER 3	On the Altars of their Idols	40
CHAPTER 4	In Dread Waters	52

Part II GODS AND MONSTERS — 61

CHAPTER 5	Scyld Scefing	63
CHAPTER 6	The Barley God	75
CHAPTER 7	Freyr	85
CHAPTER 8	The Wagon Ran After	93
CHAPTER 9	Elves and Evil Shades	101
CHAPTER 10	Choosers of the Slain	110

Part III TO KILL A KING   121

CHAPTER 11   Royal Obligations   123
CHAPTER 12   The Hall turned to Ashes   138
CHAPTER 13   The Wandering Inguz   150
CHAPTER 14   A Midwinter Game   162

Part IV BARLEY WOLF   169

CHAPTER 15   The Demon's Head   171
CHAPTER 16   The Brimwylf   183

Epilogue: People of the Wolf   196

Notes   208

Appendices
Timeline: 8000 BC–AD 1939   226
Chart 1: The Wuffingas   232
Chart 2: The Geats   232
Chart 3: The Swedes (Scylfings)   233
Chart 4: The Danes (Scyldings)   233
Map 1: Southern Scandinavia in Late Prehistory   234
Map 2: The Age of Migrations (*c.* AD 400–600)   235
Map 3: The Anglo-Saxon Kingdoms (*c.* AD 600–700)   236

Index   237

LIST OF ILLUSTRATIONS

1 Petroglyph of solar boat from prehistoric Scandinavia   71
2 Egyptian solar barque   71
3 Petroglyph of man with shield from prehistoric Scandinavia   73
4 Osiris as the growing corn   78
5 The Djed pillar   78
6 The statuette of Freyr from Rällinge   131
7 Horned figure from Gundestrup Cauldron   131
8 Boar-helmed warrior from Viking Torslunda helmet   185
9 Wolf-warrior from Vendel helmet   187
10 Wolf motif from Sutton Hoo purse-clasp   187

LIST OF PLATES

1 First page of the *Beowulf* manuscript
2 The Neolithic passage-grave at Øm, Denmark
3 Inside the grave at Øm.
4 The Trundholm sun-chariot
5 The Tollund Man
6 The remains of the girl from Egtved
7 Goddess (Nerthus?) from the Rynkeby Cauldron
8 The goddess Gefion ploughing Zealand from Sweden
9 A Valkyrie on horseback
10 The elves dancing, from an English chapbook
11 The Broddenbjerg Freyr
12 The 'drowning' scene from the Gundestrup Cauldron
13 Ritual burial monuments at Lejre
14 The site of the Viking hall at Lejre, perhaps once the site of Heorot
15 Plan of the halls at Lejre
16 The rays of the sun entering Newgrange on midwinter's morning
17 Odin as depicted on a Viking helmet
18 Odin rides his eight-legged horse Sleipnir, from the Gotland stone
19 The helmet of the Wuffinga king Raedwald, buried at Sutton Hoo

ACKNOWLEDGEMENTS

Thanks to my agent, Frances Kelly, who believed in my work and urged me to continue writing at a point I was despondent; to Michael Mann for taking a risk; to my editor Matthew Cory for his patience, his unfailingly helpful suggestions and ability to sort the wheat from the chaff; to Helga Schütze at the National Museum of Denmark who was so kind and helpful to us on our brief visit to the land of the Scyldings, and without whom we would never have found the ruins of Heorot or the tomb of the giants at Øm; to Brian Bates, Kathleen Herbert and Richard North without whose pioneering and inspiring works this book would not have been possible to write; to Paul Devereux for letting me rant; and, finally, to a certain late professor of Anglo-Saxon at Oxford, JRR Tolkien, whose books first kindled the northern-fire within me.

On a personal note, I would like to thank Heidi, for once again putting up with a husband living more in the Dark Ages than the 21st century. I hope you read this book, and see where I have been the last six months – if not, at least read the dedication. Thanks to Chloe, who took her cousin's place as 'the wolf in our living-room' when our much-missed Siri left us. Your silent companionship makes the hours of typing less lonely.

To Heidi, my Valkyrie, with love. In memory of Siri.

PROLOGUE
Where Now the Horse and Rider?

FROM THE LATE 19TH century onwards a series of archaeological discoveries were made that seemed to confirm as fact much of what had previously been thought fanciful in ancient myth and legend. In the 1870s, Heinrich Schliemann discovered the site of Homer's 'Troy' at Hisarlik in Turkey, and in 1900, Sir Arthur Evans located, near Heraklion in Crete, the mythical palace of King Minos at Knossos, whose labyrinth had reputedly imprisoned the fabled Minotaur. Not only did Evans uncover a maze of labyrinthine passages, but also evidence of a ritual (and possibly sacrificial) bull cult of which the tale of the flesh and blood monster was a dim memory. More recently, in the 1960s, Leslie Alcock's excavations at Cadbury Castle in Somerset, a site reputed by some to be King Arthur's Camelot, revealed that it had indeed been the stronghold of a Romano-British warlord. Increasingly, it seemed reasonable to consider that beneath the patina of misunderstandings and exaggerations that overlaid most ancient myths (and which had led to their dismissal as valid historical sources), there may lie an historical core and thereby clues to the beliefs of the people that had created them.

But where were the great myths of the English? Arthur, if he existed, was probably a Celt who had opposed the invading Anglo-Saxon tribes – and other English figures such as Robin Hood and Hereward the Wake were more folk heroes than the stuff of proper myth. England's mythology and the pagan religion that had produced it seemed to have been lost, the victim of conversion, invasion and suppression.[1]

England, it has been said, is the most de-mythologized land in Europe. It is also often said that it was this lack of a native English myth and tradition that prompted JRR Tolkien to write *The Hobbit* and *The Lord of the Rings* as a replacement 'mythology for England'.[2] But, as Tolkien, professor of Anglo-Saxon at Oxford, was fully aware, some tantalizing fragments of this lost tradition had survived.

Aside from the charms and the snippets of herb-lore and leech-craft that give us glimpses into the world of magic and superstition inherited from pre-Christian times, there were also a number of surviving poems. Composed after the advent of Christianity, these poems offered a glimpse into this lost pagan world through the filter of the later faith. The most important of these was an Old English poem that told of the dragon-slayer Beowulf, who single-handedly vanquished the troll-like monster Grendel and his hideous lake-dwelling mother, thus ending their 12-year reign of terror wreaked upon the mead-hall of a Danish king. This tale, set in the original homeland of the English in Denmark, told of a world in which tribal kings were buried in ships full of treasure, and where mail-clad warriors boasted of brave deeds over horns of mead. Yet, like the other extant fragments of Old English lore, this poem (not translated into modern English until 1892 – and even then regarded by scholars as a minor folktale compared to other epics) had not entered popular culture as had the Arthurian myth.[3]

The main reason for this cultural void, as far as Saxon tradition was concerned, can be traced back to the Norman conquest. Prior to 1066, tales such as *Beowulf* were the mainstay of the Old English aristocracy, but when the conquest introduced a new ruling class and a new language, the stories of Arthur, derived from Celtic oral tradition, replaced them. The figure of Arthur provided the Norman conquerors with a non-Saxon ideal of British kingship to aspire to, as depicted in Geoffrey of Monmouth's *Historia Regum Brittaniae* ('*The History of the Kings of Britain*') – a kingship which ruled an empire extending over much of northern France – matching that of the Normans.[4] Although the Old English tales no doubt continued to be told amongst native English speakers, they were never translated into Norman-French or remoulded, as were the Celtic myths, to fit in with current courtly ideals, so that in time they faded from memory.

It is probable that some of these Anglo-Saxon tales were, like *Beowulf* and the fragments of folk-magic recorded by monks, only finally to perish when the monastery libraries in which they were housed were destroyed during the Dissolution. Miraculously, the Beowulf manuscript escaped both the Dissolution and a subsequent fire – but it was the only complete epic that did. (Just two pages of one other Old English epic, the hitherto unknown tale of *Waldhere* – Walter of Aquitaine – were discovered in Copenhagen, in 1860, in the bindings of another ancient book. This is a sobering reminder of the fragility of recorded tradition.[5]) The Old English poems *Deor* and *Widsith* allude to many more such stories, some of which, like *Waldhere*, can be reconstructed tentatively from continental Germanic literature, but the majority of which, like the love story of Maethhild and Geat, are lost forever.[6] One of the handful of surviving ancient English poems, *The Wanderer*, the lament of a warrior exiled from his hall after the death of his lord, perfectly encapsulates for us this sense of loss:

> Where is the horse gone? Where the rider?
> Where the giver of treasure?
> Where are the seats at the feast?
> Where are the revels in the hall?
> Alas for the bright cup!
> Alas for the mailed warrior!
> Alas for the splendour of the prince!
> How that time has passed away, dark under the cover of night,
> as if it had never been!

'As if it had never been' – these words could have been written about the fate of Old English tradition as a whole. Tolkien adapted the lines in *The Lord of the Rings* and set them in heroic verse telling of the faded glory of the Riders of Rohan, a people he modelled on the Anglo-Saxons:

> Where now the horse and the rider? Where is the horn that was
>   blowing?
> Where is the helm and the hauberk, and the bright hair flowing?
> Where is the hand on the harp-string, and the red fire glowing?
> Where is the spring and the harvest and the tall corn growing?
> They have passed like rain on the mountain, like a wind in the
>   meadow;
> The days have gone down in the West behind the hills into
>   shadow.
> Who shall gather the smoke of the dead wood burning,
> Or behold the flowing years from the Sea returning?[7]

Beowulf and its associated lore might still be unknown to many outside academia were it not for Tolkien, who dared to stand alone from the crowd and defend its worth. In a lecture at the British academy, 'Beowulf: The Monsters and the Critics', Tolkien argued that it should be studied not only for its language, but also as a work of art in its own right; its monsters, so reviled by academia, should be regarded as central to the tale, rather than as embarrassing additions to what was essentially a saga of warring dynasties and family feuds.[8]

Tolkien's defence could not have been timelier. Just three years later, in 1939, at Sutton Hoo in Suffolk, archaeologist Basil Brown unearthed an entire Anglo-Saxon ship buried within a great burial mound with a wealth of priceless treasure.[9] This discovery, dated to the early 7th century, seemed to confirm that the boat burials and material culture such as the helmets and swords described in *Beowulf*, once thought to be imagined or exaggerated by the Dark Age poet, had actually existed.[10] Perhaps, as with Homer's *Iliad*, there was some fact to the tale; perhaps, a real-life warrior might lie behind the Beowulf of legend.

★   ★   ★

In this book, we examine whether, like the Minotaur at Knossos, there was more to the monstrous Grendel and his lake-dwelling mother of the *Beowulf* story than make-believe. Although generations of scholars have approached the poem from every conceivable angle, every facet of content and language, none has considered asking whether, like the heroes of the poem, these characters might also have had a form of real historical existence. To scholars, the monsters are either allegories or borrowings from folktale; the one thing they are not is real. In opposition to this, it will be argued in *Beowulf and Grendel* that the poem was not just a fantastical piece of fiction, composed to brighten a winter's evening, but the recounting in poetic form of a religious conflict between two pagan cults in Denmark around AD 500.

This conflict occurred because the religion of the ancestral English, rather than being identical to that recorded in the later Viking sources, differed from those of other Germanic peoples in that, above all other divinities, they worshipped a goddess in whose sacred lakes human victims were drowned in secret rites. Old English paganism had much in common with that of the ancient Britons, being similarly rooted in the ancient megalithic tradition of the Atlantic coasts of Neolithic Europe. It was a tradition based on the worship of a dying and resurrecting fertility god and his divine mother, the legacy of which was the practice of ritual regicide, and the taking of a sacred intoxicant; all this was tied in with the arcane and menacing symbolism of the wolf (from which, incidentally, the later werewolf legend was ultimately derived). And it was when this tradition encountered that of other northern tribes during the age of migration that conflict ensued.

Just as Sir Arthur Evans discovered that the Minotaur of Knossos was not a myth but the dim memory of an ancient bull-cult, so too, behind the seemingly fantastic monsters of the poem, lie the divinities of Old English paganism – a dark goddess and her son/lover. This radical interpretation not only provides a solution to the problem of why, when and where the *Beowulf* poem was written, but it also sheds new light on the coming of the English to Britain and the ultimate fate of their pagan religion.

JOHN GRIGSBY
Spring 2005

INTRODUCTION
The Keenest for Fame

THE *Beowulf* tale begins with the arrival of a mysterious child – a foundling, lacking clothing or wealth – sent over the sea to the coast of Denmark by powers unseen and unknown. But he has a name, 'Scyld Scefing' (Shield Sheafson), and in time all the kings of the neighbouring sea-kingdoms who sail the 'Whale's road' are under his lordship.

When his time comes to leave the world, Scyld's people send him back to the ocean upon a great ship, a gold standard above his head – bedecked with armour, swords and a mound of gold. He leaves his throne to his son Beow, and he in turn, to his son Healfdane – the father of four children: a daughter Ursula, and three sons, Heorogar, Halga and Hrothgar, the last a mighty warrior, who is the next king of the Scylding line when Healfdane dies.

Hrothgar, great-grandson of Scyld, decides to build a great mead-hall, greater than any known to man, named 'Heorot' (Hart). In time, it will fall to a blood feud, burned to the ground after the ending of this tale, but for the moment all is merriment – the noise of feasting, song and harp drifts from the hearth into the wilds – where it will soon fall on unwelcome ears.

For dwelling in the marshes and swamps beyond Heorot lies a monster – a descendant of Cain, kin to such evils as '*eotenas ond ylfe ond orcneas*' (ogres and elves and evil-shades). His name is Grendel. Evil swells in his breast, and, as night falls, he strides through the marshes towards the source of the merriment. The Danes are now sleeping, their mead-horns empty, and in no state to defend themselves when Grendel bursts into the hall and snatches thirty warriors, and is gone into the night – a trail of blood behind him.

The day dawns and Hrothgar sits silently in his chair, wracked with grief and shock – a position he will adopt again the following day after Grendel returns for a second night's feasting. Warriors soon learn to leave Heorot's hearthside after the evening light disappears behind heaven's bright edge. Hrothgar's great mead-hall stands empty and Grendel now has the upper hand. Not only for this night, but for the next twelve years this fiend haunts the mead-benches – his monstrous form seen at night on the 'mistige moras' (misty moors). He even rests in the hall itself, under Heorot's golden roof, the night-time ruler of Hrothgar's throne. By day, when the hall once more belongs to man, the council meets, debating how to rid themselves of this terror. Some pray at heathen shrines for deliverance, but when help does arrive, it comes, like Scyld, from over the sea.

Across the Whale's road, a day's sail north and east of Heorot, lies the land of the Geats – a land of lakes and mountains ruled by Hrethel's son Hygelac. One day, Hygelac's sister-son hears of the evil that threatens Heorot. Beowulf is the name of this man, Hygelac's nephew, a man keen for fame. He assembles a fourteen-strong crew, to sail eastwards to the land of the Scyldings.

From Denmark's seacliffs, the coastguard spots them and challenges them on their purpose in Hrothgar's land. Beowulf, son of Edgetheow, answers that they are there to aid the Shepherd of the Danes in overcoming his foe – and so the Geatish warriors, their helmets adorned with the shapes of boars, are permitted to have audience with the king.

Grey-haired and haggard, Hrothgar welcomes the Geats and their leader (whom he knew as a child). Beowulf boasts of his deeds – he has defeated giants and sea-creatures – and declares he will take on Grendel single-handed. That night, Danes and Geats together fill Heorot with song, and the mead-horns are emptied. Wealtheow,

Hrothgar's queen, toasts the Geats, and Beowulf swears on her cup to defend her people, or die in the attempt.

The sun sets, and slowly the company of Danes disappears from the hall. Hrothgar leaves, giving over control of his hall to Beowulf. And so the Geats are alone in the accursed hall, settling down to sleep, not thinking they will ever rise or see their own homes again, while across the vast dark expanses of marshland Grendel begins his approach.

The iron-clad doors of the hall fly asunder at Grendel's assault, and he looks over the hall, from his eyes shines '*ligge gelicost, leoht unfaeger*' (an unlovely light, like that of fire). Warriors he sees, and he laughs at his quarry, not knowing that his days of feasting on men's flesh will soon come to an end.

He seizes one unlucky warrior, bolts down great chunks of flesh, crunches his bones, and eats every last piece. He stretches out his hand to grasp another Geat, but his arm is wrenched aside by a grip stronger than that of any man he has met in Middle Earth. His heart sinks, and he makes to flee, but Beowulf has him in his hands. Heorot shakes at their wrestling; warriors, roused by Grendel's unearthly screams, run to defend their prince, but their ancestral swords are turned back by his enchanted flesh that magically repels all blades.

With a ripping of tendons, Beowulf tears the fiend's arm and shoulder from his body – only thus is Grendel able to flee the hall of Hrothgar and crawl back to his marshy den, where his life will soon ebb away.

Dawn comes and the monster's arm is hung from the gable of the hall as proof of the noble deed, and the trail of blood is there to be followed, leading those tracking it to the bubbling black waters of a mere, now stained with gore. Grendel has vanished beneath the water, and there dies: '*In fen freoddo feorh alegde haeddene sawle*' (in his fen-lair he has laid aside his heathen soul).

Hrothgar rejoices at the sight of the bloody limb. To the deliverer of his hall he gives horses, armour, a standard of gold and the name of 'son'. That eve the hall throngs with song and revelry, as it has not heard in twelve years. While the *scop* (storyteller) sings of the story of

Hengist and Finn, Queen Wealtheow offers Beowulf a rich collar of gold, as fine as the fabled Brising's necklace, the Brisingamen, (*see* page 50), a precious and princely gift.

But the Danes and Geats rejoice too early, for inhabiting the wastelands, doomed to dwell beneath the brackish waters of the bog like all Cain's kin, is Grendel's mother. She leaves her lake-dwelling in search of vengeance for the life of her son. When she arrives, the hall is peopled with sleeping forms on which she will exact her revenge. Unlucky it is for them that the prince of the Geats sleeps this night in separate quarters – an honoured guest; unlucky for Ashere, Hrothgar's most-loved thane, whom she drags from the hall into the night.

Hrothgar grieves for the loss of his friend, and he tells Beowulf that he knows who is behind the deed: often a pair of these creatures had been seen haunting the wolf-slopes: one mannish, the other in the shape of a woman. Her lair is a dark mere, uncannily lit at night by a fire under the water, and overhung by groves of gnarled, frost-covered ash trees. A hart pursued by hounds would rather remain on the shore and be torn apart than plunge into those waters.

Hygelac's thane sets out and soon reaches those dreaded groves and the boiling waters they encompass. Ashere's severed head by the cliff's edge marks this as the place. Beowulf, encased in mail and boar-adorned helm, takes Hrunting, his wave-patterned sword, in hand, and dives into the mere. A day's dive below is the bottom of this dank pool where the '*brimwylf*' (lake-wolf) marks his arrival, clasps him in her claws and drags him into her lair – a dry hall, lit by fire.

The water hag looms over him, Hrunting bites, but she is unharmed by its steel. Beowulf grasps her shoulder, but the water-witch throws him to the floor. Straddling his prone body she brings down her knife, but it meets his mail shirt and does him no harm. Beowulf sees, amid the weapons and armour that litter the hall, a massive sword – forged by the race of giants in ancient times. Grasping it by its golden hilt, he swings it in an arc, taking the head off the mere-wolf. (On the shore of the mere, the Danes, spying blood, presume the hero is dead, and leave.)

Beowulf finds the body of Grendel, and claims his head before he begins his ascent, the head in one hand and in the other the golden hilt of Hrunting – its coil-patterned blade having melted away like an icicle from the boiling blood of the monsters.

★   ★   ★

Beowulf returns to the land of the Geats a hero, and tells his lord Hygelac of his deeds. But a death in war awaits his liege-lord, who will fall against the Frisians and Franks on a foreign shore. Though he is offered the throne by Hygelac's widow Hygd, Beowulf declines, instead nominating Heardred, her son. But death in battle is the son's fate, too – killed by Onela, the king of the Swedes, in bloody feud, for harbouring his nephews Eadgils and Eanmund, and so the Geatish throne falls at last to Beowulf. As king, he helps Eadgils seize the Swedish throne from his uncle Onela. He rules Geatland well and wisely for fifty years, until fate sends him one last monster.

On the headland, above the breakers, lies a vast barrow – its ancient treasure hoard guarded by a dragon. All men fear to enter that place, save one – a slave, fleeing from a flogging, his hand alighting on a golden cup that will make a good peace offering for his master. For three hundred years, the dragon has watched over this heathen gold, and this theft rouses his anger. Spewing flames, the beast rises from his underground lair and ravages Geatland with his fiery anger. He burns buildings to cinders, even Beowulf's hall he turns to ash. And so Edgetheow's son, Beowulf, strides onward to meet the dragon – his shield newly forged of fireproof iron –knowing that 'wyrd ungemete neah' (fate was all too near).

From the stone arch in the barrow's curved side flickers the dragon's fire. With a war cry issuing from his throat, Beowulf rushes into the passage. Coiling and flaming, his adversary approaches, blasting fire as Beowulf's sword finds bone – but not deep enough. Flames engulf him, and all but one of his retinue flee to the woods in fear. Wiglaf, Woexstan's son, of the Waymunding line – kin to Beowulf – remains by his side. Wielding in his hands the sword he claimed as battle spoil against the Swedes, he remembers the gifts of gold given freely by his lord in his hall, and swears he would rather die alongside him than return home a coward.

The dreaded worm spies Wiglaf, and lets fly more flame, destroying his coat of mail and charring to ash his linden shield, so that he steps behind the iron shield of Beowulf for protection. Emboldened by Wiglaf's bravery, Beowulf strikes at the beast with his sword, but his arm is too strong for such a weapon, and in his ferocity the blade breaks.

The fire-drake lunges once more, grasping the Geat's neck in its fangs, drawing forth his life-blood. But it has left itself open to Beowulf's thane; Wiglaf strikes below the head, and the drake's fire falters. Released from the jaws of the dragon, Beowulf reaches for his knife and stabs the beast. Between their two blows, the dragon is killed.

But Beowulf is mortally wounded – the dragon's poison boils in his breast. He bids Wiglaf to build him a barrow overlooking the sea. In ten days, the people build a mighty barrow about the pyre on which the Geat is lain. And with him they bury the dragon's hoard. Twelve princes' sons ride around the barrow, they sing a grief stricken dirge: they praise his manhood, they raise his name.

> *cwaedon thaet he waere wyruldcyninga*
> *manna mildest ond monthwaerust,*
> *leodum lithost ond lofgoernost.*

> They said he was of all the world's kings
> the gentlest of men, and the most gracious,
> the kindest to his people, the keenest for fame.[1]

★   ★   ★

It is exceedingly fortunate that we know the story of *Beowulf* at all. Not only do no other manuscripts or poems from the Anglo-Saxon period so much as mention his name, but the one copy of his tale that has survived has done so against overwhelming odds. Written in what is known as the 'classic' Anglo-Saxon dialect of Wessex, probably in the first 15 years of the 11th century,[2] it is reasonable to suppose that for the first 500 years the manuscript was safely housed in the library of one of England's many abbeys. Like thousands of other books, *Beowulf* was kept safe and sound until the Dissolution of the Monasteries (1536–40) when many thousands of precious and unique manuscripts were destroyed – some deliberately torn apart and used for mundane purposes such as wrapping fish and as stoppers for wine kegs. Fortuitously, the *Beowulf* manuscript survived, falling into the hands of Laurence Nowell, dean of Lichfield, from where it passed into the famed collection of Sir Robert Bruce Cotton (1571–1631). In 1700, Cotton's collection was donated to the public by his grandson John Cotton and relocated to Ashburnham House in Westminster. In 1731, a fire tore through the aptly named Ashburnham collection, damaging *Beowulf* and destroying many other volumes. The manuscript survived intact (though scalded in places) by being thrown out of a window. Today, one can see that the edges of the manuscript are in a poor state – the spine has completely burned away and each leaf is now mounted on frames of paper.

Cotton Vitellius A.xv, as the manuscript is known (after its location in the Cotton collection under a bust of the Roman emperor Aulus Vitellius), contains more than the tale of Beowulf. Bound alongside the poem are another poetic work, *Judith*, and three prose pieces, *The Passion of St Christopher*, *The Wonders of the East* and *The Letters of Alexander to Aristotle*. The subject matter of the latter two pieces, with their tales of strange beasts and monsters, have led some to believe that the manuscript was put together as a kind of bestiary (*see* page 190).

While scholars disagree on most aspects of the poem, they are able to agree that it was originally an oral work, and that the author (an anonymous Christian court poet) did not invent the story but drew on an existing tale of which at least two versions were available to him at the time of its composition.[3] What is more, it is highly probable that the two sections of the poem – which might be labelled the 'Danish/Grendel' (concerned with the Scylding royal house) and the

'Swedish/Dragon' (concerned with the Scylfing royal house) sections – were also originally separate tales, to be united later by the *Beowulf* poet. But with regard to the date and place of composition of the poem, disagreement, again, is the rule.

The proposed dates of composition range from the 7th to 11th centuries, and Northumbria, Kent, Mercia, Wessex and East Anglia have all been suggested as the location of the poet. However, the pro-Danish stance of the poem suggests that it was written before the first Viking raids (late 8th century) soured the sense of kinship that had once existed between the Danish and the Anglo-Saxon peoples. This has lead to a consensus is that it was probably authored (given certain clues of dialect) in an Anglian court, possibly that of Mercia, East Anglia or Northumbria, sometime around the late 7th or early 8th century.

While most study of the poem has concentrated on its use of language and its provenance, another fascinating branch has sought to discover its historicity. Beowulf's people, the Geats, have been identified as the Götar of southern Sweden, and their king, Hygelac (Beowulf's uncle), with the Chochilaicus mentioned in the chronicles of Gregory of Tours (written around 540), who led, and perished in, an ill-fated raid into Frankish territory around 520. The Swedish king Eadgils, whom Beowulf helps to the throne, is undoubtedly an early 6th-century king named Athils, whose massive grave- mound can still be seen in the royal graveyard at Gamla Uppsala in Sweden.[4] But while such figures seem to place the poem on an historical footing, the majority of scholars agree that in all probability the hero Beowulf was not himself historical, given that his name does not follow the Germanic tradition of familial alliteration (as in Hrothgar son of Healfdeane) and that his actions are clearly superhuman.

One early theory was that Beowulf was an echo of an earlier pagan sun god and that the events of the poem were corrupted nature-myths in which Grendel represented the spring floods, his mother the sea, and the dragon the winter storms that finally overcome the power of the summer sun.[5] Others saw him as the wind purifying the pestilent marshes, with Grendel a personification of disease. More recently, the preferred argument has been that he is based on the folkloric motif of the 'bear's son' or, as it is also called, 'the three princesses'.[6]

This tale is found throughout Europe and Asia, and over 200 versions have been recorded. No two versions are alike, but a basic plot can be reconstructed. The tale tells of a prodigiously strong boy, often the son of a bear, who sets off with a number of companions, and arrives at a deserted house that is haunted by a supernatural foe. The hero's companions are worsted by the foe, but the bear's son manages to wound him and tie him up, but he escapes. The hero and his band follow the trail of his blood to a hole in the ground into which the hero jumps lowered on a rope by his friends. He defeats the foe and discovers three princesses whom he sends back up the rope, but when he comes to climb the rope, his friends drop it, seize the princesses and leave him stranded. Eventually he escapes and takes his revenge.

On the surface, the similarity between this tale and *Beowulf* are striking, and it is no wonder that scholars have argued that the Old English poem is a retelling of the 'bear's son' tale. Beowulf does defeat Grendel in a deserted hall, does follow his trail of blood, and when he is fighting beneath the water he is deserted by the Danish, if not the Geatish, troops who accompanied him there.

But the first point to note is that the three princesses are absent from the tale. If the poet had no qualms about introducing a purely folkloric character into his historical saga, why not go the whole way and include the three princesses? Why not make them Hrothgar's daughters? The obvious answer seems to be that the princess motif did not fit in with the historical tale on which these folktale elements were later pinned.

It is more likely that they were hung on the story of a real event or hero, a Geatish warrior (or warriors), perhaps, who came to Denmark to help out the Scylding dynasty, and whose historical deeds suggested parallels with the monster-slayings of the 'bear's son' story. In other words, the monster-slaying episode within Beowulf is not just an idle fancy but based on an actual historical occurrence.

The evidence to argue such a point does not appear in the text of *Beowulf* itself, but in the rites and symbols of Germanic prehistory.

For it is in seeking out the lost rites and beliefs of our Germanic ancestors that it is possible to unearth the existence of a tradition that illuminates the *Beowulf* poem and reveals that the seemingly fabled deeds of its hero were not borrowings from folklore, but were rooted in actual events. To find the first clues to this lost tradition, as a first step it is necessary to become acquainted with the peoples of pagan Germania from which the ancestors of the English people sprang.

Part I

OLD ENGLAND

·

CHAPTER ONE

CLANS OF THE SEA COASTS

Was it not Scyld Scefing that shook the halls, took mead-benches, taught encroaching foes to fear him – who, found in childhood, lacked clothing? Yet he lived and prospered, grew in strength and stature under the heavens until the clans settled in the sea coasts neighbouring over the whale-road all must obey him and give him tribute.

BEOWULF, 5–12

THE MODERN-DAY descendants of the Old English have little or no knowledge as to their own origins. Most modern history books begin their accounts of English history with the arrival of two brothers, Hengist and Horsa, on British soil (at Ebbsfleet in Kent) some time in the 5th century. But so little attention is given to where they and their people came from, that one could be forgiven for thinking that they appeared in their ships from out of the mist like the mysterious Scyld Scefing of *Beowulf*. Today, the landing point is a mile or so inland: the Wantsum Channel which once cut through north-east Kent, separating the Isle of Thanet from the mainland, has silted up since Hengist and Horsa's day.[1] The exact place of the landing is not marked with any formal monument, though a stone cross close by supposedly marks where St Augustine arrived a few generations later to convert Hengist's great-great-grandson, Ethelbert, to the new faith. Instead, away on the coast, there stands the dragon-prowed ship *Hugin* (named after one of the Norse god Odin's oracular ravens), which was sailed from the continent in 1949 to mark the 1500th anniversary of the brothers' arrival. The simple plaque on its side records where the ship, and therefore by analogy, the two brothers, left for England: Denmark, land of the Scyldings.

History books may not record the origins of the English, but for many generations after their arrival in what was to become 'England', the descendants of Hengist and Horsa continued to think of themselves as part of the continental Germanic peoples; hundreds of miles of sea were no barrier to a seafaring folk to whom the ocean was known as the 'swan's road', as accessible in their minds as a modern motorway is to us today. While it may seem strange to us that *Beowulf*, the nearest thing to an English epic, is set in Denmark and tells of the deeds of a hero from southern Sweden, to the poet and his audience, the tale would have been rooted in a tradition they considered their own, a tradition far more English than we can imagine. For the arrival of the English in Britain stands not at the start of their history, as we might presume, but at the end of their prehistory – a vast stretch of time spent in the lands the Romans knew as Germania (*see* Map 1); for the English were by origin a mix of Germanic tribes.

Germania

Like most of the non-literate inhabitants of early northern Europe, such as the Celts, we are to some extent reliant for our information on the Germans – the inhabitants of a vast swathe of territory east of the Rhine extending north into Denmark and its islands and east into modern day Poland and Hungary – from their literate neighbours, the Romans.

This source is not perfect, for the Germans both fascinated and repulsed their 'civilized' Roman neighbours, whose accounts tend towards bias in both directions. Some eulogized the Germans' uncomplicated lives (along the lines of the 'noble savage'), while others demonized a people who in the past had posed a threat to Rome itself, and might do so again in the future. In 113 BC, two nomadic German tribes – the Cimbri and Teutones – had migrated south over the Alps from Denmark and attacked northern Italy.[2] Though they were defeated by General Gaius Marius, from that time on the Romans harboured the fear that these barbarians might one day sack Rome. (The Goths did just this under their chieftain Alaric in AD 410.) Accordingly, Rome had tried to pre-empt this strike but had failed to defeat the Germans.

The nomadic tribes that constituted the Germans lived in isolated temporary farmsteads that made them a more difficult enemy to pin down and destroy than the comparatively Romanized Gauls with their static villages and defended hill forts. Caesar, having conquered the whole of Gaul, was never able to get beyond the Rhine; in AD 9, when his adopted son, the emperor Augustus, sought to annexe Germania, the result was one of the greatest military disasters in Roman history. Three legions and six cohorts (some 25,000 men), under the command of Publius Quintilius Varus, were slaughtered almost to a man in the Teutoburg forest. Stretched out in a thin line, treading a narrow path between forest and marshland, they were picked off by German natives using guerrilla tactics during a relentless and horrific three-day march.[3]

But although the Germans were the bogeymen of the Roman world, their primitive, non-urban lifestyle also provided Roman writers and critics a perfect foil to hold up against their own corrupt city life with its greed and excesses. One such writer was Cornelius Tacitus, whose *Germania* ('On the History and Geography of Germany'), written in AD 98, provides many details of the Iron Age tribes who inhabited this land. His comments are illuminating, and help support the fragmentary archaeological evidence.[4]

The name *Germania*, he explains, was not an old name but the original tribal name of the Tungri, one of the first tribes to cross the Rhine into Gaul; the name was later adopted by the Germans as a blanket term to denote all their peoples. Germania, Tacitus recorded, was a land of forbidding landscapes and an unpleasant climate, 'dismal to behold for anyone who was not born or bred there', a land of forests and marsh. And its people, like the landscape, were earthy, harsh and primal.

The Germans

The Germans, Tacitus tells us, did not live in cities, but in isolated houses built from wood. They wore no clothes except cloaks or skins fastened with brooches or thorns (only the wealthy wore tight-fitting undergarments), and were used to cold and hunger. While they did plant some cereal crops, it was not in an organized fashion, and they lived mainly off meat, curdled milk, wild fruit and ale made from barley. Though this image of the half-naked Germans living off the land is presented (save for the harsh climate) as an Arcadian idyll, Tacitus's portrait generally corresponds with what archaeologists have discovered of the culture of Germania in the Iron Age.

At most, the settlements were small groupings of farmsteads made up of basic longhouses, each divided into a living quarters around a central hearth, and a cattle byre. Cattle were clearly important in the economy, and despite what Tacitus said about cereal farming being unimportant, there is ample evidence for the growing of barley (for bread and beer), einkorn and emmer wheats, oats, millet and flax.[5] But it seems that farmland was not owned, as in Rome, by a landed aristocracy. Caesar records that land was owned by the tribe, and distributed yearly amongst kin groups to farm. Such a communal ownership prevented the accumulation of wealth in the hands of any one individual or group, and this lack of a landed aristocracy may have lead the Romans to underestimate the importance of cereals in the German diet.[6] But it also meant that if wealth was counted in terms of heads of cattle and not acres of land, then the tribal members were free to roam where they would and still maintain their social standing, unlike the Roman gentry who were tied to their land. For the most part, the Germans seemed content to stay within their tribal territories, but the freedom to move was always there. This would prove important in the later history of the Germanic peoples in the centuries following Tacitus's account, as the existence of modern-day England amply demonstrates.

The term 'German', like 'Celt', was really a linguistic tag rather than an ethnic one and denoted a shared language and culture, not necessarily a shared genetic inheritance.[7] One clue to a possible varied racial background amongst the Germanic tribes is that Tacitus divides them into three 'peoples': the Ingaevones, who inhabited the land nearest to the sea; the Herminones, who occupied the interior; and the Istaevones, who made up the rest. These three peoples were named after the three sons of Mannus, the son of the earth-god Tuisto.

As well as a shared language, one thing that did unite these people was a common set of political and societal customs, most importantly those surrounding the figure of the king. As there was no fixed line of succession, Tacitus states, the German people elected kings from amongst the nobility, and it was the people that decided matters of importance in specially convened assemblies. Such assemblies tried criminal cases and dealt out punishments. Traitors and deserters were hanged on trees, cowards, shirkers and sodomites were drowned in bogs under wicker hurdles. It is interesting to note that some of the Germanic customs noted by Tacitus continued to be practised centuries later in Anglo-Saxon England: one such was 'wer-gild' (man-price), a financial compensation to be paid by the wrongdoer to the victim or victim's family in cases of death or injury.[8]

Another custom found in England was the loyalty to one's lord in battle, a convention mentioned by Tacitus but which also appears in *Beowulf*, when Wiglaf stays beside his lord's side during his final battle with the dragon, thinking it unmanly to flee (*see* page 11). The ultimate expression of this custom is the 10th-century Anglo-Saxon poem *The Battle of Maldon* which tells of the last stand of an English *ealdorman* (literally an 'elder-man': a high-ranking chief usually in charge of a shire) named Byrhtnoth against the Vikings at Maldon in Essex in 991.[9]

In a world of limited material resources, the Germans relied on such personal acts of courage to define status, and not, as was increasingly common amongst their Celtic neighbours, through the giving of gifts received through trade. Their world was one of honour, where to make a name for oneself in battle meant everything, and in which, despite a certain boyish bravado, an almost chivalric moral code seems to have existed.

The Ingaevones

In the *Germania*, Tacitus follows his portrait of the Germans with a detailed list of the tribes who make up the country. Of particular interest is his description of the coastal tribes, the Ingaevones, for these are the 'clans settled in the sea-coasts' of *Beowulf*. The first of the coastal tribes he mentions are the Frisii and the neighbouring Chauci, who he says inhabit an area between the Rhine and Elbe on the North Sea coast in settlements extending around vast lagoons. To the east of these are the Suebi, distinguished from the others by their custom of tying their long hair in an elaborate knot to one side of the head, and who were, it seems, more of a conglomeration of tribes than an individual group. Numbered amongst them were the Langobardi[10] (long-beards) who in time would settle in Italy, giving their name to the region of Lombardy, but whose origin was in the southern region of Sweden known as *Scandza*. The most important part of the *Germania* concerning the origins of the English follows the description of the Suebi. Tacitus writes about seven tribes inhabiting an area north of the Suebian tribelands, in the region, it must be assumed, of modern Denmark:

> After them [the Langobardi] come the Reudigni, Aviones, Anglii, Varini, Eudoses, Suarines, and Nuitones, all of them safe behind ramparts of rivers and woods.

These seven tribes were an isolated population and the most important names are the Anglii and Eudoses, as these were in all probability the Angles and Jutes which the *Anglo-Saxon Chronicle* (compiled in the 9th century) records as two of the three main tribal groupings that formed the English people. The Angles, it says, came from the region known as Angulus in the neck of the Danish peninsula, (modern-day Schleswig-Holstein), where today there is a region named Angeln. Beyond them to the north, in modern-day Jutland, was the land of the Jutes. The other main tribal group that made up the English, according to the *Chronicle*, were the Saxons, though modern archaeologists would also add a contingent of Frisians and Franks to the list.

Tacitus does not mention the Saxons, but a century later Ptolemy in his *Geographia* does, locating them at the bottom of what is known as the 'Cimbric peninsula' just below the Anglii. Archaeology shows us that this Saxon culture later spread south-west to between the Elbe and Weser – the land of the Chauci. As the Chauci tribe disappears from history at this point, it seems likely that the tribes of this broad zone had united into a new confederacy under a new name.[11]

What is of particular interest about the tribes that would later become the English is that they seem to have developed in situ over a number of preceding millennia. Unlike their later history of exile and invasion, the archaeological remains of this coastal part of Germania seem to show that these tribes had been settled in Denmark and northern Germany for at least 2,000 years before Tacitus mentioned them by name. This means that though no written texts survive of their early origins, the glittering finds of prehistoric Denmark are as much the inheritance of the English as they are of the Danes.

CHAPTER TWO

·

FORMER DAYS

We have heard of the thriving of the throne of Denmark, how
the folk-kings flourished in former days.

BEOWULF, 2–4

THE HOMELAND of the ancestors of the English peoples, the
Cimbric peninsula of the Ingaevones, an area encompassing
modern day Denmark and the Schleswig-Holstein region of northern
Germany, stretched out from the top of Germany into the North Sea
to where its scatter of islands cross to Sweden. This swathe of land was
isolated from the rest of Germania and in many respects was a cultural backwater compared to some of the tribal zones to the south
that had been in direct contact with the civilizations of the Mediter-
ranean. However, in prehistoric times, long before the founding of
Athens or Rome, it lay at the centre of many of the long- distance
trade routes that had connected the cultures of northern Scandinavia
and the coasts of the Baltic to the Bronze Age centres of power such
as Mycenae and Crete. Indeed, in former days there had been a
'Golden Age' in this region of Scandinavia, unknown to Tacitus but
remembered by the Germanic peoples themselves.

For them, this area, Scandza, was seen as the birthplace of their
tribal ancestors: the Christian Goth historian Jordanes in his *Getica* (a
history of the Gothic peoples written in 550) referred to Scandza as

'*vagina nationum*' (the womb of nations).[1] His own people, the Goths, had probably originated on the south-west coast of Sweden – an area still known as Götland – crossing the Baltic to present-day Poland by the time Tacitus was writing. It is likely that part of the tribe remained behind to become the Geats of Beowulf. The Langobards and Burgundians, too, claimed an origin in Scandza, though it is not clear whether these tribes all originated in this area, or whether the 'Golden Age' provided them with an idealized past. Either way, from the start Scandza was unique both geographically and socially.

Denmark, its islands and the southern tip of Sweden had probably formed a cultural whole soon after the ending of the last ice age (*c.* 8000 BC) when we see evidence of Mesolithic (middle Stone Age) hunter-gatherer groups inhabiting its coasts and wooded river valleys, such as the Gudena river in Jutland. These groups moved from camp to camp, following the herds of wild game as the seasons dictated. This was happening all over Europe, but there was something about coastal people, as opposed to those living inland, that helped forge a sense of community and connectedness with the land: the ocean. To an inland group, the massive wildwood that covered much of Europe was without boundaries, but to those dwelling on the Atlantic coasts (including those of northern France and the British Isles) the knowledge that the land was limited, that one could not simply push forever onwards, created a difference. Here land was scarce, and so it was important to mark it out as belonging to one's kin or extended family, to defend one's territory, to define boundaries.[2]

It may be that it was here that tribal identities first began to form in earnest, and there is certainly archaeological evidence that might suggest this in the cemeteries, such as those at Vedbaek (near Copenhagen) on the Danish isle of Zealand (Sjaelland) and across the water at Skateholm on the southern tip of Sweden. The cemeteries show that a similar material culture existed in this region at this time, yet they also show remarkably different methods of burial rite and grave goods (the Skateholm people, for instance, buried their dogs with grave goods, affording them the same honours as humans). Such differences have allowed archaeologists to postulate the existence of three major 'tribal' zones in Mesolithic Scandza: one in Jutland, another on the Danish islands, and another in southern Sweden.

Houses of the Dead

It is probably this well-defined sense of tribal identity and land ownership that explains, in Scandza as well as in Britain and northern France and Spain, the appearance of great megalithic structures during the following Neolithic Age (New Stone Age). The Neolithic Age saw the arrival of farming practices in northern Europe (around 4200 BC), ultimately from the Middle East, where crops were first grown around 5,000 years earlier.

Farming societies were much more tied to the land than their hunter-gatherer ancestors, enabling each member of the tribe to help on the farm whatever their age or ability. The development of farmsteads and villages in place of seasonal shelters and camps must also have had an impact on the nature of society. The more settled community could now concentrate more effort into expressing its tribal and ancestral identity and the house of the ancestors – the tombs for the dead – provided such an expression.

These tombs were usually placed in highly visible positions, defining tribal boundaries – the ancestral bones within them demonstrating the occupation of the land by that tribe. But the building of these tombs seems to have gone far beyond the need to establish land ownership. The whole tradition shows a preoccupation with the ancestors and their connection with the earth that was almost fanatical in its fervour. The fact that such effort was put into making these structures out of the hardiest materials says much for the motivation of these people, whose own dwellings have long since vanished. Such tombs were not mere reliquaries but formed the centre of tribal life. The bones of the ancestors were not hidden away; instead the doors to these 'houses of the dead' (often mimicking the houses of the living in design) frequently remained open, with the bones of the dead being carried out for use in certain rites. Thus the ancestors could be taken from the tomb to be present at special occasions – marriages, perhaps, or alliances and feasts. And supplications and offerings were made to the ancestors to ensure the fertility of the land over which they presided.

The worlds of the dead and the living overlapped. When an individual died, his body would be dismembered and placed anonymously into the tomb where he would become one with the amorphous throng of ancestors – perhaps, who knows, one day to be reborn into the tribe.

In Denmark, two major types of mortuary structure once dominated the landscape. The earliest were the great dolmens (*dysser*) which consisted of a small burial chamber formed from three or four upright stones capped with a massive monolith: 3,500 of these are to be found on the Danish islands alone.[3] It is thought that such structures developed from earthen long-barrows with wooden mortuary chambers, and that the dysser were originally contained within low mounds. In time, another type of tomb emerged, the passage grave, of which 600 examples have so far been discovered. Thought in later times to have been the work of giants – hence the term *jaettestuer* (giant's graves) – these passage graves allowed access to the remains of the dead.

The tombs reveal the use of both individual and communal burial traditions, and have been associated by modern authors with the belief in the 'great goddess'[4] – the tomb within the green rise of earth representing the pregnant belly of the goddess into which the dead were placed for rebirth. While it is not known which gods, if any, were worshipped at such times, there is ample evidence for ancestor worship. Indeed, it may be that their beliefs and rituals were not centred on any specific divinity, but rather on the throng of ancestral spirits who made the tombs their home.

Stone Age Ceremonies

While little is known of the rites of the megalith builders, archaeology does provide us with some clues as to the nature of the ceremonies with which they were associated. In Denmark, the building of the megaliths coincided with the arrival of a type of pottery vessel known as 'funnel-necked beakers', long-necked gourd-shaped vessels which may have been used in a drinking ceremony that accompanied the newly introduced rites of farming. This is only supposition, but evidence does exist in Britain, where the first grain to be found was not grown locally but imported from the continent, and was used not to make bread, but, so it seems, a kind of ritual drink. Evidence from Skara Brae, a Neolithic village in the Orkneys, and two other ritual sites in Fife reveal that barley grain was brewed into a hallucinogenic beer containing meadowsweet for flavour, and deadly nightshade, known in Old English as *dwale* (trance), along with henbane, both of which contain psychoactive alkaloids. It may be that the brew (such 'drinks' were in reality more like a kind of fermented porridge than modern beer) once drunk from the funnel-necked beakers was similarly spiked.[5]

At Tustrup in East Jutland, we get some idea of the ceremonies that may have once accompanied the taking of this hallucinogenic 'drink'. Built around 3200 BC, Tustrup appears to have been a kind of necropolis consisting of three tombs (two dolmens and a passage grave) and a temple, all in use during a single period within one community – a fact that argues against different grave types being indicative of different eras or tribes.[6] The temple complex fell within the triangle formed by the three tombs; it was a horseshoe-shaped structure of stones forming a 5-m sq internal area open to the north-east. The whole structure may have been roofed, with its apex on a massive pillar at the centre of the open end – an opening whose orientation suggests it was built to face the rising sun on the morning of the summer solstice, or the setting sun of winter solstice for those looking towards the temple, as was the case at Stonehenge. The temple may have been a mortuary temple, perhaps where the newly dead were placed before joining the rest of the ancestral bones in the tombs. At the centre of horseshoe was a pit surrounded by 28 vessels and 100 vessels were found around entrances of the tombs.

The tradition of leaving offerings to the ancestors may have continued well into the modern age – the Danish archaeologist PV

Glob reports that even in the last century, at the passage grave at Øm near Roskilde, farmhands were sent to clean out the passage at midwinter so the farmer's wife could leave a bowl of porridge for the 'giants and the spirit that dwelt there'.[7] Similar observances survived into the last century in connection with the so-called 'cup-markings' – shallow bowls carved into Neolithic and Bronze Age stone monuments, which were used as depositories for food or drink for 'the elves' (*see* page 102).

What is intriguing is that these temple structures were ritually burned: that at Turstrup was burned after a single rite, while there is evidence that a temple site at Ferslev was cleared and re-used a second time before being burned. It is here that we may see the first expression of the custom of lighting midsummer and midwinter fires that continued to be practised throughout northern Europe until recent times.[8]

The collective burial of nameless individuals found in the majority of megalithic tombs is often seen as evidence of a kind of Neolithic 'communism', but the fact is that the number of bodies accounted for in the tombs can only have been a small percentage of the total population; there was clearly some kind of 'selection' process at work, although it is not possible to say whether this was political or if it points to the existence of an elite. Whatever its origins, around 2000 BC the communal burial rite comes to an end and we begin to see a rise in the number of individual graves.

Beakers and Battle Axes

Much argument has raged over whether the change in burial traditions found throughout Europe at this time was brought by a new invading population or whether it was the result of a shift in ideas. In recent times, the latter view has become predominant. Although there was undoubtedly some movement of individuals, including, no doubt, skilled artisans bringing new ideas and techniques with them, there was not a huge migration of people. And since there is no evidence for any major incursions of peoples into Denmark after this point (until a possible invasion of the Danes around AD 300), it is safe to assume that the people who were buried individually in low round mounds in wooden coffers were: a) the descendants of the builders of the megaliths, and b) the ancestors of the English people. In other words, like the Celts who are now their neighbours, the English were in origin a megalithic people.

To archaeologists, the individuals who are found buried in single graves are known as the 'Corded Ware' people after their innovative pottery that was decorated by making elaborate impressions with hemp cords (that some suggest betray the contents of these drinking vessels: a cannabis-based brew).[9] This solitary inhumation did not necessarily mean that the ancestors were no longer important to man; on the contrary, it may have been that the nameless throng of ancestors had been joined by *named* individuals who could be supplicated directly by their descendants. These named ancestors who, in time, would perhaps be able to grant their people supernatural help, when all personal memory of them had faded and they had begun to acquire superhuman attributes, became what might be termed 'gods'. (Hence the idea of being able to trace one's lineage back to a god, as reflected in Anglo-Saxon genealogies that link the royal houses back to the Germanic god Woden, or, in Christian times, to a biblical figure such as Adam.)

The new pottery and funerary techniques seem to have spread across western Europe in two main 'waves' – those of the Corded-Ware (or 'Battle-Axe' cultures as they are also called) to the north, and the 'Beaker traditions' (which saw the drinking of alcoholic beverages and the first use of metalworking), to its immediate south. While the Beaker cultures to the south began to use metal, crafting the first bronze swords and daggers, and forming a military elite to use them, the peoples of Scandza were left out on a limb. With no sources of metal of their own, they exported the amber that was washed up on their beaches and maybe fur in return for a few items of these new and highly-prized crafts.

With so little disposable wealth and prestige goods, the tribes of Scandza developed no real warrior aristocracy, their chieftains remained just heads of families, of the farming landscape, and their power lay in the wealth of the soil. Hence the terms 'lord' and 'lady' in Old English were *hlaford* (loaf-guard) and *hlafdige* (loaf-kneader).

However, the developments of new trade links during the Bronze Age changed all this. Denmark suddenly found itself at the crossroads of a massive increase in trade between the Baltic and the Rhine, Danube and Oder rivers. For one short Golden Age, the chieftains of Denmark, the middlemen in this trade, were buried in huge domed round mounds, kitted out with swords and spears.

The Mound People

The 'Mound People'[10] as PV Glob termed them, flourished for some 200 years around 1500 BC. And, luckily for us, the construction of their domed tombs, made from layers of turf and clay, protected them from the elements and kept them hermetically sealed so that many of them are well preserved today. Among them are the 'family' from Borum Eshøj, in East Jutland, whose burial goods were not the richest ever found, but whose unity in death presents us with a glimpse of an ancient 'English' family.

Buried within a massive earthen mound in split and hollowed oak trunk coffins, the old man, woman and possibly their son had been preserved by the tannic acid in the oak bark that had leached into the waterlogged graves. The old woman had been buried in a long woollen skirt, an elaborate hair net on her head, and with bronze jewellery and a dagger. Her husband, aged in his late 60s, was simply buried wearing a woollen skullcap, a cape and a loincloth. Their son (whose wisdom teeth were just emerging) was buried with greater wealth, wrapped in a hide shroud with a bone comb, in his scabbard a six-inch dagger – his sword, it is supposed, inherited from his weaponless father and passed on to the one who ordered the mound to be built and who led the funeral rites. Although by some standards these were not rich goods, the sheer volume of earth in the mound that enclosed them was a testament to their status.

Ancestors of the Anglii tribe were also found preserved in their graves. Perhaps the most interesting find was that of a 'princess' of the Mound People from Egtved in the neck of the Cimbric peninsula (*see* plate 6). She was aged 18–20, 5 ft 3 in tall, with a 23-inch waist, sported a shoulder-length blond bob, and a corded short skirt with no undergarments beneath. At her side lay a bucket of wheat and honey beer flavoured with cranberries. A beautifully engraved circular bronze disk lay on her otherwise bare belly, and some yarrow flowers lay at her left knee, showing she died in the summer. At her feet lay the body of a girl aged about 9 or 10, possibly a serving girl robbed of her young life to accompany her mistress into the world beyond.

It is likely that her revealing attire with the solar symbol over her womb was a type of ritual costume – similarly dressed Danish figurines have been found, depicted leaping and dancing (from Grevensvænge, South Zealand, and Kaiserberg in Holstein). The sun image is found on many items from the Bronze Age, most impressively borne on a model wagon drawn by a bronze horse from Trundholm, Zealand (*see* plate 4). In later Norse myth, we find the image of the sun drawn across the heavens by a horse, so it is possible that this image appeared in their rites. These people were the children of the sun – and the myriad carvings they made on rocks throughout Scandza give some fleeting idea of their rites: there are images of a circle with a cross inside (symbolizing the sun), the horse and, above all, the ship. There are also figures playing huge curved trumpets (*lurs*) and what seem to be men and women engaged in sexual acts to promote fertility.

At Kivik in Sweden there is a rare stone sarcophagus carved with images of darker rites associated, most probably, with the funeral of the individual whose grave it is. Figures in long robes process towards a large vat or altar, while bound figures are being led by a swordsman, perhaps to be sacrificed. There is an open grave, a chariot, stallion fights, the blowing of lurs, and drumming.

After only a few generations, the Mound People declined and cremation in urns became the normal rite of burial. But even though their Golden Age was brief, the aristocratic Mound People presaged the later Iron Age 'Folk-Kings' such as Hrothgar. Quite why the Golden Age ended is open to question but it is most probably linked with the general collapse, occurring around 1200 BC, that saw the fall of many of the great Bronze Age civilizations, including those of Minoan Crete, Mycenae and, further afield, the Indus Valley. Whether the collapse was brought about by a deterioration in the climate or another factor, the knock-on effect for a powerful ruling class founded ultimately on trade was catastrophic. But, for the majority of the farming peasantry, little would have changed. It was at this period that the Trundholm sun-chariot (*see* page 34) was placed in a bog, suggesting that the deposition of the chariot may have been a supplication to the gods for the return of a stable climate. By Tacitus's time, the ritual deposition of goods (mainly weapons) in lakes and bogs had become the main ritual expression of northern Europe.

Folk on the Move

During the closing years of the Bronze Age and the following Iron Age there was less emphasis on building communal ritual structures and instead the widespread emergence of more defensive structures as populations grew and pressure on land increased, so leading to inter-tribal tension. It is during this period (perhaps catalyzed through trade with Rome) that we first begin to see the mass relocation of tribes from overpopulated areas, including that of the Cimbri and Teutones, possibly from Denmark. And it is was as a result of their contact with a literate civilization that their names began to be recorded, although we will never know how far back these tribal names went.

Tacitus mentions seven tribes in Denmark (*see* page 24), whereas later Anglo-Saxon records identify just the Danes, Angles and Jutes, with the Saxons to their south. In all probability this was due to the formation of larger tribal units; it may have been that, in a growing population, small tribes of extended kin were no longer able to exist independently within the same landscape. This was especially the case as there were major folk movements from the east, where tribes were being driven westwards by nomadic interlopers such as the Huns, who were pushing eastern Germanic tribes, such as the Goths, into Roman territory.[11]

It is not clear whether the appearance of a people named the Danes, Hrothgar's people, in former Anglian territory was due to an influx of new people, perhaps from the southern tip of Sweden, or whether, like the Saxons, they were essentially a later confederation of aboriginal tribes. That Hrothgar appears in *Beowulf* under the title 'Lord of the *Ingwine*' (friends of Ing) could support either theory; his people were either descended from the Ingaevones (which means the same as *Ingwine*) or they achieved dominance over them. Archaeologically, there is increased evidence of prestige goods (especially gold) associated with trade in Denmark around the 4th and 5th centuries, as well as a massive increase in iron production that went beyond local demand. This could be taken as evidence that a number of tribes in this area became, as had the Mound People before them, middlemen in trade between the Roman provinces and the Baltic, and developed into a rich confederacy we know as the Danes. If this is the case, it may be that these Danes put pressure on the Jutes and Angles, forcing them either to join their confederacy or leave their homeland. This is clearly suggested in *Beowulf*: Scyld, it says,

> ... shook the halls, took mead-benches, taught encroaching foes to fear him ... until the clans settled in the sea coasts neighbouring over the whale-road all must obey him and give him tribute. (*Beowulf*, 5–12)

It addition, there was also an element of environmental pressure on the coastal tribes at this time. Archaeologists have shown that during this period the sea levels were rising, and that many coastal sites, such as the Saxon village of Feddersen Wierde,[12] at the mouth of the Weser, were abandoned (*c.* 450). With the sea encroaching on one side, and nomadic warring tribes on the other, it is no wonder that the now inadequately defended Britain to the west seemed a more than tempting proposition.

The *Anglo-Saxon Chronicle* for the year 449 records:

Martianus and Valentinian received the kingdom and reigned for seven years. In their days the Angles were invited here by King Vortigern, and they came to Britain in three longships, landing at Ebbesfleet. King Vortigern gave them territory in the south-east of this land, on the condition that they fight the Picts. This they did and had victory wherever they went. They then sent to Angeln, commanded more aid, and commanded that they should be told of the Britons' worthlessness and the choice nature of the land. They soon sent hither a great host to help the others ... Their war leaders were two brothers, Hengest and Horsa, who were Wihtgils' sons. First of all they killed and drove away the King's enemies; then later they turned on the King and the British, destroying through fire and the sword's edge.[13]

This part of English history is relatively well known. The coming of the Anglo-Saxons (*Adventus Saxonicum*) to Britain, has been much discussed by historians, and for the most part their theories have been confirmed by archaeologists, who have been able to show that material goods from the relevant tribal regions of Germania match those of the respective parts of England. Types of brooches common in Jutland, for example, appear in Jutish Kent; Saxon pottery found in Wessex matches exactly that of Saxony (some examples may even have been the work of the same potter).

No contemporary records for this period exist, the nearest being that of the West Country monk Gildas, whose *De Excidio Britanniae* ('*The Ruin of Britain*') was written in the second quarter of 6th century, and whose descriptions of the *Adventus Saxonicum* were written in a deliberately apocalyptic style.

The arrival of the Anglo-Saxons was probably a gradual affair.[14] Saxon pirates had been harrying British shores for at least a couple of hundred years, prompting a number of defensive shore forts to be built along the Channel coast around AD 280. In 407, the would-be emperor Constantine III left Britain, taking the remaining Roman legions with him in an attempt to stabilize the western Empire, but his defeat in 410 meant the troops never returned, leaving a vacuum. The Saxons, pressured by loss of land in their homeland, but also other more local barbarian peoples, such as Irish and Pictish raiders (from Scotland), took advantage of this.

Eventually, under tremendous pressure from continued barbarian attacks, the Christian Roman ruling class, headed by an individual bearing the title Vortigern (Celtic for 'Overlord'), made the decision to grant a number of Germanic warriors land in Kent in return for acting as federate troops (*foederati*) to defend against the Picts. These warriors were led by the Jutish Hengist and Horsa mentioned by Bede, and are represented by a number of Germanic military-style burials found in the south-east dating from the mid-5th century. That there seem to have been earlier burials in this area suggests that in reality Vortigern was not granting new lands to the Anglo-Saxons but legitimizing land that had already been occupied by them after 407.

This measure, probably based on established Roman policy, seems to have been effective, as after this date the Picts are not mentioned as a problem. However, it also had the result of establishing a strong Germanic warrior presence in the south-east, so that when the *foederati* did rebel (perhaps over the payment of food rations) they were already armed and established in prime military positions. It was at this point that the major Anglo-Saxon advance took place, checked for half a century around 490–500 when the Britons were able to win a major victory at a place called *Mons Badonicus* (Mount Badon), probably under a leader named Ambrosius Aurelianus (though legend would attribute it to King Arthur). The rest, as they say, is history.

Although the general picture of the *Adventus* that portrays Saxons replacing Britons is a massive oversimplification of a long process of piecemeal settlement, integration, acculturization and some violence, by the 7th century most of lowland Britain was speaking a Germanic tongue within one of seven Germanic kingdoms. In time, the varied tribes that made up the *Adventus* – Saxons, Jutes, Frisians, Franks and Angles – would take the name of the latter, then the most powerful faction, and become the *Angelcyn* – the English.

To all intents and purposes, the period between the 5th and 6th centuries saw the pagan Germanic inhabitants of Denmark and north-west Germany shift a few hundred miles westwards over the sea, bringing their culture and language with them. It was a land not unlike their old one – a maritime province that once had formed part of the megalithic zone of the Atlantic coasts. But the centre of their imaginative world remained in Germania, in 'Old England', and would continue to do so for many generations, and it is there that *Beowulf* is set.

CHAPTER THREE

.

ON THE ALTARS OF THEIR IDOLS

They prayed aloud, promising sometimes on the altars of their
idols unholy sacrifices if the Slayer of souls would send relief to
the suffering people. Such was their practice, a heathen hope;
Hell possessed their hearts and minds: the Maker was unknown
to them, the Judge of all actions, the Almighty was unheard of,
they knew not how to praise the Prince of Heaven, the Wielder
of Glory.

BEOWULF, 173–82

As the *Beowulf* poet was aware, his tale was set in the pagan days
before the Word of God had been spread north beyond the
lakes and forests and into the land of the sea-going Ingaevones. And
though willing to tell of the pagan virtues of heroism and personal
glory, the Christian poet had no desire to fill his work with details
of the idols to which the Danes offered sacrifice in return for protection against foul Grendel. It is therefore necessary to turn to other
sources gain some idea of the lost rites that the Anglo-Saxon tribes
practised in their original homeland and brought with them across
the North Sea.[1]

Although the Anglo-Saxons, like their cousins the pagan Celts,
possessed a written alphabet (*see* page 98), its use seems to have been
mainly for magical purposes such as casting spells and divination.[2]
Tacitus notes that the Germans committed information to song

alone, and there may in fact have been certain prohibitions regarding the committal of these traditional songs into writing. Accordingly, such records came into being only after the religion that informed them had been cast aside, meaning that no pre-Christian vernacular source for Old English paganism exists.

The surviving vernacular literature, dating to after the conversion, is fragmentary (*see* pages 2–3) but is bolstered by evidence from church laws (dictating what practices were no longer acceptable under the new religion), genealogies, and the magical and medicinal charms found in a number of magico-religious manuscripts dating to around 950–1050.[3] Archaeology provides us with some limited clues, and place names provide another kind of evidence, although, as the English were mostly converted within just 200 years of St Augustine's arrival in 597, such names are limited.

Our only written sources on Germanic paganism are the scant commentaries of the Romans, written 500 years before the *Adventus*, and the Icelandic literature written some 500 years after. And, since they reflect an unwritten set of beliefs amongst a fluid population within a massive territory over a period of 1,000 years, the portrait painted by each is markedly different. Our first shard of evidence – that of the heathen calendar – comes from the very end of the pagan period in the writings of the 8th-century monk Bede. The 'Venerable Bede' as he is known, was born in 673 on monastic land at Wearmouth, Northumbria, and at the age of seven he was sent for education with the local abbot. He later moved to the monastery at Jarrow, where he spent the rest of his life. Bede is best known for his *Ecclesiastical History of the English People*, which he completed around the age of 60, and which is our main source for the early history of the Anglo-Saxons, especially their conversion to Christianity. It also provided the details of the *Adventus* in the Anglo-Saxon chronicle.

The Pagan Year

Bede's comments on the heathen calendar are found in *De Temporum Ratione*, a work dealing with the calculation of Christian feast days.[4] It was never Bede's intention to describe Old English paganism; in fact, he only gives what information is necessary to put over his point. His real aim was to describe the difficult process of calculating the Christian festivals such as Easter by reference to the old pagan year.

According to Bede, the year started on 25 December in the month of *Æerra-Geola* (Before Yule) with a festival Bede records as *Modranicht* (Night of the Mothers), but of which he gives no details. January was *Æftera-Geola* (After-Yule) and February *Sol-Monath* (Mud(?) Month), when, he records, cakes were offered to the gods. March and April, *Hreth-Monath* and *Eostre-Monath* respectively, were named after a pair of goddesses, and May was *Thri-Milce* (Thrice Milking), the month when in former times cattle could be milked three times a day. June and July were *Æerra-Litha* (Before Litha) and *Æftera-Litha* (After Litha) – the meaning of Litha not being explained; August was *Weod-Monath* (Weed Month), September *Halig-Monath* (Holy Month) and October, *Winterfyllith* (Winter Full-Moon): the first full moon of winter. Lastly, came November, *Blot-Monath* (Blood Month), when cattle were offered to the gods.

The heathen year, Bede records, was split into two halves, summer and winter, the latter starting in October, and the former, we must assume, in April. This corresponds closely to the Celtic 'Coligny calendar', found near Marseilles, which divided the year into dark and light halves.[5] But it seems clear that each of the two seasons was subdivided into six 'moons' apiece, the year being seen to hinge on the two major festivals in December and June, namely *Geola* (Yule) and *Litha*. 'Yule' (*Jol* in Old Norse) may be related either to the Old English *hweal* (wheel) or to the modern word 'jolly'. The Icelandic scholar Snorri Sturluson, writing in the 13th century, recorded it as a three-day feast beginning on midwinter's night. The name might refer to the concept of the turning wheel of the year or, perhaps, to the sun or the moon, which sometimes were thought of as wheels rolling across the heavens. With regard to the opposing summer festival, it can be surmised that *Litha* means 'moon' from the name of October – Winterfyllith – that is Winter-fyl-lith – 'Winter Full-Moon'.

Aside from the major festivals, the rest of the calendar reflected the farming year. The cakes given to the gods at *Sol-Monath* were probably interred in the first furrow when ploughing began in February. This rite is recorded in an 11th-century charm known as *Aecerbot* (field-remedy), as part of a complicated, and only nominally Christian, ritual to restore fertility to the land (*see* page 96). There are also reflections of the farming year in *Halig-Monath* (Holy Month) – no doubt a time of rejoicing over the harvest – and in *Blot-Monath* (Blood Month), when surplus cattle were slaughtered to provide meat for winter. Unsurprisingly, it is a calendar that reflects a close relationship with nature.

The name of Hreth, (or Rheda), goddess of March, can be linked with the Old English word *Hreth* (triumph or glory), this being the month of the spring equinox, the triumphal return of vegetation and the sun's victory over winter. *Eostre-Monath* stems from a linguistic root that gives us both 'east' and the Greek *eos* (dawn); it also gives us the present-day word 'Easter'.

But, although useful, Bede's calendar presents us with an anomaly. Neither Rheda, Eostre nor the 'Mothers' worshipped on *Modranicht* are to be found in any later written source. Instead, there is a very different pantheon that does not appear in the calendar at all, but it is one for which there is ample evidence, both in place names and in the names given to the days of the week.

Groves and Gods

When the Anglo-Saxons came to 'translate' the days of the Roman week into the vernacular, it has been assumed that they substituted the names of the Roman gods with those of their own gods that seemed to fit best with the qualities of the other. Thus, *Dies Solis* (Sunday) and *Dies Lunae* (Mo[o]n-day) are obvious equivalents; the next, *Dies Martis* (the day of Mars), became Tuesday, dedicated to Tiw, whose rune, tiwaz (↑), is found on weapons – hinting that, like Mars, he was a god of war. *Dies Mercurii* (Mercury's day) became Wednesday – Woden's day; *Dies Jovis* (Jupiter's day) became Thursday – Thunor's day (Thor in Norse); and *Dies Veneris* (the day of Venus) became Friday

– Frig's day. As *Dies Saturni* (Saturn's day) remained as Saturday, it may be that the Saxons had no equivalent to this god.[6]

  This presents us with the names of four divinities whose functions can be guessed at: Tiw, a war god; Woden, a god of trade and perhaps of the dead; Thunor, a storm god, like the thunderbolt-wielding Jove, and Frig, a goddess of love and fecundity. Each of these god's names occur in heathen place names and this is significant because such place names usually contain two elements – not only the name of a possible divinity associated with the place but also the *type* of shrine, for instance, whether it was a natural grove or a man-made shrine. There are found to be at least four main types of site in evidence:

1 *Hearh/Hearg* – a hilltop sanctuary;
2 *Leah* –a clearing or grove in a wood;
3 *Weoh* – a holy place;
4 *Ealh* – a wooden temple.

The most widespread name associated with holy sites is that of Woden, commonly associated with mounds or earthworks, such as Woodnesborough (Woden's barrow) in Kent and the Wansdyke (Woden's dyke or ditch) in the vale of Pewsey, Wiltshire, and numerous places named Grimsdyke after 'Grim', a nickname for Woden meaning 'the hooded one'. Thunor is found at Thunoreshlaew (Thunor's mound) in Thanet, and Thundersley (Thor's grove) in Essex, to name but two of the many places containing his name that attest to his popularity. Tiw can be evidenced at Tuesley (Tiw's grove) in Surrey; and, finally, Frig, the goddess, may be remembered in Froyle (Frig's hill) and Freefolk (Frig's people) both in Hampshire, and Friden (Frig's valley) in Derbyshire.[7]

  As their Celtic neighbours, it seems that it was natural features that provided the Anglo-Saxons with their places of worship – a worship, as St Gregory put, it 'of sticks and stones'. Later Church law forbade anyone to practise divination or 'evocation' at springs, stones or trees, and so it follows that they must have played a part in the Old Religion. This seems to fit in with what Tacitus wrote about Germanic paganism:

They judge that the gods cannot be contained inside walls ... they consecrate groves and woodland glades.

One such grove, in the territory of the Suebic Semnones tribe, was the site of bloody human sacrifice, possibly dismemberment, 'for the public good'. It was not permitted to enter the grove unless bound, and if one fell during the rites (possibly hinting at the use of trance states), one could not attempt to stand up within the grove, but had to roll out of it. Tacitus says this grove was the cradle of the race, and the dwelling place of the 'supreme god'.

Of the *ealh* (wooden temples) – only two place names survive (both in Kent) – but the remains of such a structure have been excavated at Yeavering in Northumbria, a 17 x 35 ft rectangular timber building, with three post-holes near the entrance, perhaps for idols.[8] Bede refers to 'idols' associated with heathen temples (possibly akin to the crudely carved phallic figure found at Broddenbjerg in Denmark, made of a forked oak branch – *see* plate 11) in his description of the destruction of a shrine at Goodmanham in Northumberland by its own high priest, Coifi. Bede writes that Coifi offers to destroy the old shrines and the 'pagan idols' that have done him no favours:

So he formally renounced his pagan superstitions and asked the king to give him arms and a stallion – for hitherto it had not been lawful for the Chief Priest to carry arms or to ride anything but a mare – and, thus equipped, he set out to destroy the idols. Girded with a sword and with a spear in his hand, he mounted the king's stallion and rode up to the idols. When the crowd saw him, they thought he had gone mad; but without hesitation, as soon as he reached the shrine, he cast into it the spear he carried and thus profaned it. Then, full of joy at his knowledge of the true God, he told his companions to set fire to the shrine and its enclosures and destroy them.

If they were anything like their Norse counterparts, such temples would have been quite plain. They were empty save for a ring (probably an arm ring) on which to swear oaths, a bowl to hold the blood of sacrificed animals, and a switch of branches to scatter the blood on either the congregation or the idols.[9] Evidence is sparse, but it is possible some were re-used, as suggested in the letter of Pope Gregory to Abbot Mellitus in 601 with instructions on conversion for St Augustine. Gregory had come to the conclusion that:

> The temples of the idols should on no account be destroyed. The idols are to be destroyed, but the temples are to be aspersed with holy water, altars set up in them, and relics deposited there. For if these temples are well-built, they must be purified from the worship of demons and dedicated to the service of the true God. In this way, we hope that the people, seeing that their temples are not destroyed, may abandon their error and, flocking more readily to their accustomed resorts, may come to know and adore the true God. And since they have a custom of sacrificing many oxen to demons, let some other solemnity be substituted in its place ... on such occasions they might well construct shelters of boughs for themselves around the churches that were once temples, and celebrate the solemnity with devout feasting.

Archaeology has shown the nature of the sacrifice at such sites. Adjacent to the Yeavering temple was a pit full of ox skulls (and some other bones), and Harrow ('*Hearg*') on the Hill similarly had a pit containing more than 1,000 ox skulls. As to the identity of the idols that Gregory wishes to be destroyed, Bede does not mention their names. But generations of scholars have sought for clues to these lost gods within the medieval Norse sources that, unlike their English counterparts, survive in good order in the prose sagas, historical sagas, and mythological poems that were written down in Iceland between the 11th and 13th centuries.[10]

The Norse Gods

First among the gods of the Norsemen was Odin (the Old English Woden), described as blue-cloaked, grey-haired and one-eyed; he held a spear, Gungnir, or a staff in his hand, wore a wide-brimmed hat on his head, and on his shoulders perched two ravens, Hugin and Munin – 'thought' and 'memory'. Odin was known as All-Father, a hint at his role as an ancestral figure and chief deity of the family of the gods, the *Aesir*. A god of battle, and of poetry and inspiration, his name means 'mad', 'inspired' or 'seer'. Odin's chief act was to sacrifice himself to himself on the World Tree, Yggdrasil, around which hung the three worlds: the underworld, *Niflheim* (the world of the dead), 'Middle Earth', *Midgard* (our own world), and the upper world, *Asgard* (the dwelling place of the Aesir, the gods). This is pure shamanic imagery, and it is clear that Odin, able to journey through the worlds on his eight-legged horse Sleipnir and gain occult knowledge, bears many traits of a shaman.

Odin's wife is Frigg (Frig), daughter of Fjorgynn, Mother Earth, and their son is Balder the beautiful, who was killed with a mistletoe spear by his own brother, the blind god Hodr, at the instigation of the trickster god Loki, and sent to the underworld. The goddess Hel, Loki's daughter, agreed to release Balder if all creation wept, and all did, even the trees and rocks – save for a giantess named Thokk – who proved to be Loki in disguise. Balder remains in hell until Ragnarok, the final battle between the gods and monsters, when the wolf Fenrir will break his bonds and destroy the world, whereupon a new world will be ushered into existence.

Thor (Thunor), probably the most popular of the Aesir with the majority of worshippers, is depicted as red-haired, bearded, and immensely strong. Thor wrestled with Jormagund, the oceanic serpent that encircled Middle Earth, and fought giants with his hammer Mollnir. The rumbling of his wagon across the sky was the sound of thunder.

Tyr (Tiw), like Thor, was a son of Odin. Originally a god of battle, he became one-handed as a result of helping bind the wolf Fenrir. He placed his hand in the wolf's mouth as a guarantee that when the gods bound him they would release him afterwards. Of course, the gods did not intend to, and so Tyr lost his hand.

The Icelandic literature that depicts these gods was heavily influenced by other European literature and tradition. The Norse gods were not portrayed as forces of nature but as heroes who might not seem out of place in one of Homer's epics – indeed the Icelandic poet and statesman Snorri Sturluson (1179-1241),[11] whose works provide us with perhaps the greatest insight into Norse myth, says in his *Prose Edda* (*c.* 1220) that Thor was King Priam of Troy's grandson. In this way, the gods were humanized – Odin is said to have come from Asia (an attempt to explain away the term Aesir) – and thus rendered valid for a Christian world. Snorri presents a divine family more like the figures of a modern soap opera than forces of nature. But we are not to see the real divinities of Germanic paganism in this light – indeed just the opposite. As Tacitus writes:

> The Germans do not think it in keeping with the divine majesty to confine gods within walls or to portray them in the likeness of any human countenance. Their holy places are woods and groves, and they apply the names of deities to that hidden presence which is seen only by the eye of reverence.

Even so, one may give a name to an elemental force such as thunder and conceive of it in human form without believing it to be in any way human or placing an image of it in a temple. However, it does seem likely that in certain areas of Germania, if not all, some of these elemental forces were beginning to be depicted in human form by Tacitus's day.

The Influence of Roman Religion

The origin for the personification of elemental forces may have sprung from contact with the Romans or the neighbouring Celtic tribes.[12] There have been many debates on the differences between the Germans and the Celts, but in reality these peoples seem to have been closely related both genetically and culturally, their chief difference being one of language. Their minor differences were exaggerated when the Celts established close trade links with Rome and, subsequently, their territories became part of the Empire, leading them to develop a more affluent and urbanized culture than the Germans.

The Celts, like the Germans, seemed to possess a nature religion of polymorphous deities until they were influenced by the Roman cosmology. Caesar wrote that the Celts did not depict their gods as human forms, but the hundreds of images from the Roman period testify that this was soon to change. What is more, the many hundreds of different god names from cult statues and shrines show the rigid Celtic 'pantheon' of medieval Welsh and Irish literature to be a literary conceit.

Caesar's description of the Celtic gods is very close to Tacitus's list of Germanic deities. Mercury, Caesar records, is their chief god, followed by Apollo, Mars, Jupiter and Minerva. Apart from Apollo, these seem very close to Woden, Tiw, Thunor and Frig. The Celtic Mercury was in all probability a god named Lug – depicted with ravens, he was a god of magic and the underworld and he possessed a magical spear. In one Irish epic, he stands on one leg and closes one eye – a druidic posture that might explain the single eye of Odin (*see* page 46). This divine figure was most likely the same god as Odin, a fact that has prompted some to speculate that Odin was borrowed wholesale from Celts.[13] But such supposed 'borrowings' were in all probability based on an underlying similarity of god-concepts between the two peoples. The Gallic Jupiter, for instance, named *Sucellos* (the 'good striker') and depicted with a hammer, was known in the Rhineland as *Taranis* (the thunderer) mentioned by the Roman poet Lucan as one of three main Celtic deities. Taranis is undoubtedly the same being as the Thunor/Thor of Germanic myth.

However, whether gods were borrowed or not, it was perhaps the Romanized Celtic influence in the Rhineland that catalyzed the Germans to begin personifying their deified natural forces, for the early Germanic religion seems to have been an animistic nature religion devoid of such imagery. As Caesar writes:

The only beings they recognize as gods are things that they can see, and by which they are obviously benefited, such as Sun, Moon, and Fire; the other gods they have never even heard of.

This seems to reflect Bede's calendar, with its solar and lunar empha-sis, more than the gods of Asgard found in Norse literature. But perhaps the fact that such elemental forces of nature and fertility seem so at odds with the later Norse pantheons is because they were actually an *entirely different* family of gods. It might be that Bede's Anglo-Saxon calendar with its sun and moon worship and its unique goddesses were a survival from isolated Denmark of an older order of worship.

The Vanir: the Older Gods

The Norse myths inform us that the Aesir were not the only divine beings in the cosmos. There had once existed an earlier race of gods, and especially goddesses, known as the *Vanir*. The Vanir were gods of joy and fertility, of the earth and waters; of growth and increase. The Vanir and Aesir, so the legends say, were once at war, but hostages were exchanged and peace was made; indeed many of the Aesir took brides from the Vanir.[14]

First amongst the Vanir were the twin gods Freyr ('Lord') and Freyja ('Lady'), said to be the twin children of Njorthr, a god of the oceans. Freyr owned a magical ship and a golden boar, and rode around the countryside on a wagon bringing fertility. His sister (said to be his lover) was a mistress of magic; about her neck hung the fabled necklace of the Brisings – the Brisingamen. Freyr ruled Vana-heim (home of the Vanir) but was also linked to Alfheim (the home of the elves), the elemental or ancestral spirits of the landscape. These were not gods 'up there' but forces in the natural world – the sort of numina one might perceive in a grove of trees or a spring, forces of the fructifying earth: Caesar's 'things that they can see, and by which they are obviously benefited' (*see* pages 44–45).

Given the evidence of the Anglo-Saxon calendar, with the god-desses and 'Mothers' not found in the later Norse Aesir pantheon, it might be that the Aesir played a relatively minor role within the Old English religion, and the religion of the seven tribes of the Cimbric peninsula. The ancient paganism of the Old English, who were less culturally forward than their southern German (Roman-influenced) neighbours, is likely to have been more concerned with the Vanir and with rites to ensure a good harvest, at least in Tacitus's day, than with gods of battle. The festival of Modranicht (Night of the Mothers) certainly suggests this: The Vanir had among their ranks goddesses with names that can be translated as 'the giver' such as *Gefn* (another name for Freyja) and *Gefion*, (also likely to be Freyja in another guise). This same element has been found in the names of a number of goddesses to whom shrines were set up in the Roman period in the eastern Rhine area (and in Celtic areas, too). Bearing titles such as *Gabiae* (richly giving), the images carved of them usually show three beings, often associated with horns of plenty and fruit, known collectively as '*Matronae*' (the Mothers).[15] The Modranicht mentioned by Bede suggest that in the Old English religion it may have been the 'Mothers', the giving goddesses of the Vanir, who had the upper hand.

If the Aesir were indeed the foremost gods amongst the warrior aristocracy which constituted a small percentage of the invaders, at the same time countless anonymous shrines may have existed to other tutelary deities whose names we do not recognize as those of gods, such as the mythical giant Wade whose name probably lies behind Watling Street. Alternatively, it might be that Woden, depicted by Snorri as a latecomer to the Norse pantheon (as was his Celtic counterpart Lugh in Irish myth), arrived in England later than the Vanir cult.

In either case, the presumed Vanir religion of the Anglo-Saxons is one that can be traced back to their continental ancestors who, in turn, were the descendants of the mound-builders of the Neolithic and Bronze Ages. As Tacitus pointed out, there was something unique about the religion of the tribes of Old Denmark that set them apart from their contemporaries – and this something was of great import to the themes of *Beowulf*.

CHAPTER FOUR

•

IN DREAD WATERS

> Grendel's mother herself, a monstrous ogress ... had been
> doomed to dwell in dread waters, in the chilling currents,
> because of that blow whereby Cain became the killer of his
> brother ... to inhabit the wastelands.
>
> BEOWULF, 1258–65

To THE AUDIENCE who first heard *Beowulf* as a spoken poem in its native tongue, the land of the sea-coasts of Denmark and its inhabitants would have been as familiar as the characters in modern soap-operas are to us today. This early English audience still considered themselves a Baltic people – the centre of their world was Old Germania, its stories were their stories, and the *Ingwine* were their own ancestors. Accordingly, they would have been intimate with the background details of the tales which are no longer available to us. And elements of the poem that would have seemed obvious to them may go unnoticed by us – ironies and puns that pass us by might have left them gasping or howling – and this might include the original identity of the lake-dwelling fiends of the poem.

In the poem, Beowulf journeys to Denmark and encounters two monstrous creatures whose abode is a dark, mysterious body of water. This lake, over which bend ash trees thick with hoar frost, is littered with discarded armour and weaponry, with which Beowulf is able to kill Grendel's mother. While these could simply be imagined locations and creatures – the invention of the *scop*, the storyteller – what Tacitus tells us of rites of the Ingaevones makes this doubtful; the audience are likely to have known of such weapon-filled lakes (*see* page 35) and the major part they played in the heathen rites of their Vanir-worshipping forebears, so recently put aside.

According to Tacitus, the Anglii and their neighbouring six tribes, isolated behind their ramparts of rivers and woods, had something in common that made them stand out from the other tribes of Germania:

> They share a common worship of Nerthus, or Mother Earth. They believe that she takes part in human affairs, riding in a chariot among her people. On an island of the sea stands an inviolate grove, in which, veiled with a cloth, is a chariot that none but the priest may touch. The priest can feel the presence of the goddess in this holy of holies, and attends her with deepest reverence as her chariot is drawn along by cows. Then follow days of rejoicing and merrymaking in every place that she condescends to visit and sojourn in. No one goes to war, no one takes up arms; every iron object is locked away. Then, and then only, are peace and quiet known and welcomed, until the goddess, when she has had enough of the society of men, is restored to her sacred precinct by the priest. After that, the chariot, the vestments, and (believe it if you will) the goddess herself, are cleansed in a secluded lake. This service is performed by slaves who immediately afterwards are drowned in the lake. Thus mystery begets terror and a pious reluctance to ask what that sight can be which is seen only by men doomed to die.

Roman writers have often been accused of fabricating or exaggerating accounts of barbaric atrocities, most often by those seeking to remove their perpetrators (most usually the Celts) from any reports that might tarnish their idealized image.[1] Perhaps because writers on Germanic paganism have never been inspired to filter out the atrocities of these peoples in order to make them more palatable to a modern audience, the accounts of Germanic sacrifice found in contemporary sources have never really been questioned – and probably rightly so. In Uppsala in Sweden, according to the 11th-century Adam of Bremen, sacrifices were held every nine years in which nine of every kind of animal was sacrificed; he reports seeing dogs, horses and men hanging in the same bloody groves. A similar rite is recorded in Denmark: every nine years, reported Thietmar of Merseburg, possibly aping Adam's numbers, ninety men were offered with horses, dogs and cocks to the powers of the underworld at a site known as Lejre, on Zealand.[2] This site, which had been an important centre of ritual activity since the megalithic age, had later become the capital of the Scylding dynasty, according to Danish legend. This is supported by excavations of massive feasting halls dating from the early Viking period. It will become evident why there is good reason to connect Lejre with the location of the hall of Heorot in *Beowulf* (*see* page 7).

The Bog People

The remains of numerous Iron Age bodies recovered from the 'dread waters' of peat bogs throughout Denmark suggest that Tacitus's reference to the drowning of the slaves who took part in the Nerthus rite was based on reality. Such individuals are preserved by the acidic tannins in the peat bogs: although often dissolving the bones, they cure the skin into a leathery hide. The soft tissue is preserved to the extent that not only can the features be distinguished, but also the hair, expression and fingerprints; indeed, save for the bronzed colour of the skin, these individuals would look as if they were sleeping peacefully – were it not for the evidence of ritual murder.[3]

The serene expression of the man found at Tollund in Jutland in 1950 (*see* page 5) belies the fact that he died a violent death: a 5-ft noose was plaited about his neck, from which he was hung before being placed in the bog. Tollund man allows us to come face to face with what is probably a Jute, an ancestor of the men of Kent. He was found lying on his side, wearing nothing but a leather girdle, the noose about his neck, and a pointed leather cap, like that of a pixie – a bog elf. He was clean shaven, his chin and top lip peppered with red stubble; his short hair hidden by the cap. The hair of such 'bog-people' is usually a fiery copper or red, tanned like the skin, against which it shows up well. Indeed, the figure of Iron John in the Grimm's fairy tale of the same name, with rust-red hair, found when a pool in a forest is drained, suggests that such remains have turned up throughout history.[4]

After the discovery of the Tollund man, PV Glob (already mentioned in connection with ancestor veneration and with the Mound People; see pages 30 and 33), an archaeology professor from Aarhus University, was called to the scene. He describes in his book *The Bog People* how the man was placed in a wooden case and lifted on to a horse-drawn cart from where he journeyed by train to the National Museum of Denmark at Copenhagen. The box was very heavy, and one of the workers collapsed with a heart attack. Glob writes:

> The bog claimed a life for a life; or, as some may prefer to think, the old gods took a modern man in place of the man from the past.

Glob was also called in two years later, following the discovery of another body, found in Nebel Mose by workers from Grauballe (after whom he is named). Initially, Grauballe man was just a head sticking out of the peat, his features twisted, throat slit from ear to ear, nearly severing the gullet. He too was naked. He has recently been carbon-dated to 291 BC.

Of the many hundreds of bodies that have been found, some were strangled and cut – such as the man at Borremose, who was buried in an old peat cutting in a cross-legged position: he had a triple-knotted hemp rope around his throat, severe injuries to his skull and a slit jugular; this mirrored the death of the Lindow body, found in Cheshire, which revealed this also to have been a rite amongst other Iron Age north-west European peoples.[5]

Debate has continued over whether these people were the victims of human sacrifice or had died from other causes. Clearly, some of the many remains found in peat bogs would have been victims of accidental drowning or of crimes of passion, or even offerings to the gods of prisoners of war (such as the severed head from Osterby, Old Anglia, wearing the knotted hairstyle of the Anglii's southern neighbours and foes, the Suebi). Others, like the girl found at Windeby in Schleswig Holstein, blindfolded and drowned with half her hair shorn, might have been victims of capital punishment. Tacitus records that if a wife was found to be adulterous, her husband shaved her head, stripped her naked and flogged her through the village. Both the Windeby girl and the remains of a man nearby were pressed down into the bog with birch branches, matching what Tacitus records as the punishment for a sexual crime. Alternatively, some have suggested that her blindfold marks her out as a seer, a shaman. There are, however, a number of distinguishing signs that point to possible victims of sacrifice. They are usually naked, often exhibit more than one single method of death and, pointing away from them being common criminals, the victims have smooth hands. This lack of the calluses associated with either manual work or the use of weapons (at least not for some time prior to their deaths) points either to an aristocratic or a priestly caste, rather than slaves as Tacitus described.

The Last Supper

One final but significant clue that these victims have in common is a shared 'last meal'. Analysis of the stomach contents of some of the more recent bog finds shows that their last meals consisted of a vegetable gruel made from grains and seeds.[6] As there were no traces of fruit in this porridge, it is widely assumed that these people did not die in the spring, summer or autumn. They had met their deaths in the winter, perhaps at the midwinter festival itself. One other substance of note discovered in the stomachs of both Tollund and Grauballe man was a large amount of a poisonous parasitic fungus named ergot (*Claviceps purpurea*). This fungus grows on barley and rye in regions with a damp climate, and not only gives the seeds an unpleasant look, but, more importantly, it is so toxic as to cause vasoconstriction, sensations of burning and, if ingested in any quantity, death. Major outbreaks of ergotism, as the illness caused by this fungus is known (or 'St Anthony's fire' as it was called in the Middle Ages after the horrendous burning sensations its sufferers experienced), were once common in the past. In 994, some 40,000 people died in Aquitaine alone after eating bread made from ergotized grain. Those who did not die experienced convulsions and massive vasoconstriction leading to gangrene and the loss of limbs. The toxins also produced mind-altering effects such as the sensation of flight or of changing into an animal. This was due to the hallucinogenic alkaloids the fungus contains, including lysergic acid (LSD). The fungus was not only ingested accidentally. In the medieval period it was used to induce labour, or, in greater doses, abortion.[7]

The presence of ergot in the stomachs of the bog victims brings to mind a number of intriguing possibilities. Were these people purposely sedated before being killed? Did the inclusion of the toxic grain suggest a failure of the harvest for which reason the individual was being offered up to the gods to solicit their help? Or was the ergot taken specifically for its hallucinogenic qualities? (This last question is examined at some length later; *see* page 82.)

Glob was adamant that the 'bog people', as he called them, were the 'slaves' reported by Tacitus as meeting their end in the rites of the goddess Nerthus. Putting aside for the moment their possible identities, there is more evidence for this cult than the bodies alone – the peat bogs of Denmark have also offered up the very wagons on which the goddess was processed throughout the land.

The Wagon Goddess

The most striking of these ritual wagons are from Dejbjerg on the west side of Jutland, where two wagons were discovered in a bog in the 1880s – and thought to date to around AD 200.[8] The bronze mountings and fine detail on these wagons show that they were not used for transporting grain or for casual farm use. One wagon contained an elaborate alder-wood stool for the 'goddess' to sit on, and part of a loom was found in one of the many pots deposited with the vehicle, suggesting a female occupant or, at the very least, female symbolism.

Another richly ornamented wagon was found accompanying the 9th-century boat burial of a high-ranking lady, together with a female attendant, at Oseberg. Found with nuts and apples, items commonly depicted in the laps of the divine 'Mothers', this was accompanied by tapestries depicting a man and woman standing beside a wagon.

But it was at Rappendam in the north of Zealand that the greatest deposit was found. This major find consisted of 28 wheels and 13 hubs deposited over a period of time and was associated with the remains of a male skeleton and the bones of animals, including cattle, horse, wild pig and sheep. Near to the Rappendam lake is a place named Jørlinde, which perhaps derives from the name Njorthr – the father in Norse myth of Freyr and Freyja, the chief gods of the Vanir. Njorthr was also a fertility deity associated with water, whose name is directly related to Nerthus (*see* page 53). Another place name on Zealand – Niartharum (modern-day Naerum, north of Copenhagen) – also suggests a connection with this deity.[9]

Zealand is mentioned in the Norse *Edda* of Snorri Sturluson in a tale named *Gylfaginning* (the trickery of Gylfi). Gylfi was a Swedish king who offered a vagrant woman, in exchange for 'entertainment', as much land as she could plough with four oxen in one night. Unbeknown to Gylfi, this lady was the goddess Gefion (possibly a form of Frejya, *see* page 51). She took four magical oxen from the land of the giants in the north (they were her four enchanted sons from a union with a giant), and they drew a plough that cut so deep that it separated the land from Sweden, the land floating west to form Zealand. Here she is said to have lived with Skjold, son of Odin, at Lejre; Skjold being the same figure as Scyld Scefing of *Beowulf* – head of the Skjoldung dynasty of Denmark (*see* chart 4). It seems that Gefion's Lejre, where Thietmar of Merseburg reported mass sacrifice (*see* page 54), may have been the cult capital of Nerthus's island, and that Nerthus and Gefion were one goddess – Gefion ('the Giver'), like Freyja, ('the Lady'), being a title rather than a personal name. Also, the name Gefion is related to the Old English *geofon*, a word used to suggest bodies of water such as rivers, lakes or the sea. It is feasible that this word was derived from the title of the lake goddess in the same way that our modern word 'ocean' is derived from the fish-tailed Titan Okeanos of Greek myth, who controlled the seas.[10]

Anyone studying *Beowulf* cannot help wonder whether the dread lake of Grendel and his mother into which Beowulf dives might not be such a sacred lake or bog as we find both in Tacitus's written record (*see* page 53) and archaeologically in the ritual depositions of Old Denmark. Intriguingly, the poet himself seems to leave us a veiled clue to this possibility: Before Beowulf sets off to seek Grendel's mother, the Geatish hero comments that even though she may try to hide he will find her. He describes the locales she will flee into:

> I can promise you this, she will not protect herself from hiding in any fold of the field, in any forest of the mountain, in any dingle of the sea, dive where she will! (*Beowulf*, 1391–4)

But the actual words the poet uses, translated here as 'dingle of the sea', are *gyfenes grund*, a phrase that could literally be translated as 'Gefion's ground', in other words the abode of the water goddess. The use of this turn of phrase may provide evidence, albeit in the form of a pun, that the lake-abode of Grendel and his kin were the same sacred lakes of the goddess Gefion/Nerthus and that the Beowulf poet and, perhaps, his audience, knew enough of the old religion to make sense of this.

★　　★　　★

In Part I we have seen how the English people, amongst whom the tale of Beowulf developed, were immigrants from Denmark and the German coasts – members of a tribal network known as the Ingaevones – and that their ancient religion seems to have been more goddess-oriented than that of the later Vikings as suggested by Norse myths. They celebrated an ancient festival called 'Night of the Mothers' within a ritual calendar dealing with the farming year, connecting them both to the 'triple mothers' of archaeology and to a family of gods known as the Vanir, who seem to have been more ancient divinities than the Thor and Odin of later Norse myth. Cut off from the rest of Germania by forests and streams, it seems that the Vanir cult had remained strong amongst the 'English' Ingaevones. And ritual sites, such as the lake of the wagons at Jørlinde, point to the fact that just 250 years before they crossed the channel and entered the history of the British Isles, the English were still taking part in sacrificial rites to an ancient Vanir goddess whose sacrificial victims may have been hung and drowned at midwinter.

But what were the origins of this Vanir cult and what is its importance to the tale of Beowulf's struggle with Grendel and his mother in the ancient goddess lakes of Old Denmark? Might the heroic elegy that is *Beowulf* really be concerned with the cults and gods of a long-lost religion? The first clues to such a possibility come in the form of the figure of Scyld Scefing, with whom the poem starts and who, in Norse tradition, was husband of Gefion. And it is the true identity of Scyld Scefing – who was not really a mortal hero at all – that tells us much about the real background to *Beowulf*.

Part II

GODS AND MONSTERS

CHAPTER FIVE

·

SCYLD SCEFING

SCYLD (SHIELD), the child brought by the sea to the shores of Denmark, appears in Beowulf as the eponymous ancestor of the Danish royal line, the Scyldings. It is with him that the poem begins, setting the scene for the events of his great-grandson Hrothgar's rule (*see* page 7).

He who arrives from the sea eventually returns to it – his body set adrift in a boat, surrounded by swords and armour; on his breast great treasures; above his head a gold standard. Thus he returns back to those mysterious and unnamed powers that set him adrift many years before.

The image of the wave-born prince is a powerful and dramatic one. It is thought that Tennyson made use of it in his *Idylls of the King* when he imagines Arthur arriving at Tintagel on the Cornish coast not from the womb of Ygerna, but from the dark sea itself;[1] and, in his hour of passing, when his body is taken away by ship, Sir Bedivere hears this mysterious phrase:

From the great deep to the great deep he goes.

From the start, the figure of Scyld, like that of Arthur, seems to possess a quality more than human. Scyld, at least in the manner of his arrival into and departure from this world, was no mortal man. There is something mythical about him and clearly we are not intended to take *Beowulf* at face value and see Scyld as simply a warrior ancestor, a man under whose rule the Danes achieved dominance over the kings of neighbouring tribes. Fortunately, the name and deeds of Scyld do appear outside of the poem, and what they suggest is most intriguing.

In King Alfred's day, during a renaissance in education and learning, the royal genealogy of Wessex was extended so that it contained as many generations as that of the house of David, thereby enabling the royal house to trace its ancestry all the way back to Adam rather than to the god Woden of their heathen forefathers.[2] To achieve this, the original list had to be extended and numerous gaps in the royal Wessex line somehow filled. To this end, figures from existing Anglo-Saxon tradition were used – figures who were considered worthy enough to be described as ancestors of the king. The three figures that topped the list of newcomers were the strangely named *Scef* (Sheaf), *Scyld* (Shield) and *Beow* (Barley).

The proximity of this list to the genealogy of the Scyldings in *Beowulf* is clear – here, too, Scyld (Scefing) is the father of Beow. But who is *Scef* (Sheaf), whose name appears above that of Scyld in the Wessex family tree? A 975 gloss on this figure, found in the genealogy of *ealdorman* Aethelweard, contains some details about him:

This Sheaf came to land in a light boat, surrounded by weapons, on an island in the ocean which is called Scani. He was indeed a very young child and unknown to the folk of that land. However they took him up and looked after him as carefully as if he were one of their own kin and afterwards elected him king.

From this it is apparent that the figure called *Scef* (Sheaf) in the Wessex genealogy fulfils the same role as attributed to Scyld Scefing (Shield *Sheafson* in *Beowulf*). It seems that the son has inherited the father's myth – a myth that was cunningly used to link him into the biblical family tree, by recording that Scef had been born in Noah's Ark.[3] In 1140, William of Malmesbury recorded a little more about the figure he also calls 'Sheaf':

He was brought as a child in a ship without oars ... he was asleep and a sheaf of corn lay at his head. Therefore he was called Sheaf ...

William records how Sheaf was brought to an isle of Germany called Scandza and went on to reign in Hedeby in Old Anglia: '... from it the Anglii came to Britain.' In other words, Scef was an ancestor of the English, too.

But although the characters of Scef and Scyld seem to share a common story, Scef's absence from *Beowulf* is remarkable. To explain this, it has been suggested that perhaps he was merely an invention. And at first glance, it is tempting to conclude that he was indeed an invented character. Scyld in *Beowulf*, as we have seen, bears the second name *Scefing* – a name that can be interpreted as meaning 'with a sheaf'. However the suffix '-*ing*', in both Old English and the early Germanic languages, can also play the same role as the word '*mac*' or '*mab*' in the Celtic languages; it was the patronymic, meaning 'son of'.[4] In other words, *Scef-ing* can be read as either 'with a sheaf' or 'son of Sheaf'. So it is possible that the royal genealogist (the *thylas*) who constructed the Wessex genealogy interpreted his source as meaning the latter, and inserted at the head of the list a wholly fictitious Scef.

Such an argument would be convincing if it were not for two things. Firstly, would a completely fictional character, invented through a linguistic slip-up, have been allowed to head a royal genealogy if it were common knowledge (at a time when the English oral tradition was still strong) that it was Scyld who was truly the progenitor of the Wessex line? Secondly, the poem *Widsith* (predating *Beowulf*), mentions one *Sceafa* as an ancestor the Langobards, who believed their origins also lay in Scandinavia (*see* page 27).[5] From this early clue, it must be supposed that the Wessex *thylas* was correct and was drawing on ancient traditions when he made Scef and not Scyld the progenitor of their royal line.

In the case of *Beowulf*, the poet (or his immediate source) has deliberately removed the name of the original foundling-hero Scef/Sheaf in order to fit his story into what was known of the Danish sources, which, like *Beowulf*, do not mention Scef. Their version of Scyld, known in Danish as 'Skjold',[6] does not arrive or depart on a boat: the primary role of this thoroughly land-locked youth is that in childhood he wrestles with a bear and is said to be either the son of a man named Dan (the progenitor of the Danes – likely to have been invented solely for this purpose) or the god Odin.

Crying the Neck

The names Scef and Beow suggest these characters are not human ancestors at all but, instead, some kind of personification of the crops: the sheaf of barley, which when cut down at harvest-time yields the seed from which next year's barley will grow. In practical terms, the harvested sheaf really is the 'father' of next year's barley crop.

Until recent times, in farming communities in England and northern Europe, the last sheaf of corn or barley to be cut during the harvest was regarded with a certain reverence, or played a role in one of many farming customs.[7] Often the sheaf was shaped into a basic human form and dressed as a person, or as an animal (such as a wolf), and regarded as the personification of the 'spirit of the corn'. Sometimes the sheaf was kissed as it was placed on the cart that would bear it to the farm, or regaled with song and merrymaking. In parts of England, where this sheaf was called the 'neck', it would be sung to in a ceremony known as 'crying the neck' ('neck' stemming either from the idea of the resemblance of the sheaf to a neck and head, or from the Norse word *'nek/neg'* meaning sheaf).

Sometimes the personified sheaf was burned or thrown into water; a custom that may have been a faded memory of a pagan rite concerning a divinity of the crops. It is reasonable to speculate that the last sheaf in ancient times may have been similarly regarded with special favour as the spirit of the crops, thus entering the imagination and, in time, becoming a deity itself – whose life story mirrored the seasonal death and rebirth of the corn. We find such a personification of the sheaf in the folk song *John Barleycorn,* which is worth quoting in full as it contains many significant images and themes:

> There was three kings into the east,
> Three kings both great and high,
> And they hae sworn a solemn oath
> John Barleycorn should die.

They took a plough and plough'd him down,
Put clods upon his head,
And they hae sworn a solemn oath
John Barleycorn was dead.

But the cheerful Spring came kindly on,
And show'rs began to fall;
John Barleycorn got up again,
And sore surpris'd them all.

The sultry suns of Summer came,
And he grew thick and strong,
His head weel arm'd wi' pointed spears,
That no one should him wrong.

The sober Autumn enter'd mild,
When he grew wan and pale;
His bending joints and drooping head
Show'd he began to fail.

His colour sicken'd more and more,
He faded into age;
And then his enemies began
To show their deadly rage.

They've taen a weapon, long and sharp,
And cut him by the knee;
Then ty'd him fast upon a cart,
Like a rogue for forgerie.

They laid him down upon his back,
And cudgell'd him full sore;
They hung him up before the storm,
And turn'd him o'er and o'er.

They filled up a darksome pit
With water to the brim,
They heaved in John Barleycorn,
There let him sink or swim.

They laid him out upon the floor,
To work him farther woe,
And still, as signs of life appear'd,
They toss'd him to and fro.

They wasted, o'er a scorching flame,
The marrow of his bones;
But a Miller us'd him worst of all,
For he crush'd him between two stones.

And they hae taen his very heart's blood,
And drank it round and round;
And still the more and more they drank,
Their joy did more abound.

John Barleycorn was a hero bold,
Of noble enterprise,
For if you do but taste his blood,
'Twill make your courage rise.

'Twill make a man forget his woe;
'Twill heighten all his joy:
'Twill make the widow's heart to sing,
Tho' the tear were in her eye.

Then let us toast John Barleycorn,
Each man a glass in hand;
And may his great posterity
Ne'er fail in old Scotland!

So powerful is the imagery that perhaps Scef/Sheaf and Beow/ Barley were originally vegetation gods rather than human ancestors. Such vegetal connections were clearly known to the *Beowulf* poet, as demonstrated by the subtle pun he uses concerning Beow, Scyld's son (ln 18):

Bēow wæs brēme, blæd wīde sprang

Beow was renowned, far and wide his **glory** spread

This may also be rendered as:

Barley was renowned, far and wide his **leaf** spread

There are a number of possible traces of a 'barley spirit' in myths. In Norse myth, there is a figure known as *Byggvir* ('Barley man') who is mocked by the god Loki for being a parasite 'by Freyr's ear', by which it appears that the Vanir god Freyr was conceived of as wearing a barley wreath on his head in which the barley spirit dwelt. The cult of this otherwise unheard of figure may have moved with scattered Norse settlers into Finland, where a figure named *Pekko* appears (related phonetically to *Byggvir*) who promoted the growth of barley. Depicted as a child in a corn bin, a wooden image of Pekko was taken into the fields at sowing time. Pekko had two feasts, on moonlit nights in spring and autumn, reminiscent of the *Litha* feast of the Anglo-Saxon calendar. Also, in the Finnish epic *The Kalevala*, there is mention of a character named Sämpsä Pellervoinen, a vegetation deity recorded as coming as a boy from an isle in the ocean, in a 'corn-boat' – just like Sheaf.

It seems likely that Scef and Beow were related to these mythological figures and were personifications of a corn spirit. If this is the case, the question remains as to what Scyld (Shield) was doing between the two in the later genealogies, and why he came to supplant his father in Danish tradition, and as a result, in *Beowulf*. The answer may lie in a long-forgotten ritual and image.

The Sheaf on the Shield

During the reign of Edmund I (941–6), a dispute over a certain piece of land the monks of Abingdon Abbey claimed as theirs was resolved in a very odd manner:

> Appealing to the Judgement of God, the monks put a sheaf of corn, with a lighted taper at its head, onto a round shield and launched the shield into the Thames.

The shield with its sheaf on board circumnavigated the disputed lands (which had flooded) and this therefore 'proved' the land belonged to the Abbey.[8] Not only was this a remarkable way of settling a land dispute, it is also a clue as to how the confusion over Scyld and Scef may have arisen. The ceremonial act undertaken by the monks at Abingdon may have originated in the ancient iconography of the arrival of the corn-spirit. If this is the case, there is a valid reason why a figure named 'Shield' should be associated with these cereal deities, for it refers not originally to a person, but to the mode of transport of the god. But why should the corn deity be imagined as arriving on a boat or shield at all?

There is a possible literal interpretation, in which this deity is somehow connected with the arrival of farming traditions during the Neolithic period, bringing with him the knowledge and practice of cereal farming. Such a god could easily be imagined as arriving by boat, and in the case of the Danish islands and much of Scandinavia, and Britain, this is exactly how knowledge would have arrived. Boats would have sailed from the continental mainland with their hulls full of seed – exactly as in the *Kalevala* myth.

The Solar Boat

There is perhaps an alternative, more symbolic meaning to the image of the shield. In Part I, it was shown that rock carvings in Scandinavia depict the ship above all other religious symbols (*see* page 34); this image clearly had a religious function. The ship often is accompanied by the 'solar disc' pattern – a circle with a cross inside. A similar motif appears in Egyptian iconography, where it represents the solar and lunar barques that sail across the sky bearing the heavenly bodies. While there is an obvious connection between the sun and the growing of the crops, there is also a connection in ancient thought between planting and the phases of the moon, and this was demonstrated by the use of the moon to calculate dates of planting. The crops can, therefore, be said to be *brought by the sun or moon*, in a process depicted figuratively as the plant arriving in the solar or lunar barques – crossing the blue waters of the heavens.

In a similar fashion, the arrival and departure of the sea-born hero in the boat mirror the daily rising of the sun and its setting. This is a

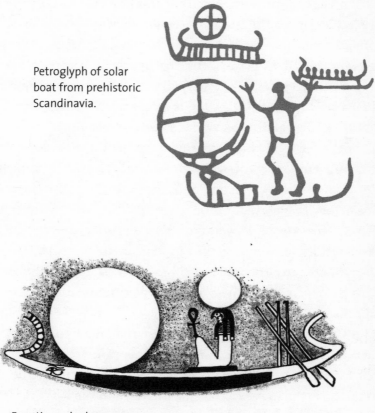

Petroglyph of solar
boat from prehistoric
Scandinavia.

Egyptian solar barque.

particularly strong connection to those living in a coastal zone, such as Scandinavia, where the sun seems to rise from the ocean itself and return thence at night: *from the great deep to the great deep he goes.*

The image of the solar boat helps explain the manner of the cereal god's arrival, but not, at first sight, the use of a shield as a boat. One obvious connection is that the shield in shape does resemble a boat – especially a coracle. In Sumerian myth, the moon god Sin was said to traverse the heavens in an early type of coracle known as a *quffah* which is hemispherical in shape. His choice of the *quffah* as a symbol is apparent to anyone who has seen a half moon sailing over the horizon. If the solar and lunar barques were originally conceived of as hemispherical *quffahs*, in later times, or in distant regions where such craft were unknown, this hemispherical transport could be imagined as a shield.[9, 10]

But the link between the shield and heavenly barque is not mere conjecture: indeed, it seems to be an ancient image, for the solar symbol found on the ships in ancient Scandinavian rock art also appears carried as a shield by the figures of male warriors. This ship–shield connection is also found in northern myth: in the *Edda*, Snorri tells us that 'Ull's ship' is a *kenning* (a poetical image) for a shield, as Ull, a Norse god, *used his shield as a boat.* In Welsh myth, King Arthur's shield bears the same name as his ship, '*Prydwen*': *Prydwen* meaning 'fair aspect' or 'white/shining face', a suitable name for the lunar/solar disk. The name of Arthur's ship appears in Taliesin's poem *The Spoils of the Abyss* (*see* page 130),[11] in which Arthur and his men sail into the underworld to rescue a prisoner and to steal a wondrous cauldron. Similarly, in Egyptian myth the solar barque was thought to enter the underworld in the west each night, do battle with the forces of darkness and emerge triumphant at dawn in the east the next morning.

All these parallels seem to suggest that the figures of Scef and Beow at the start of *Beowulf* were not human ancestors but ancient fertility gods and that the figure of Scyld, as found in the Danish genealogies and in *Beowulf* itself, stems from the image of the heavenly shield-boat that brings the crops.

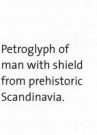

Petroglyph of
man with shield
from prehistoric
Scandinavia.

Rejecting Sheaf

Scyld rather than Scef seems to be the 'invented' figure: an anthropo-
morphized image of the corn-bearing ship. But why did the Danes
not recognize the figure of Sheaf in their genealogies? It seems as if all
notion of Sheaf the fertility god was erased deliberately from the
Danish version of the Scylding family tree and in his place there was
elevated the 'invented' figure of Scyld (Skjold, son of Odin), whose
name suggested a more fitting ancestry for the military aristocracy of
the Danes.

When the English *Beowulf* poet draws on Danish tradition he is in
a position to know all about Scef and the true ancestry of Scyld as the
vessel in which the corn god arrived, but rather than impose his own
country's traditions on to those of the Danes, he makes a compromise.
He too makes Scyld a man, the ultimate ancestor of the Danes, but he
gives him Scef's sea-borne arrival, referring to the veiled existence of
Scef by calling Scyld the 'Scefing'. And, in time, when the Wessex
genealogist compiles his new family tree, he reinstates Scef to his true
position, but follows *Beowulf* in giving Scyld a human identity.

This foray into the quagmire of genealogical invention and corn
gods (what Tolkien referred to as 'a most astonishing tangle')[12] helps
us conclude that although influenced by Danish tradition, *Beowulf*

begins with the veiled tale of the arrival and departure of an ancient god, a cereal deity known as an ancestor by the peoples of Scandinavia, including the English, but whom the Danes had purged from their royal family tree.

While on the surface this may not seem relevant to the deeds of the monster-slaying *Beowulf*, in the next chapter it becomes apparent how the worship of Scef/Sheaf was based on an ecstatic Neolithic farming religion whose use of a sacred intoxicant reveals parallels with the last meal of the bog men and the wagon ritual of Nerthus. In fact, the rites of Sheaf have *everything* to do with the dreaded lakes of pagan Denmark, and there is good reason why the Danes sought to distance themselves from this deity.

CHAPTER SIX

·

THE BARLEY GOD

T HE FIGURES OF SHEAF and his offspring Barley of Old English
tradition are not alone in myth as personifications of cereal gods.
A number of divinities in the ancient world had lives mirroring the
seasonal death and rebirth of vegetation. Complex mythologies grew
up around these divine figures, but they all keep to the basic pattern
found in the folk song *John Barleycorn* (*see* page 66). The earliest
recorded forms of the Barleycorn myth are in the Mesopotamian
story of Tammuz and Inanna (or Ishtar), in which the young god
Tammuz is killed, bringing on the winter, and prompting his wife
Inanna to descend into the underworld to beg for his release.[1]

This motif reappears in the search of the Egyptian Isis for her
green-skinned husband Osiris, and in the Greek goddess Demeter's
search for her daughter, Persephone (revealing that the vegetation
spirit was not necessarily a male figure). What is known of Tammuz's
rites shows that they were accompanied by a great public outpouring
of grief, a fact even mentioned in the Bible (Ezekiel 8:14):

> Then he brought me to the door of the gate of the Lord's house which
> was toward the north; and, behold, there sat women weeping for
> Tammuz.

The myth of Tammuz closely resembles that of the Norse Balder (*see*
page 47). Balder (whose name also means 'lord' as well as, possibly,
'the swollen one'), son of Odin and husband of Nanna, is slain by his

blind brother Hodr, resulting in the loss of Earth's fertility. Hel, the goddess of the underworld, agrees to release him if all creation weeps for him, but Loki in disguise does not and he remains Hel's prisoner until the day of doom.

One of the best-known forms of the vegetal god is the Greek Adonis – from the Phoenician *Adon* (Lord) – a Middle Eastern god who entered Greek myth as the lover of Aphrodite. Adonis, normally represented as a beautiful youth born from a myrrh tree, was gored in the thigh by a boar while hunting on Mount Lebanon and sent down into the underworld. The land above, however, became blighted in his absence, and following the outpourings of grief by all creation, he was allowed to return to the upper world for a period of each year but must return to the underworld every winter.[2]

The Phrygian form of Adonis was the goddess Cybele's castrated son/spouse named Attis, who was either killed by a boar or self-emasculated while standing under a pine tree. His death and resurrection were celebrated in ancient Rome at the spring equinox (21 March) when a pine tree was brought in from the woods, bedecked with flowers, and an image of the god placed on it. On 24 March, the god was seen to die, symbolized by his priest (named Attis after the god) drawing blood from his arms. On 25 March, Attis was seen to rise again, so providing later Christians with the traditional date of Easter.[3]

Farming Metaphors

The origin of the imagery found in these myths is clear. The wounding of the god in the thigh or his self-emasculation (like Attis) is derived from the act of harvesting the corn: it is the separation of the generative organ (the seed) from the main plant. (Just as John Barleycorn is cut down 'at the knee', so the wound dealt to the god is to the thigh.) When the god is in the underworld (the seed in the soil), the land lies barren for the winter. The image of castration is perhaps the earlier image, arising as it does from the idea of a self-seeded plant. The wounding of the god by the tusks of the boar is a later farming-based metaphor, the curved tusk of the boar representing the curved blade of a sickle.

It is important to recognize that while the folk song *John Barleycorn* was simply a metaphor for the crops, the gods of the ancient fertility religions were more than symbols for vegetal growth: they were the forces of nature – the force of continued creation itself. Ancient man did not worship the corn but rather the spirit that animated it, the same spirit that animated the ever-turning sun, the waxing and waning moon, and, ultimately, the death and resurrection of mankind.

Osiris is the most evocative of vegetal deities, perhaps because of his numerous portrayals in Egyptian art as green-skinned and serene, seated on his throne, with a tall white crown on his head. With his wife, his twin sister Isis, he is said to have brought the gift of cereal farming to mankind, journeying around the world (presumably by boat) spreading the knowledge of farming and of pacifism. His demise comes when he is tricked into a coffin by his jealous brother Seth and cast adrift on the Nile. The coffin washes ashore at Byblos in Syria and grows into a sycamore tree that is cut down and used as a pillar in a local palace. When Isis discovers its whereabouts, she travels to Byblos and becomes the nurse to the young prince of the palace. By day, she secretly burns the prince in a fire to give him immortality, while at night she flies in the form of a hawk around the pillar containing her husband. Eventually, she obtains his release, takes his body and hides it in the marshes of the Nile, begetting by it the hawk-headed god Horus. The evil Seth, however, stumbles upon his brother's body while hunting a boar during the full moon and dismembers the corpse into 14 pieces, which Isis collects in a *corn sieve* and puts back together. Using her magic, she resurrects her husband, who goes on to rule in the underworld, where he becomes the judge of the dead.[4]

Like those of Attis and Adonis, the rites of Osiris are reminiscent of the Germanic Sheaf. His annual festival began with the ploughing of land and, after his death, on the third day of the festival a boat was taken down to the waters of the Nile, and a golden vessel filled with

Osiris as the growing corn.

Nile water. A paste was made out of this water and a certain type of vegetable mould, and fashioned into a sickle shape, which was then clothed, placed in the boat, and brought back to the temple, whereon all shouted 'Osiris is found!' The resurrection of Osiris, whose prone body is often shown with corn springing from it, was symbolized by the erection of the *Djed* or 'stability' column, a symbolized *bound sheaf of corn*, showing that in Egypt, as amongst the Germans, honour was given to the newborn 'sheaf' in a boat.[5]

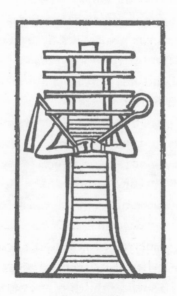

The Djed pillar.

While these gods may appear far removed from the Dark Age Beowulf and the monstrous Grendel and his mother, there is no doubt that Osiris and the rest have a great affinity to the figure of Sheaf/Scyld. The similarity is more than coincidental. As this mythology is clearly linked with the practice of growing crops, we can surmise that its observance spread with farming and arrived in Scandinavia from the Middle East in the Neolithic age. The well- documented cults of the Middle East provide us with a window into the rites that would have been practised in the prehistoric chambered tombs of Denmark by the ancestors of the Ingaevones. We can almost be sure that the families of the Mound People and the girl at Egtved (*see* page 34) would have known a form of this myth; the solar disk on her belly and the barley drink by her side indicate this. But it is the Greek god Dionysos who reveals that there was a link not just between this cereal deity and Sheaf but also the wagon-borne Vanir goddess Nerthus, whom the Mound People's descendants worshipped in the Iron Age.

Dionysos

Dionysos (the Bacchus of the Romans), whose cult reached classical Greece from Anatolia, was a god of wine and ecstasy. Born of the goddess Semele (a name related to an old Greek word for earth) and Zeus, he was torn apart by the Titans and his body parts boiled in a cauldron. Subsequently, he was rescued and reconstituted by Rhea, his grandmother. Other versions of the myth call him 'son of Demeter', and state that it was she who brought him back to life.[6]

Dionysos was credited with the invention of wine on Mount Nysa in Libya, and was depicted as an effeminate man with flowing curly locks. He was driven mad and wandered throughout Asia *on a chariot* accompanied by wild women named maenads, and by satyrs, spreading knowledge of winemaking just as Osiris had spread knowledge of cereal farming. He journeyed to Egypt, India and, eventually, Boeotia and then to Thebes, where King Pentheus opposed him and tried to imprison him, but ended up being rent apart by the possessed maenads – his head torn from his body by his own mother Agave.

Dionysos continued his journey through the Aegean, now on board a ship, and caused the oars to become serpents, himself a lion, and a vine to grow up the mast. Eventually, he ascended to heaven to live amongst the immortals, the Olympian gods.

The origin of Dionysos is complex. In the person of the god of wine, he is a late arrival in classical Athens, though it seems that he and his cult of ritual intoxication were ancient. What was new was his championing of the sacramental vine, for he had existed much longer as a cereal god. Some scholars have traced his worship back to Neolithic Crete, where he was known as Zagreus. When Arthur Evans excavated the site of Knossos, he unearthed small cups decorated with ears of barley which may have been used in ceremonies to Zagreus. It is clear that barley beer preceded wine as the ritual drink of the 'mysteries', as the rites of these dying and resurrecting gods were known; this was the same cereal intoxicant found in Skara Brae and in the beakers of megalithic Europe. The connection between Dionysos and the cereal intoxicant is indicated in a number of his epithets, including 'Bromios' and 'Sabazios'. *Bromios*, often thought to mean 'fire-born' actually means 'oat-born' or 'wheat-born' and *Sabazios*, so the Greek historian Amianus Marcellinus tells us, is derived from *Sabaia*, a barley intoxicant.[7]

Scholars have long held that the rites of Dionysos – performed before an audience – were the true origin of theatre, the word 'tragedy' stemming from the word *tragos* meaning goat, after the goat-satyrs who accompanied him on his revels. But a more plausible suggestion, especially in view of the fact that the satyrs were latecomers to the god's cult, is that the word stems from another meaning of *tragos*, 'spelt', which is a cereal, a relative of wheat, used at the time for brewing. In reality, the tragedy was the ritual enactment of the life and death of the cereal god.

It is plain that the original Dionysos was not the son of Zeus and Semele but, as the god of cereals and intoxicating cereal drinks, the son of Demeter. The name Demeter most likely derives from a Cretan name, 'Deo-Meter' (barley mother), and her rituals provide us with a striking connection between the fertility religions of the Middle East and the Nerthus rites of the Ingaevones.

The Mysteries

The mysteries of Demeter and her daughter Persephone were cele-brated annually at Eleusis near Athens for some 2,000 years, until Alaric the Goth sacked the sanctuary in AD 396. The myth behind the rituals that were performed followed the same basic divine pattern: Persephone is abducted by Hades, lord of the underworld, and her mother Demeter goes to find her so that the winter that has descended on the world might end. Like the Egyptian Isis, Demeter becomes the nurse of a child (here named Demophoön) whom she burns in a flame in order to endow him with immortality, and is even-tually successful in freeing Persephone, at least for a portion of the year. The mysteries at Eleusis make clear that the rites of the corn deity were not simply enacted to guarantee a good harvest, but they also appeared to grant a personal spiritual revelation, offering a sense of immortality to their celebrants.[8]

Although it will never be known exactly what this experience was, it was achieved during the observation of a ritual drama based on the death and rebirth of the god, and by performing a ritual act involving sacred objects. What may have played a part in this trans-forming experience, however, was the mental state caused by a nine-day preparatory fast followed by the taking of the ritual drink called *kykeon*. The initiates spoke the following words of this act:

> I fasted; I drank the kykeon; I took out of the chest; having done my task, I put again into the basket, and from the basket again into the chest.

What exactly did the initiates put into the 'basket'? The most proba-ble explanation is that it was a symbol of Dionysos, a wooden phallus. While this might seem slightly laughable, to the ancient Greeks the image was suggestive of a lot more than lewd humour. The phallus in the basket is better understood when it is realized that this was a *win-nowing basket*, known in Greece as a *liknon*, the corn sieve in which Isis assembled the dismembered body parts of Osiris. The winnowing basket was used in farming to separate the seed from the chaff, and it contained the new seed reaped from the body of the parent plant; it was also commonly used as a cradle for newborn babies. The phallus placed in the basket by the initiates at Eleusis was the 'seed' of the cereal god, threshed from the sheaf, and represented the new life come from the death of the old. In his reborn form, Dionysos was known as *Liknites,* 'he of the winnowing basket', and was depicted in Greek religious art as a newborn baby sitting in the basket accompanied by the cereal crop.

The winnowing basket was a shallow *shield*-shaped object, and this in itself suggests that the idea of the arrival of the newborn Sheaf in the shield/boat may also have been derived in part from this ancient farming practice of winnowing.

Ergot

There is further evidence to link the practices at Eleusis with those of ancient Denmark aside from the obvious link between Sheaf and *Liknites.* The *kykeon* ('mixed drink') drunk by the initiates at Eleusis was more than a simple barley beer. Evidence suggests that it had an active ingredient that aided the initiates to see more in the winnowing basket than a simple wooden object. It is known that the secret of Eleusis was linked to the kykeon, as some of this drink was stolen by Alcibiades in 415 BC and served to his dinner guests – an act that was seen as both scandalous and sacrilegious.

It is now thought that the kykeon was made using *ergot* – the toxic fungus containing hallucinogenic alkaloids that grows on barley and rye grains (*see* page 56). Ingestion of ergotized grains was very dangerous, but in small, measured, doses the kykeon may have offered its imbibers quite a 'trip'.[9]

Large doses of ergotized grains were also found in the stomachs of the Danish bog men, those individuals who may have died as sacrificial victims to the wagon-deity Nerthus in her sacred lake (*see* page 57). Together, this constitutes firm evidence that the ancestors of the English were worshipping the same kind of gods as the more 'civilized' peoples of Rome and Greece far to their south. Where they may have differed, however, is in how these gods were represented.

Wagons, Ships and Drownings

In their rites, the fertility gods of the Near East were usually depicted by wooden images: Attis was a carved wooden figure hung on a pine tree, Osiris was either a wooden statue or a carved Djed pillar, and Dionysos was also either a wooden carving or a phallic pillar. What links these gods more firmly with the Nerthus rite described by Tacitus is the way these images were carried.

In Athens, the wooden image of Dionysos was paraded through the streets on either a common cart or a ship on rollers – as befitting a god who spread the knowledge of wine by both land and sea – and in Eleutherai (a village on the Boeotian border), a phallic cult symbol representing the god was pulled through the streets in a wheeled ship. Osiris, like all Egyptian gods, when represented in the form of a cult temple image was placed inside a portable model barque housed within a shrine representing the primeval mound that had first arisen from the primal lake at the start of creation. It seems as if ship and wagon were interchangeable symbols; this is significant because not only does it suggest that the wagon-borne divinity and the boat-borne Sheaf may have been equivalent images but also it helps explain something Tacitus writes about the Seubic tribes to the south of Denmark, some of whom later became the Saxons.

> Some of the Suebi sacrifice also to Isis. I do not know the explanation of this foreign cult; but the goddess's emblem, being made in the form of a light warship, itself proves that her worship came in from abroad.

It may be that what Tacitus was recording amongst the Suebi was a variant of the worship of the wagon-borne Nerthus of the Ingaevones, who like Dionysos could have been depicted as travelling in both types of transport. And though, technically, he may have been right in suggesting the Suebic 'Isis' had come from abroad, since this boat-born fertility deity had arrived in Scandinavia from the Middle East some 4,000 years before he wrote his account, it could hardly be called 'foreign'. The 'light warship' was undoubtedly an indigenous vessel, the ancestor of the Viking warships of the Dark Ages.

What makes Tacitus's description of the Nerthus rite stand out is its description of ritual drowning, but a look at the life cycle of the Near Eastern fertility gods shows that this was a motif in their myths too. In one myth, Dionysos is said to have drowned in the Alconyian lake – and was summoned reborn from the water with trumpet blasts. Osiris is said to have been drowned by Seth in the Nile.[10] Adonis was also said to have drowned and in his rites, the image of the slain god was either set adrift in the sea or placed in the waters of a spring – just as the harvest sheaf was drowned in English farming customs. But perhaps the most clear link between the fertility gods of the Near East and the Nerthus rite is the fact that three days after the ritual death of Attis, the image of his mother/lover, the goddess Cybele, and the bullock-drawn cart in which she sat were ceremonially washed in the river Almo – an act reminiscent of the washing of Nerthus mentioned by Tacitus (*see* page 53).

The fertility gods of Greece and Rome, paraded on boats and carts and then cast into the waters, were represented by wooden images. In stark contrast, the lakes of ancient Denmark, littered with human corpses, bear witness to a more macabre offering. It seems that in ancient Scandza, isolated and out on a limb, an older form of the fertility cults had survived; a form in which men, not images, embodied the gods. And the chief of the Vanir deities of this region was the barley-wreathed god Freyr, the brother/lover of the fertility goddess Freyja, whose myths appear to support the idea that in the dark northern forests and wind-tossed seas of Scandinavia the fertility god once lived and died in the form of flesh and blood men.

CHAPTER 7

·

FREYR

Archaeologists had discovered that the final meals of the victims preserved in the Danish bogs comprised the same hallucinogenic barley brew as used in the mysteries of Eleusis. The existence of this ritual drink provides physical proof that the ancestors of the English were practising an ancient fertility cult, derived from the Middle East, concerning the life cycle of a barley deity who, as late as the 9th century, appears prominently in Anglo-Saxon genealogies as Scef. The ceremonies connected with this god included the bearing of his/her image on a wagon/ship, its drowning in sacred waters and an act of ritual washing – all of which are suggested in the Tacitus's *Germania* as applicable to the rites of the Danish goddess Nerthus, in whose sacred lakes, the *Beowulf* poet hints, Grendel and his mother dwelt. However, unlike the wealth of accounts concerning the gods of Greece, Rome and Egypt, the only contemporary written evidence concerning the Danish rites is the single paragraph in Tacitus (*see* page 53) and he makes no mention of a dying and rising god accompanying the wagon-rite.

However, the later Norse myths mention a deity named Njorthr – the father of the chief Vanir deities, Freyr and Freyja. Not only is the name Njorthr the exact form the name of the Danish goddess would be expected to take (minus its suitably Latin ending) were it to be written in Old Norse, Njorthr is referred to in the Icelandic Snorri Sturluson's *Skáldskaparmál* (*The language of poetry*) as 'the god of wagons'.

Njorthr, so Snorri informs us, was associated with the oceans and ocean-going vessels; his home was Noatun (ship enclosure, harbour) and he controlled the winds and the fruits of the sea. Immediately, then, it is possible to link him to the ship-borne deities such as Sheaf and Dionysos. Snorri writes of him: 'To him one must pray for voyages and fishing'. Njorthr seems to have been worshipped along coasts, fjords and also inland lakes and waters, some of which were associated with sacred islands much like that of his Danish name-sake. His name was most probably derived from the Indo-European root word *ner* meaning 'below' that appears as an element in the modern words 'be*neath*' and '*neth*er'. This is an apt name for a divinity who dwelt under the waters of the world and, if he was akin to Dionysos/Osiris, may have lived part of the year in the underworld, the land of dead – and who was connected to the underworld through his daughter Freyja, who possessed the ability to raise men from the dead.

Given that the names Nerthus and Njorthr are identical forms of the same name, some scholars have assumed that over time the Iron Age goddess Nerthus underwent a change of gender to appear in Viking times as a god.[1] But this may be an unnecessary complication. The farming rites of the Near East suggest that the fertility gods were always depicted in pairs, such as Attis and Cybele, Isis and Osiris, and so the wagon that toured the land may originally have been occupied by embodiments of both the god and goddess (which would explain why the tapestries of the wagon in the Oseburg ship showed both a man and a woman beside the vehicle (*see* page 58). And besides, the seeming change from one sex to another over time might simply be explained as a result of a misunderstanding on the part of Tacitus.

The word *Nerthus* is actually a masculine noun, and this has led some to believe that Tacitus's source (possibly an earlier Greek work) mentioned *two* divinities: a god Nerthus/Njorthr who was paraded around the countryside in a wagon like Dionysos, and a goddess 'Mother Earth' who was, like Cybele, washed after the procession in the sacred lake. The suggestion is that Tacitus misunderstood the source and attributed the name of one to the other. Such confusion might have been compounded by the fact that the Germanic deities often had very similar names.[2] For instance, the name of Thor's mother, Fyorgynn (earth/mountain) was almost identical to that of Fyorgyn, his father; and Freyr is not far away from Freyja. In a similar fashion, the name of Njorthr's partner 'Mother Earth' might have been almost identical to that of her husband, so allowing a confused Tacitus to record *her* as Nerthus and ignore the presence of the god, believing that the 'Nerthus' borne about the land and the similarly named 'Mother Earth' washed in the lake were a single entity. Such a mistake may have been coloured by Tacitus's own religious background.

Tacitus was a priest of the goddess Cybele, whose wagon-borne image was bathed in the river Almo on 27 March. Given the similarity of the rites, it would have been easy for him to colour unconsciously the Danish rite with what he knew of the Roman one.[3] In this final ceremony in the rites of the castrated Attis, the god did not play any role at all (having already been killed and resurrected) and so Tacitus would already have had preconceived notions *that the god would not be present* in the equivalent Danish rite. Having already confused the god's name with that of his wife, his knowledge of the unaccompanied bathing of Cybele meant that even had mention been made in the earlier Greek source of the *god* Nerthus's presence in the lake ceremony, he would have read it as referring to the goddess.

Arguably, the god *was* present, and like his Near Eastern counterparts was drowned, but Tacitus, accustomed to wooden depictions of deities, failed to see the drowning of the 'slaves' (whose preserved bodies show no sign of having performed manual labour) as in any way connected with the drowning of the god.

The masculine ending of the word *Nerthus* gives some weight to the theory that the god Njorthr was present, if unseen, in Tacitus's account of the wagon rite. (For clarity's sake, the name Nerthus will continue to be used to refer to the goddess whom, as suggested, may have borne a very similar name to her husband.) Either way, there is no confusion if it is accepted that on the tour of the land to promote fertility, the wagon ritual was enacted by the necessary pairing of divinities: a god later known as Njorthr and a goddess who may have had a similar name, but equally may have been known as Gefion or Freyja (*see* page 51), but recorded simply as 'Mother Earth'. It was a sacred marriage of earth and sky, of sun and land, of grain and soil through the uniting of male and female.

It is Njorthr's son, Freyr, however (whose name, like that of Adonis, simply means 'the Lord'), who provides the closest parallel to the wagon-rite of Danish prehistory and the cereal gods, as he is also associated with a wagon tour around the land. Indeed, since the epithet 'wagon god' applied to his father in the *Edda* is more applicable to the son, it suggests that the two were not originally separate entities at all but differing aspects of what may originally have been a single deity.

God of the World

Snorri makes it clear that Freyr was principally a 'fertility god':

> He decides when the sun shall shine or the rain comes down, and along with that the fruitfulness of the earth, and he is good to invoke for peace and plenty.

Freyr – 'god of the world' as Snorri calls him – was principally a deity of the sun and of the fertile earth, of peace and prosperity. From the start an affinity with the Middle Eastern vegetation gods is suggested, but a closer look at his attributes makes it plain that Freyr can be no other than the north-west European equivalent of Osiris or Dionysos. The solar nature of Freyr is reflected in his two cult animals: the horse (which drew the solar chariot across the sky), as stallion fights and horse sacrifice were part of his worship; and the boar.[4]

The boar might seem an odd animal to connect with the sun, although in the barley god's myth it does play the part of the creature that gores him in the thigh. Freyr's boar, however, was a magical creature named Gullinbursti (golden bristles), fashioned for him by the dwarves, which accompanied him in his chariot. The boar was said to shine brightly, especially its golden bristles, and could outrun a horse and 'ride across the sky'. This boar was clearly a solar symbol, its bristles being the rays of the sun.[5]

This solar connection no doubt led to the boar being the sacrificial offering made at the midwinter solstice amongst the Germanic tribes. Norse warriors swore oaths concerning the coming year at Yule over a sacrificed boar – the origin both for our New Year's resolutions and the medieval 'boar's head feast' still celebrated at Queen's College, Oxford.

But perhaps the most important connection between Freyr and Sheaf, suggesting that the two were a single deity, is that Freyr was depicted as a child journeying over the sea on a boat and returning thence after death. Snorri records that Freyr had a magical ship *Sk'öblaðnir* that could house all the gods yet which could be folded up like a cloth and kept in a pocket when not in use. This suggests that this was either an image of a ship on cloth or a wooden cult-image of a ship like the ritual barques kept in the temples of the Egyptian gods. This connection is only one amongst many:

1. Like the Egyptian god Osiris, who lived on 'after death' within his tomb, Freyr was also believed to live on after his death within his burial mound. He was reported to have been buried in a great burial mound with a door and three windows: one for offerings of gold, one for silver and another for copper. It was said the people continued to give him offerings, believing he was still alive within the mound.

2. Just as Osiris was associated with spreading the idea of pacifism, so Freyr's temples were free of weapons; it was illegal carry weapons into them, let alone to shed blood in them or in the sacred fields that stood nearby. Indeed, at Ragnarok – the final battle where the gods are destroyed before the world is renewed (*see* page 47) – Freyr has no sword. When he fights a figure named Beli, he does so using a stag's antler.

3. Like Dionysos, who was often depicted as both phallus and snake, Freyr was associated with the serpent and portrayed in a state of

sexual excitement. Aldhelm of Sherborne, in the 8th century, mentions pagan shrines in Wessex where:

> Once the crude pillars of the same foul snake and the stag were
> worshipped with coarse stupidity in profane shrines.[6]

Since Freyr's weapon was the stag's antler, it is a possibility that this shrine mentioned by Aldhelm was sacred to him. Adam of Bremen writes that the statue of *Fricco* (Freyr) at the great sacrificial temple at Uppsala was 'indecent' (in other words, phallic). And his sexual nature is also borne out in his name which, though meaning 'Lord', is also connected to the Sanskrit word *priya* (the beloved), and the English word 'prick'.[7] An image possibly of Freyr survives in a statuette from Rällinge in Sweden which dates from around 900. It depicts a male figure sitting cross-legged, with an erect phallus, with one hand stroking his beard. He is also wearing a pointed hat like a gnome or, perhaps significantly, like that worn by Tollund Man. Another image, found on a cauldron (possibly of Thracian origin but depicting north European cult images) discovered at Gundestrup, Jutland, depicts a similarly cross-legged figure bearing antlers and holding a snake – the two animals mentioned by Aldhelm (*above*). Normally regarded as depicting the Celtic horned god Cernunnos, given its location the figure might just as easily be a depiction of Freyr (*see* page 131).[8]

4. Like those Dionysos, Freyr's rites were accompanied by some kind of theatre or mime, which the Danish historian Saxo Grammaticus (Saxo the Learned, *c.* 1150–1220) describes as obscene, with much 'ringing of bells' and 'effeminate gestures'. Such mimes (possibly the ultimate origin of the dances of mummers and morris dancers, which often involve death and rebirth symbolism) may have been the northern equivalent of the ritual drama of the god that in Greece became the theatrical 'tragedy' (*see* page 80). Just as morris dancers often include cross-dressing men, so too the priests of Freyr, like those of Attis, were seen as sexually ambivalent and 'uncanny'.[9]

5. Like the vegetation gods of the Middle East, Freyr was believed to have died. Unlike the later Aesir (with two notable exceptions) and the Greek Olympians who seemed neither to mature nor age, having appeared almost 'fully formed', the Vanir gods seemed to undergo birth, growth and death. This is their enduring characteristic.

6. Freyr's death may have been accompanied by weeping, as was that of Adonis, Tammuz and their ilk: Freyja, Freyr's sister, is said to have cried tears of gold at the death of her husband, a mysterious deity named Od. And, since Norse myth suggests that Freyr and Freyja, though sister and brother, were, like Isis and Osiris, lovers (and like Isis she could assume the shape of a falcon),[10] it is likely that Od and Freyr were one and the same.

7. Freyr was associated with a ritual wagon tour of the land (*see* page 50).

A cursory examination of Freyr's attributes reveals that Freyr and the Vanir were undoubtedly derivatives from the same prehistoric farming cults celebrated throughout Europe and the Middle East in the Neolithic age. They survived well in Scandza, not only because of its isolated location from the rest of Germania, but also maybe because the megalithic landscape still connected its people to the ancestral spirits of the land. In fact, Freyr's burial mound with its open door and windows strongly evokes the passage graves of Neolithic peoples with their open doorways that allowed communication with the ancestors. It is entirely possible that the Norse Freyr had been worshipped in the north, relatively consistently, for some 5,000 years, this worship coming to an end only shortly before Snorri composed his *Edda*.

The Wooing of Gerthr

Despite their great age, by the time most of the Norse myths were recorded, the worship of Njorthr and his children Freyr and Freyja had been superseded by the cults of the Aesir. Only a single myth concerning Freyr appears in Snorri's *Edda*. *Skírnismál* (*The Lay of Skírnir*), tells of Freyr's seduction of the giantess Gerthr, the daughter of Gymir, and their tryst in the grove of Barri (barley).[11]

Gerthr ('enclosed field/farm') is first seen by Freyr as a great shining light far to the north, as he sits on a high throne in the land of the gods. Immediately, Freyr falls for her. He gives his stallion and sword to his servant Skírnir ('shining one') and sends him to woo her for him. Behind this charming tale, it is possible to discern a farming metaphor – the preparation of the field, the fertile earth ready for planting. Gerthr is initially wary, and Skírnir threatens her with a kind of possession, a 'love-sickness', and so she yields, agreeing to meet Freyr in nine days time in the barley grove. The poem ends with Freyr musing on the length of those nine days, when but one day seems to him a month.

This single surviving myth of Freyr is important, as it suggests the enactment of a fruitful union between the god and the earth goddess that caused the crops to grow. And there is evidence from other Viking sagas that suggests this 'sacred marriage' played a major part of the wagon tour of the god.

CHAPTER EIGHT

·

THE WAGON RAN AFTER

THE BEST EVIDENCE for the sacred marriage and the wagon tour of Freyr is found in the sagas of the Norwegian king Olaf Tryggvason (968–1000).[1] Tryggvason played an important part in Anglo-Saxon history; according to the *Anglo-Saxon Chronicle* he was the leader of the Viking fleet that attacked Maldon in Essex in 991. *The Battle of Maldon*, after *Beowulf* perhaps the most famous Anglo-Saxon poem, tells of the last stand of the Saxon nobleman Byrhtnoth, its theme being the willingness to die alongside one's lord in battle that we find at the end of *Beowulf* (*see* pages 11–12).

Although Olaf's presence at Maldon is the subject of some dispute, he was definitely in England in 994 at the head of a fleet of 94 Viking ships. Around this time, Olaf was converted and baptized in England, under the sponsorship of King Ethelred II ('the Unready') and he swore no longer to raid England. Instead, he married the wife of the deceased Viking king of Dublin and divided his time between Ireland and the north of England. While in Dublin, his royal relatives in Norway sent news that in his absence an earl named Hakon had reverted to paganism and seized the throne, taking many women as concubines. Olaf returned to Norway to oust him, only to find the job done already – Hakon's disgruntled subjects had murdered him. Olaf was asked to occupy the throne in his stead.

Olaf comes across in the sagas as a fair and politically adept king, ending his life heroically during a sea battle at Swold. He was attacked at sea by Svein Forkbeard, king of Denmark, and Earl Eric, the murdered

Earl Hakon's son. When Olaf saw he was outnumbered and the battle lost, he jumped from his ship *Long Serpent* into the sea, putting his shield over his head so that his enemies could not pull him from the water.

During Olaf's reign (995–1000), according to the *Heimskringla*, a subject named Gunnar Helming fled from Norway after being accused of murder, and his exploits in neighbouring pagan Sweden tell much of the worship of Freyr that was still popular at this time – only 70 years before the Norman conquest of England, and some 500 years after the English themselves had converted to Christianity.

The story[2] is told tongue in cheek, written to satirize the provincial pagan Swedes, but its contents rest on some truth. Freyr was worshipped as an idol through which 'the devil' was said to speak. He had also been given a pretty young priestess who had 'dominion over the temple' and it was believed they were lovers. On arriving in Sweden, Gunnar asks for shelter in Freyr's temple; the priestess warns him her god does not like him, but he can stay three nights. Gunnar's charms, however, begin to win her over and he is allowed to stay for a little longer.

> After some time, he talked again with Freyr's wife. She said: 'People like you well, and I think it is better you stay here this winter and accompany us when Freyr makes his annual journey.' ... Gunnar thanked her well ... Now the festival time came, and the procession started. Freyr and his wife were placed in the carriage, whereas their servants and Gunnar had to walk beside.

Journeying through the mountains, the cult-wagon and its party become trapped in a snowstorm during which the servants of the god flee to find shelter. Gunnar and the priestess, however, remain with the vehicle. Gunnar tires of driving the cattle when there is a perfectly good seat beside the priestess, so he gets into the wagon, which angers Freyr so the two begin to fight. As the pair wrestle, Gunnar calls on King Olaf's Christian god, promising that if he gives him victory he will renounce his pagan ways, return to Norway and be reconciled with Olaf. With this, the 'spirit' of Freyr is seemingly exorcised from the wooden idol, and Gunnar and the priestess decide that Gunnar should now impersonate the god, so he dresses in its clothes and takes his place beside her for the rest of the ritual progress.

The gullible Swedes are happy to see their god looking so well and happy:

> They wondered how he went about among them and talked like other men. Thus Freyr and his wife spent the winter going to festivals. Freyr was not more eloquent towards people than his wife, and he would not receive living victims, as before, and no offerings except gold, silk and good clothing.

They also noticed the priestess had become pregnant, which was a good sign for their crops. Indeed, the land had never been so fruitful. News of Freyr's miraculous vigour spreads to Norway where King Olaf begins to suspect what is really happening. Olaf now knows that Gunnar did not commit the murder and sends Gunnar's brother Sigurd to Sweden to fetch him back. Gunnar, his wife and newborn child flee to Norway with the god's offerings and are baptized.

Although satirical, the story of Gunnar's deceit provides a number of startling links with the Nerthus rite of a millennium earlier: the yearly sacred progress of a deity in a cattle-drawn wagon associated with fertility of the land. Behind the humorous façade lie traces of a misunderstood rite in which, on certain specific occasions, the god Freyr may have been represented by a mortal man. Such an epiphany would be quite understandable – if the spirit of Freyr could enter a wooden image then it could also enter a man.

We know that Freyr was associated with wooden images as two are mentioned in *Ynglingatal* as being kept in Freyr's grave mound. These 'wooden men' were taken out of his tomb and carried to a shrine in Sweden and another at Trondheim in Norway, perhaps as part of a ritual progress. In design, the wooden idols may have been akin to that found in the bog at Broddenbjerg (*see* page 45), with its huge phallus and its legs formed from two roots (*see* plate 11). Just as in Gunnar's tale, the idols were seen to be possessed by the spirit of

Freyr, so in *Flateyjarbok* King Eric of Sweden was able to detect the presence of a wagon-borne god named *Lytir* by an increase in the weight of the god's sacred wagon. The name of the god probably stems from the Old Norse *Lyta* meaning 'disgraceful', and is likely to be a Christian appellation for a god thought to be obscene – the sexually promiscuous and possibly ambivalent (given the effeminacy of his priests, *see* pages 191) Freyr.[3]

Blessing the Fields

The tour of the land by the divinity meant that the act of sacred consummation could be enacted in many locales; the farms and fields of every region could be blessed, the marriage celebrated in every first furrow that was ploughed. We get an idea of these rites from a very late 'ceremony' enacted in Anglo-Saxon England under the eyes of the church, but whose symbolism is far from Christian.

This was the *Aecerbot*, a 'field remedy' which was an early 11th-century charm used to help improve fields that yielded poorly.[4] The enactment of this charm was a day-long affair which begun with four sods being cut from the four quarters of the field at night, and then taken to church for a mass to be sung over each. Prior to this, a porridge containing yeast, honey, oil and milk, together with a part of all species of plants from the locality (save buckwheat and all hardwoods) was applied three times to the underside of the turfs – a mixture evoking the plant-rich porridge of the Danish bog men. Having been returned to the field before sunset, each bearing a wooden cross, the turfs were then sung over by a healer who faced the direction of the rising sun, turned three times clockwise, and called on the 'holy guardian of the heavenly kingdom' to 'fill the earth' and make the crops grow. A plough was then anointed with a 'hallowed' mixture of oil, paste, frankincense, salt and fennel, and a chant sung over them including these words:

Erce, erce, erce eorþan modor

Erce, erce, erce, Mother of Earth!

(The word *erce* may mean 'great', being probably linked linguistically to the word 'arch' as in 'archbishop').

> Great Mother of Earth, may the Almighty, the eternal Lord, grant you fields growing and thriving, increasing and strengthening, tall stems and fine crops, both the broad barley and the fair wheat.

Then the field was ploughed, as these words were recited:

> *Hal wes þu, fira modor,*
> *Beo þu growende on Godes fæðme,*
> *Fodre gefylled firum to nytte.*

> Hail to you, earth, mother of mortals,
> may you grow big in God's embrace,
> filled with food for the use of humankind.

Then the healer placed a loaf made of every type of grain into the first furrow. Despite the Christian imagery, the rite was pagan in origin, and made use of the symbols of the marrying of the solar god with the earth mother to make the fields fruitful. Similar rites, though possibly enacted sexually between the god and goddess in human form, probably accompanied the wagon tour of Nerthus and Freyr amongst the continental ancestors of the English country folk who used the charm.

Ing

The rites of Freyr in turn of the millennium Sweden closely resembled those of Nerthus 1,000 years earlier, thus providing a significant clue to the rites of the ancient English – the members of the Ingaevones whose descendants were the original audience of *Beowulf*. For the very name of these coastal tribes – the Ingaevones – betrays the presence of Freyr in Denmark.[5]

Freyr was known as *Yngvi-Freyr* in Sweden, where he was seen as the progenitor of a line of Swedish kings called the *Ynglinga* – 'the sons of

Yng/Ing' – and the name Ingaevones contains a reference to the same god.[6] The Roman historian Pliny the Elder (AD 23–79) offers an alternative spelling of Ingaevones – *Ingvaeones* – and it is probable his form is the correct one, for minus its Latin ending it yields Ingvaeon, the same word as *Ingwine* ('friends of Ing') used in *Beowulf* to denote these tribes. The word *ing*, as well as forming the patronymic ('son of', *see* page 65), is thought to be derived from *ingwaz*, a proto-Germanic word for man.

Ing appears in a fascinating set of verses known as *The Old English Rune Poem* found in George Hickes's *Thesaurus of the Old Languages of the North* (1705). Though the original poem has long disappeared, linguists have been able to suggest a date of composition some time around the 9th century.

Runes, at least in common parlance, were the angular characters of the Germanic alphabet – (known as the *futharc* from its first six characters f, u, th, a, r and c) that were principally used for rituals and divination. (The word 'rune' is really a term meaning 'magic' and it was not originally applied to the letters themselves.)[7] The first documented use of runes seems to have been in Jutland, where runic amulets dating to around AD 250 have been uncovered. Rune poems have been found throughout the Germanic world, and they usually give the meanings of each rune, which seem to be symbols for all manner of pagan and natural imagery. In *The Old English Rune Poem*, a composition in which the various properties, origins and meanings of the runes are discussed in verse, however, all pagan reference seems to have been removed, or cunningly hidden in puns – save for the verse concerning Ing. It reads:

Ing waes aerest mid Est-Denum
Gesewen secgum, oth he siddan est
Ofer waeg gewat; waen aefter ran;
Thus heardingas thone haele nemdun'

Ing was among the East Danes
first seen among men, till he later departed [east? back?]
over the sea; the wagon ran after
thus the hard-men [warriors?] named the hero.

This short verse proves most illuminating. Ing, like Sheaf, was first seen by mortal men in the territory of the East Danes – arguably the isle of Zealand, sacred to Nerthus/Gefion. The words 'first seen', however, point to the fact that subsequently his cult and influence had spread, perhaps to England. His return journey east over the sea followed by his wagon is once again suggestive of the return of the wagon to its sacred precinct after the completion of the Nerthus rite, as well as the mysterious nautical peregrinations of Sheaf. The word for the direction of his return is, however, ambiguous. *Est* can mean either 'east' or 'back' (as in the words 'aft' or 'astern'). Either way makes sense, as it could refer to his return to his shrine, or, if we see Ing as the sun rising from out of the east and traversing the sky in a wagon, returning back to the eastern horizon to rise again the following day.

If the verse does obliquely refer to a god once found in east Denmark moving from Scandza to England, the presence of this deity might have been allowed to remain in the otherwise Christian poem on the grounds that by this time Ing was regarded (as in some Anglian genealogies) as a great continental ancestor. *Ingui*, for example, appears in the royal genealogy of Bernicia and was probably once seen as the progenitor of all Anglian kings.[8]

The English could be said to have enjoyed a particular relationship with this god in both their continental homeland, where they formed part of the confederacy known as the 'friends of Ing', and in the new lands they migrated to in the 5th and 6th centuries. In time, they would name these lands Angle-land, and it is tempting to speculate that the word Angle was derived from, or thought of as a pun on, the name of Ing.

Such a special connection might shed light on why the figure of the boat-borne baby Sheaf, ultimately derived from Freyr/Ing, played such a major role in English tradition, while the Danes themselves had already replaced him with the bear-killer Skjold in their royal family tree.

The question remains as to why the Danes may have wanted to purge the figure of the fertility god from their genealogy. The most obvious clue is the fact that the sacred lakes of the land of the Ingaevones, so intimately tied in with the rites of the wagon-god and goddess, were depicted in *Beowulf* as the abode of a pair of horrific monsters. Where we would expect to find the presence of two fertility deities, a god and goddess associated with sacred waters and wagons along the lines of Attis and Cybele, as suggested to us by Roman sources, comparative myths and archaeology, the *Beowulf* poet instead provides us with two superhuman blood-curdling fiends. This suggests two possibilities: firstly, that Grendel and his mother were purely poetic inventions and had no connection with the old gods save for a coincidental use of the same subaqueous dwelling place (*Gefion's ground*); or, secondly, that there was perhaps a more sinister side to this ancestral farming religion (as its practice of human sacrifice suggests) and that these Vanir deities possessed a darker side that was correctly remembered in the poem.

CHAPTER NINE

·

ELVES AND EVIL SHADES

So the company of men led a careless life, all was well with
them: until One began to encompass evil, an enemy from hell.
Grendel they called this cruel spirit, the fell and fen his fastness
was, the march his haunt. This unhappy being had long lived in
the land of monsters since the creator cast them out as kindred
of Cain. For that killing of Abel the eternal Lord took
vengeance ... From Cain came down all kinds misbegotten –
ogres and elves and evil shades.

BEOWULF, 99–112

ONE OF THE MOST interesting facets of *Beowulf* is that it presents
us with a glimpse into the world of the Anglo-Saxons for whom
it was composed and who, having only very recently left paganism
behind, lived in a very different world from us. Despite their conversion to Christianity, mentally they still dwelt in the Middle Earth of
their forebears, a world, like that popularized by Tolkien, populated
with 'ents' (giants), elves, dwarves and 'orcs' (evil shades). Belief in the
unseen forces of nature did not vanish overnight – indeed aspects of
such beliefs continued in rural areas into modern times – but what
had changed was the way such beings were conceived.

Beowulf provides us with the re-categorization of these supernatural creatures within a Christian framework. Formally, the origin of
such beings had been firmly explained in myth: the dwarves were
created from the maggots bred in the flesh of the frost giant Ymir;

giants themselves were formed from the primal ice that co-existed with the primal fire at the start of creation; man himself had been licked from the ice by a cow named Audumla.[1] None of this cosmology fitted in with the events of Genesis, and so for the converted Old English the universe had to be re-visioned.

This re-visioning is painted clearly in *Beowulf*. Far from dismissing such supernatural creatures as superstitious nonsense, the metaphysical creatures of the Germanic heathen world were given a make-over, enabling them to slip effortlessly into the Judeo-Christian world as 'fiends from hell', devils and demons. They were re-imagined as the descendants of Cain, the brother-killing son of Adam, and like this outcast, exiled from man for his heinous deed, the heathen monsters were cast into the wastelands on the edge of society in dark forests, misty moors and haunted meres.

For the original audiences who first heard the poem, the 'orcs' and 'elves' it mentions were no fairytale creatures but actual entities which everyone present would have both believed in and feared. Perhaps the same was true in relation to Grendel and his mother, who were clearly thought of by the *Beowulf* poet as kin to these other 'kinds misbegotten'. If these monsters were considered to have been real rather than mere fictional creations intended to amuse and entertain, it may be that Grendel and his mother were dim memories of ancient pagan divinities. And there is good evidence that the Vanir gods of the old cults underwent such a relegation in status to be numbered amongst the descendants of Cain, for Norse mythology makes clear the Vanir were also known as the *alfar* – they were the elves.

The Shining Ones

To the pagan Germans, elves were not the flimsily-clad cherubs with bluebell bonnets of Victorian romanticism, nor the playful sprites of medieval fairy lore, but powerful spirits that could appear in many shapes and guises. The word 'elf' comes from the Indo-European *alba* (white/fair) and these 'shining ones' were the spirits of the landscape, the forces of nature, the fertility gods themselves.

In Norse myth, the elves are associated with Freyr: he is said to have been given *Alfheim*, the home of the elves, as a gift from the Aesir when he cut his first tooth, and throughout the *Edda* the customary phrase 'Aesir and Vanir' is often rendered as 'Aesir and Alfar'.[2] Once accepted, the link between the elves and the Vanir becomes obvious. The Vanir's dislike of weaponry (Freyr allowed no weapons in his temple) and the dislike of iron (in Nerthus's rites all iron was locked away) led to a belief that carrying iron averted the elves and other fairy beings.[3] (From here on, the term 'elf' is used for Old English/Scandinavian derived spirits and 'fairy' for Celtic and later generalized folkloric spirits, amongst which the elves were numbered but not exclusively.) The Vanir were widely perceived as collective beings, a fact supported by the numerous shrines to the 'Mothers' that tend to depict these beings in groups (usually twos or threes), often accompanied by small, hooded beings known as *genii cucullati* (hooded spirits).[4] Similarly, the tribes of British and Danish elves and fairies are seen as collective in nature: in Britain they are most commonly depicted as dancing in groups, forming fairy rings, which is of interest given the collective burial rites of the Neolithic ancestor cult from which the Vanir cults may have been derived (*see* page 31).

The connection between elves and the '*Matronae*' (the Mother Goddesses of the Vanir) is especially clear in Celtic fairy lore: in Wales, the fairies were known as *Bendith y Mamau* (the Mothers' Blessing). And in Ireland they were said to be descended from a prehistoric divine race, the *Tuatha De Danann* (People of the Goddess Danu).

There is one school of thought that argues that these spirits, who are sometimes depicted in folklore as 'fallen angels', were originally seen as elemental spirits of landscape. They appear in certain Anglo-Saxon treatises as *wudu-elfen* (wood elves), *wæter-elfen* (water elves), *dun-elfen* (hill elves), *sæ-elfen* (sea elves) and *wylde-elfen* (moor elves), thus emphasizing their connection with the natural world.[5] This derivation of the elves is certainly supported in Icelandic saga, where we hear of *landvaettir* (land wights), the spirits of the landscape, who were thought to have inhabited Iceland prior to the arrival of man.[6]

In addition, there is strong evidence to suppose the elves were connected with the human dead. In British fairy lore, elves and fairies are often associated with hills and mounds (*see* plate 10), especially prehistoric burial mounds, which suggests that the elves were, at least in part, derived from the spirits of the ancestral dead. In Irish fairy lore, after their defeat at the hands of the incoming Gaels, the *Tuatha De Danann* were given the *sídhe* – the burial mounds of Ireland – as dwelling places, having had to relinquish the 'upper world'; again, this is suggestive of an origin as tomb-dwelling ancestral spirits. In time, they became synonymous with the mounds themselves and took their name: they became the *sídhe* – the people of the hills.

People of the Hills

The chief god of the *Tuatha* was called the *Dagda* ('Good God': indicating great versatility, not morality). After their defeat by the Gaels, he was said to be have been given the most splendid *sídhe* of them all: *Brugh na Boinne* (Palace on the Boyne) which is known today as Newgrange, in County Meath. Newgrange is a massive Neolithic passage grave, whose spectacular corbelled passage is aligned to allow the first rays of the midwinter sunrise to penetrate a slot above the doorway and send a beam of light into the burial chambers. This seasonal use of the chamber is reminiscent of the passage grave at Øm on Zealand, where two farm workers were sent to clear the passage annually at midwinter, and left porridge there for 'the spirits' (*see* page 31).

The Dagda can be closely linked with Freyr. He was a sexually prodigious and overtly phallic deity who mated with a nightmarish goddess named the *Mórrighan* (great queen) over a stream, just as the phallic Freyr enjoyed a union with the giantess Gerthr (*see* page 92), a form, perhaps, of the watery Nerthus. Freyr, like the Dagda, lived within a burial mound with its doors and windows left open for 'offerings', and the orientation of the 'sun window' at Newgrange links the Dagda to the solar imagery we find in Freyr's rites. The Dagda has also been connected to the Celtic horned god of plenty, Cernunnos, who is possibly depicted on the Iron Age Gundestrup cauldron seated cross-legged (like the Rällinge Freyr; *see* page 131), holding a snake and wearing stag's antlers, both symbols sacred to Freyr (see pages 89–90). The Dagda and Freyr seem to have been cast in the same mould.

If the Vanir were the spirits of the dead, how did they become conceived of as deities? One possibility is that this was a gradual process over time as the personalities of the ancestors faded from memory to be replaced by the idea of a collective ancestral being. However, an example found in Norse tradition shows that the process of the dead becoming *alfar* might have been more direct. It concerns a Norwegian king named Olaf who, following his death and burial, is said to have lived on within his burial mound, continuing to exert an influence on the affairs of men and the fertility of the land: offerings were made to him as supplications so that he might favourably influence events. Within a very short period of his death, Olaf was already conceived of as an elf, becoming known as the 'Elf of Geirstad'.[7]

Such deified ancestral spirits would then have the potential to become tribal and even national gods. This brings into question whether the fertility cults that arrived with the practice of farming necessarily brought with them the idea of a 'god' in the form of a non-human entity, rather than the concept of the deified ancestor. This might then explain the sudden adoption of the megalithic rite and the massive expenditure in terms of labour and resources in the building of houses for the dead. To the Neolithic people of the Atlantic coasts, whose lives were relatively short and hard, it is small wonder that effort was deployed on the houses of eternity than those of the living. They would inhabit their earthly homes, built of wood and thatch, for a much shorter period.

This may have been of even greater significance if they also believed in a form of reincarnation, as is suggested by an anecdote concerning the 'Elf of Geirstad'. This appears in the *Saga of St Olaf of Norway* (King Olaf Haraldson) who owned the sword of the earlier King Olaf, Elf of Geirstad, as it was taken from the latter's grave on the birth of the saint. St Olaf's followers, when passing the mound of the elf, asked St Olaf whether he had been buried there, which Olaf, being a Christian, denied. That such a question might be asked, suggests that reincarnation was deemed a possibility, and, despite the saint's protestations, the fact that he had been named after the earlier Olaf, and had been given his sword, suggests that at least *someone* had this idea.

The strong links between the fairy lore of Ireland and the Vanir cult of Scandinavia comes as no surprise when a number of common features shared by these locations are taken into account. Both were located on the Atlantic coasts, where their megaliths had been crafted in stone, remaining as permanent features of the landscape, and both were isolated geographically, neither having been conquered by Rome. Even so, it does come as a surprise just how strong these ancestor cults must have been to survive, in the guise of the fairy traditions, the introduction of a new religion. Their demise was eventually brought about, not by religious intolerance or deliberate suppression, but through the urbanization and industrialization of the last century, divorcing the population from their agricultural heritage.

Alfablot and Elfshot

One of the last vestiges of the fairy faith was the leaving of milk or porridge for the fairies. This took many forms: the pouring of milk into 'cup' marks on prehistoric stones, the leaving of foodstuffs in the fields or by the hearth, especially on special days such as Halloween, Midsummer's Eve and Christmas Eve.[8] The act appears to have been a debased version of a rite once called *alfablot* (elf-blood), when the blood of sacrificed animals, or ritual cereal brew, was left at megalithic tombs for the spirits (as with the multitude of vessels left for the dead at the Tustrup necropolis; *see* page 30). In the Icelandic *Cormac's Saga* we find a description of *alfablot*:

> There is a knoll a little way from here where the elves dwell; thou shalt take hither the ox that Cormac slew, and sprinkle the blood of the ox on the outside of the knoll, and give the elves a banquet of the meat; and thou shalt be healed.[9]

The idea that the elves could affect the health of individuals is one that survived into the Anglo-Saxon age; though with a negative slant as elves were seen to cause certain illnesses. In Christianized medico-religious manuscripts, elves are identified as the cause of such colourful illnesses as *alfsogodda* ('elf juice': possibly dyspepsia or hiccups) and 'water-elf-sickness', the symptoms of which included localized swellings on the skin suggesting it may have been measles. These diseases could be warded off or cured by the reciting of charms and the taking of herbal remedies.

In the charm for use 'against a sudden pain' (*wið færstice*) found in the *Lacnunga* manuscript, a 10th–11th-century document containing healing lore (now housed in the British Library), we see both elements of this healing. To cure the illness – caused by invisible spears cast by a group of supernatural women – the patient had to take a potion containing feverfew, nettle and plantain (all have spear-shaped leaves) boiled in butter, and to repeat a verse that would counteract the effect of the 'spears' by removing them from the body and casting them back at the hags.

> Loud they were, lo, loud, when they rode over the burial mound;
> They were fierce, when they rode over the land.
> Shield yourself now so that you this evil attack might survive.
> Out, little spear, if here any be within.
> I stood beneath a linden-shield, under a light shield,
> Where the mighty women revealed their power,
> And they, yelling, sent forth spears;
> I to them another one back will send,
> A flying arrow straight towards them.

The connection in the charm between this group of women and the burial mound clearly suggests they were Vanir spirits – elves. Indeed, the charm ends with a rousing plea to be made safe from the *'elves' arrows'*.

Despite what might seem to be the 'quack' nature of this remedy, there are some significant insights into disease: the advised use of feverfew, for instance, does have a real effect on fevers by reducing the temperature, and the idea that disease was caused by invisible entities attacking the body, is paralleled by our present knowledge of infections. Also, the use of the charm seems akin to the modern technique of 'visualization', a mental tool used to help overcome certain illnesses (such as some cancers), by which one visualizes the disease as a foreign entity being overcome by one's (personified) immune system.

Although this wholly negative portrayal of the elves may have been promulgated by the Church in order to curtail the continued pagan worship in rural areas, it is probable that the elves were thought capable of bringing bad luck even in pagan times. That the elves were given offerings to help heal an individual clearly shows they were conceived of as having power over disease, and so, by extension, they might also have had the propensity to harm. Spirits of the dead in all cultures are things to be feared and placated, but this does not mean the Vanir were 'evil' – more that they were morally ambiguous, beneficial if appeased but vengeful if ignored or offended.

Elves were thought to be behind a number of aberrant mental states such as madness and 'demonic possession', and this may offer a clue as to the original nature of their rites and the behaviour of its celebrants. To the early Christian Church such illnesses may have been linked to the elves as they bore a great resemblance to the *deliberately* invoked trance or possession states that seem to have played a role in the rites of the *alfar*.

Possession

As the word itself explains, the Old English adjective *ylfig*, for instance, roughly translatable as 'elfy' or 'elfish' and meaning mad or deranged, was seen as a state of mind caused by elves.[10] Was this in origin the state of being possessed by the *alfar* – perhaps deliberately invoked through the taking of the sacred cereal intoxicant? This is also suggested in the word 'giddy' – meaning light-headed or dizzy, but which originally was '*gidig*' – the feeling of being possessed by a '*gid*' (god). This ritual potion is likely the reason the worshippers in the grove of the Semnones may have fallen, giddy, to the floor in their groves (*see* page 45).

Another term for possession that is found in the Old English 'leech-books' is *aelfsiden*.[11] The word *siden* is related to the Old Norse *seithr*, a word denoting a magical tradition based on elements of shamanism and clairvoyance, said to have been taught to the Aesir by Freyja and practised by the priestesses of the Vanir. The practitioners of this Vanir-based tradition, like the maenads, traditionally were groups of women known as *Volva* who toured the land *in wagons*, once again linking them with the fairies, who also tend to appear in folklore as groups of females rather than individually or as males. In fact, the wagon-borne Volva may represent the last remnants of the fertility goddess's progress around the land.

The main role of these *seithr* priestesses was to foretell the future.[12] The term *seithr* is related to the word 'seat' – it was a sitting, a séance. A Volva is usually portrayed as going into a kind of trance, like a modern medium, answering the questions of the crowd who assembled around the platform on which she sat.

With such abandoned states at the heart of the Vanir cults, it is small wonder that they were rejected by Christian Church, and that the gods of this religion, the elves, were deliberately demonized as descendants of Cain, associated with ills and evils until they faded into demons haunting the old monuments, to be propitiated and feared, but not worshipped. But, while this may indeed have been the case, these creatures may have possessed a darker side from the very start, and that it is in this 'alter-ego' that we at last get to the heart of the monstrous lake-mother of *Beowulf*.

CHAPTER TEN

.

CHOOSERS OF THE SLAIN

NUMBERED AMONGST the descendants of Cain in the Christian-ized Anglo-Saxon cosmology found in *Beowulf* were the gods of the old heathen religion. Since the poet makes it clear that Grendel and his mother are amongst such fiends, it can be deduced that this pair of monsters were originally divinities too – namely the fertility god and his lover/mother of ancient Denmark. At first glance, the idea might seem preposterous. Grendel and his dam are described using horrific imagery: they are 'cursed spirits', 'demons', 'shadow-walkers'; he is 'God's adversary', she is 'monster of the deep', 'water-witch'. Though in the shape of man and woman, these beings are man-eating demons that either gobble down their prey immediately or drag them back to their watery lair. Yet a closer look at the Vanir reveals a darker side to these divinities that in every way matches the description and the modus operandi of the two nightmarish creatures.

The Keres

The first clue to the dual nature of the Vanir comes from the parallel traditions concerning similar 'spirits' in Greece. Early Greek religion recognized spirits known as *Keres* (singular: *Ker*) that, like the elves, were in origin spirits of the dead.[1] The Keres were depicted on Greek vases (our best source for Greek religious imagery) as small winged beings, akin to the winged sprites of later fairy lore. Like the Egyptian

Ka with which they are linked, not least linguistically, the Greek *Ker* – the inner fate or 'genius' of the individual – was seen to live on in the underworld or the burial mound after death. The Keres were offered food, usually barley grain in the form of a porridge named *pelanos*, linking them with the porridge left for the fairies in Irish tradition. As with all spirit beings of this kind, as long as they were honoured and placated all was fine – but the problem was that they were easy to offend.

As with the elves of north-west Europe, we can trace the development (or rather the demise) of the Keres. In pre-classical times, the Keres were conceived of as the spirits of the dead, but in due course the idea arose that they were sinister entities that brought illness and disease as well as madness, blindness and nightmares. There are portrayals on vases of heroic figures such as Herakles fighting Keres (where they appear as diminutive, ugly, winged creatures), and the *Hymn to Herakles* reads very much like the Anglo-Saxon charm against illness:

> Come blessed hero, come and bring allayment of all diseases. Brandishing thy club, drive forth the baleful fates; with poison shafts banish the noisome Keres far away.

It is interesting that these spirits were reduced to being carriers of disease from the lofty state of ancestral souls not by Christianity, but by the Olympian religion of the Immortals that preceded it. Like the Aesir, with whom they have much in common, the worship of the Immortals of Mount Olympus clashed with the aboriginal farming cults that involved the worship of local spirits in local shrines – a clash represented in myth by the victory of the gods, led by Zeus, over the monstrous Titans, whom they cast into the underworld (*see* page 189).[2] In these clashes, the old gods lost the fight and were relegated to the position of nightmarish bogeys. They haunted the grave mounds of yore like the Irish *sídhe*, still sensed by the people closest to the land, but now feared more than before.

The transformation of the Keres into the stuff of nightmares was not a difficult process as it seems they were already associated with bringing death. The winged Keres were perceived as coming to take

the spirits of the recently departed to the grave. As Odysseus says of
them in the *Odyssey*:

Howbeit him whom the Death-Keres carried off to Hades' House.

From this image stemmed many of the 'monsters' of ancient Greek
myth – the winged Furies, Harpies and Sirens – creatures that would
lure you to your doom. The monstrous water-witch and her son in
Beowulf seem to have been of similar pedigree.

The Valkyries

The Keres were shown hovering around battlefields waiting to satiate
themselves on the blood of the slain and in Norse myth we see identical spirits, the Valkyries, who we can confidently link with Freyja. The
Valkyries, meaning 'choosers of the slain', were often imaged as
armoured women riding through the sky on horses or wolves, or as
ravens, bearing the souls of those killed in battle to Valhalla, the 'Hall
of the Slain' (*see* plate 9). The Valkyries' names associate them with
spears – 'spear goddess', 'spear brandisher', 'spear of battle'.[3] They are
the same grave spirits casting their spears in the charm against a sudden stitch, yet in their true guise before the new religion had demoted
them from goddesses to disease-bringing sprites. The role of choosing
the slain on the battlefield originally belonged to Freyja (*see* page 50)
and it is likely the Valkyries, in later myth depicted as Odin's daughters, were originally an aspect of the Vanir goddess herself.

In Irish tradition, the equivalent of the Valkyries is the *Mórríghan*;
the name given both to an individual, the mate of the Dagda (*see* page
104) and a trinity of battle goddesses who appeared on the battlefield
as winged ravens that took the souls of those slain in battle to the
otherworld. (She later appears in Arthurian lore as Morgan le Fay – *the
fairy* – who with two other queens bears the wounded Arthur to
Avalon.)

In origin, the animal attributes of both the Mórríghan and the
Valkyries originated in the carrion-eating ravens and wolves that

visited the battlefield and devoured the slain. In an age when it was believed that by eating something one absorbed its 'essence' or 'soul', it was natural to see a blooded crow or wolf as an emissary of the goddess, come to take the soul of the dead to the underworld. And scavengers such as dogs and pigs enjoyed a similar status.

The idea of these goddesses as death omens was just one short step further. If such beings took away souls then it was logical to believe that to see one of these spirits presaged a death – perhaps one's own or a family member. In the *Vita St Gregory* that tells of the conversion of the Northumbrian King Edwin to Christianity (whose chief priest, Coifi, destroyed his own shrine, *see* page 45), an incident is related in which Edwin and his men hear the cawing of a crow 'from a less propitious corner of the sky' and presumably take this as a death omen. Bishop Paulinus, who is with them (and is in the process of converting them), has the bird shot with an arrow.[4] He says:

'Since that insensate bird did not know how to avoid death for itself, still less might it foretell men anything of the events to come.'

In Irish lore, there is the image of the 'washer at the ford' – a vision dreaded by warriors for it was of the raven-goddess Mórríghan[5] washing the clothes of those who were to be slain in the forthcoming battle (*see* page 112), and even today belief in the banshee as an omen of death persists in Ireland. The Valkyries also seemed to act as death omens. In *Njals saga*, relating to the battle of Clontarf at Dublin in 1014, we hear of three hideous women seen before battle weaving on a loom made of the entrails of slain men and weighted with severed heads; while they weave they sing how the 'Valkyries have power to choose the slain'.

These three goddesses were known among the Norse as the Norns or 'daughters of the night', who spun the life-threads of mortals.[6] One sister wove the thread, another measured it, and the last, named Skuld, cut it – bringing death. These were the three 'wyrd' sisters who appeared to Macbeth in Shakespeare's play to foretell his destiny, which is what *wyrd* means. The pieces of a loom found with the ritually deposited chariot at Dejbjerg (*see* page 57) suggests a link between such death-heralds and the goddess Nerthus.

Black Dogs and Blue Hags

It is significant here that the Greek Keres of the battlefield are referred to as the 'hounds of Hades', for the phantom black dogs of English folklore are also thought of as omens of death. These large black shaggy hounds, the size of calves, with huge glowing eyes, go by many different names depending on the locality: Black Shuck, Skriker, Bargest and Padfoot, to name a few.[7] Dogs regularly appear in mythology as being connected to the land of the dead, either as guardians or as psychopomps (soul-guides), so there is a tradition that following a black dog is, in effect, following the path to the underworld. In Egyptian myth, the dog-headed god Anubis acts as a psychopomp, and in Greek myth the three-headed dog Cerberus guards the entrance to Hades. In view of the honour granted to the dogs buried at Skateholm in Sweden during the Mesolithic period (*see* page 27), this tradition is one of utmost antiquity. Black dogs, like ravens, crows and wolves (from which they are descended and who are the carrion eaters *par excellence* of the Norse world), are connected to the idea of carrion eaters who have, by extension, become omens of portending doom.

When such carrion-eating spirits were depicted in more human form they yielded the image of cannibalistic hags. The Black Annis of Leicestershire, a lean, blue-faced hag with long iron fingernails who lived in a cave in the Dane hills and stole (and then ate) children who slept near open windows can be traced back to such beginnings. Not only is blue-black the colour attributed to the death-Keres in Greek tradition, but it is also the colour of the plumage of the raven. The cannibalistic blue-black hag is surely an extension of the fused concepts of the carrion-bird and death-Keres, a fact seemingly compounded by the Germanic hag figures known as *Frau Holda* or *Frau Perchta*, which are depicted with huge hooked iron noses suggestive of beaks.[8]

Such hags abound in British folklore. In Scotland and Ireland she is known as the *Cailleach* (Old Woman), a goddess closely associated with winter, being reborn at Halloween and blighting the land with frost and snow. On May Eve she turns to stone, awaiting rebirth at the summer's end. In some versions of the story she is transformed in the spring into a beautiful maid – in other words, the barren, blighted winter earth becomes transformed into the abundant spring soil, ready for impregnation. The Cailleach as 'mother nature' has two sides – summer and winter, death-bringing and life-restoring – like Freyja, who is both goddess of the fruitful earth (the earth as womb) and the chooser of the slain (the earth as tomb).

The hag is associated with open water, wells and streams. One such water-hag is Jenny Greenteeth, said to haunt the streams of Lancashire and to drag down children who get too close to the edge. The hag of the river Ribble was known as Peg O'Nell (who was said to claim a victim every seven years), while that of the river Tees was Peg Powler; but in Yorkshire she went by the familiar-sounding name of Grindylow.

It has been suggested that these nightmarish creatures are merely 'nursery bogeys' – monsters invented to scare children from playing near deep water or from wandering off alone. Now while there may be some truth to this, the question arises as to why they are all women and display such unified characteristics. An alternative explanation would be that these water-hags are pagan deities in origin, fertility goddesses like Nerthus, in whose lakes men were ritually drowned.

The Devouring Goddess

Just as the Keres of Greek tradition and the elves/Vanir gods possessed a dual nature, it is probable that since the Danish Nerthus was a fertility goddess cast in a similar mould, one would expect to find that she, too, possessed a negative side. This darker aspect would be associated with the infertility and barrenness of winter (when we know her victims died, *see* page 56), and, coloured by the symbols of carrion animals, it would find expression as a bloodthirsty cannibalistic monster dragging men to their watery deaths. Arguably, the figure of Grendel's mother as found in Beowulf was the sinister side of such an ancient deity – the winter aspect of the fertile earth; she was the tusked sow who cuts down the barley god and devours him (*see* page 76) – a role remembered in *Syr* (sow) one of Freyja's many alternative names.

Although at odds with our modern concept of how a divinity should look and behave, the description we find in *Beowulf* of the Valkyrie-like 'bone-cruncher' that is Grendel's mother does not exclude her in any way from being of divine origin – in fact, precisely the opposite.

Nowhere is this devouring attribute made clearer than in the Welsh tale of Taliesin. This story tells of a witch named Ceridwen, who *dwelt under a lake* (Llyn Tegid) with her husband, Tegid Voel. There, using her magical arts, she brewed a cauldron of '*awen*' (inspiration) for her ugly son Morfran, while a young lad named Gwion Bach tended the fire. While the potion was being stirred, three drops flew onto this lad's finger, burning him. Without thinking, he placed them in his mouth, and received the inspiration intended for Morfran. In her anger, the goddess chased him, but using the magical knowledge acquired from the cauldron, Gwion transformed himself into a hare and sped away. Ceridwen, however, became a greyhound, and each shape he took she followed him until finally he became *a grain of corn* and she a hen; she *ate him*, and nine months later gave birth to him. Unable to harm him, she *sent him adrift on the ocean in a leather bag or a coracle*. He was found in a salmon trap by a man named Elffin who named him *Taliesin* (radiant brow), and in time he became the foremost bard of Britain.

Though a relatively late tale (first appearing in medieval Welsh poetry), the myth of Taliesin preserves a number of interesting parallels with Sheaf: he is a grain of corn (Sheaf/Beow) set adrift on the waters as a newborn baby – having been devoured by the water-goddess. Not only does his tale recall the floating of the corn on the shield, and the drinking of the initiating *kykeon* of the mysteries, but his name 'radiant brow' is also suggestive of the 'shining face' of the sun. Most intriguing in light of *Beowulf* is the reference to a cannibalistic witch and her ugly son dwelling under the lake. This tale captures the essence of the dual goddess myth.

The rebirth of the 'radiant brow' from the mother reveals that solar symbolism also became associated with the carrion-goddess. The sun, plunging into the underworld at night, was also seen as entering the maw of a giant monster. In Norse myth, this monster was usually the wolf, as in the myths concerning Ragnarok, the final battle in which the gods are slain. Not only are the sun and moon swallowed by a pair of wolves, but Odin is swallowed whole by the giant wolf Fenris. The motif of the man between two wolves on a purse, in the Sutton Hoo find, is suggestive of this myth (*see* figure 10, page 87). It seems to represent a solar being between two wolves with open jaws – the sun escaping at dawn only to be swallowed again at night.

The Welsh figure of Ceridwen suggests that the ancient Earth-mother, the wife of the barley god, did have such a negative side. Though there is no direct connection made between her and the winter earth, the fact that Taliesin is born on May Day suggests he was in the womb all winter, having been eaten at harvest time. This wintry aspect, however, is better illustrated in a myth concerning the Greek barley goddess Demeter. In this, we hear how Demeter is chased by the god Poseidon and hides as a mare amongst horses, but Poseidon finds her and mates with her as a stallion. This violation infuriates her and she takes on the aspect of '*Demeter Erinys*' (Demeter the Fury).[9] She wears black and retires to a cave on Mount Eleaus in western Arcadia where she was known (and worshipped) as the Black Demeter of Phigalia, and depicted as having a mare's head (a symbol associated with kingship and sovereignty; *see* page 126).

During Demeter's sojourn in the Phigalian cave, the earth goes black and all fertility ceases – clearly the Black Demeter, like the Cailleach, is a metaphor for the dark barren winter earth. This vengeful, dark goddess is only calmed from her terrible fury when she is bathed in the waters of a local river (the Ladon).

This myth illuminates much about what is going on in the Nerthus cult of old Germania. It is significant that Demeter's 'husband' is Poseidon – god of the *sea* – whose name simply means 'husband of the lady': he is an exact equivalent to the Germanic Njorthr. What is more, her rage and her hiding away in a cave in the mountains to become a winter goddess might explain the actions of one of Njorthr's wives, the goddess Skathi (ski-goddess) who, unable to bear living in Njorthr's coastal home, returns to the cold mountains, leaving her husband behind.[10] It seems that Skathi was in fact the winter aspect of the goddess Nerthus. It is possible that the ritual bathing of Nerthus in the sacred lake after her 'secret rites', as reported by Tacitus (and linked to the bathing of Cybele after the death of Attis), was like that of Demeter in the river Ladon, an act to calm and cleanse this vengeful mother after the act of love.

Demeter's myth bears all the traits of the winter goddess, although the cannibalistic motif is missing. It does, however, appear in the tales of other horse-Keres – as such entities might be termed. In the Dionysos myth, one of his maenads, *Leucippe* (white-mare), kills and eats her son *Hippasos* (foal), for which punishment she and her three sisters are turned into birds.[11] And in Welsh myth, the horse-goddess Rhiannon (associated with the underworld and with three magical birds) is accused of eating her son Pryderi. This connection to horses also appears in the triune Irish Mórríghan, who included in its trinity a goddess named *Macha* (Battle), a horse-goddess who dies giving birth to twin foals. The devouring horse-Keres, it would seem, is a potent figure in European myth, not least in the carrion-goddesses of the north, the horse-riding Valkyries.

Hag-riding

Unsurprisingly, there is also negative imagery concerning the horse and the goddess in Norse myth. It is often to be found with regard to the acts of the priestesses of the Vanir, the Volva (*see* page 109). As well as acting as clairvoyants and seers, when these women took on the *seithr* power of the goddess Freyja, it could be put to malevolent use. We find them connected to hag-riding – a terrifying nocturnal assault said to have been caused by a witch; it was an event also linked to the

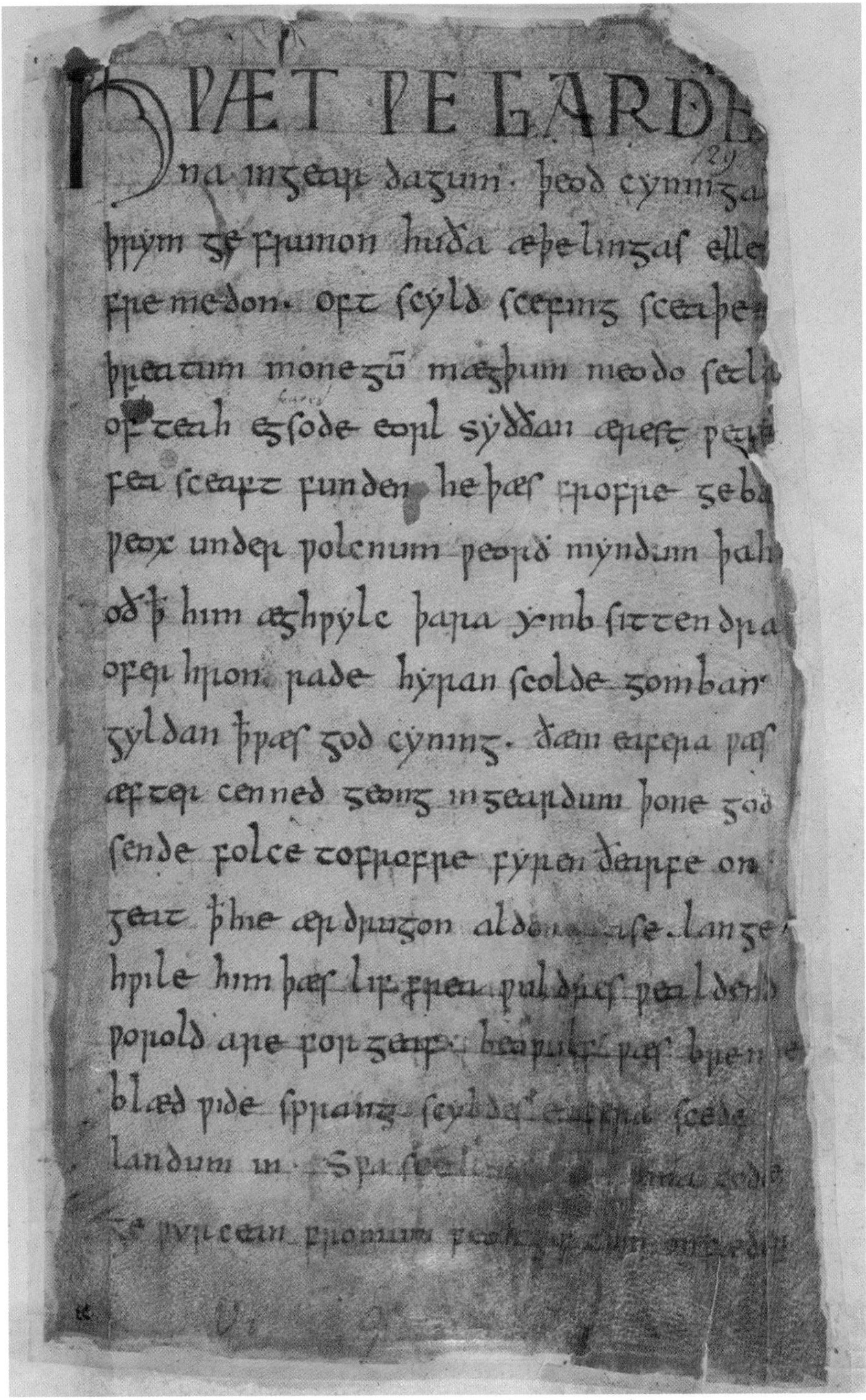

Plate 1. The first page of the *Beowulf* manuscript – the only surviving source for the deeds of England's oldest hero. (*Trustees of the British Library.*)

Plate 2 (left). The Neolithic passage-grave at Øm, Denmark. Such sites were the abode of ancestral spirits that played a major role in the fertility religion of the ancient English peoples. (*John Grigsby.*)

Plate 3 (above). Inside the grave at Øm. Offerings were left here at midwinter for the spirits until recent times. (*John Grigsby.*)

Plate 4. The Trundholm Sun-Chariot. The symbols of sun and steed were paramount in the pagan fertility religion of Denmark, from where the ancestors of the English originated. (*National Museum of Denmark, Copenhagen.*)

Plate 5. The Tollund Man – archaeological evidence of the sacrificial cult of the goddess Nerthus, as reported by the Roman historian Tacitus? The sacred intoxicant he had taken before his death yields clues as to why he died. (*John Grigsby.*)

Plate 6. The remains of the girl from Egtved – a Continental ancestor of the English people. (*National Museum of Denmark, Copenhagen.*)

Plate 7. A goddess (Nerthus?), from the Rynkeby Cauldron. Is the terrible Grendel's mother in *Beowulf* a dim memory of this lake-dwelling goddess? (*John Grigsby.*)

Plate 8. Two faces of the goddess: 1. The goddess as giver – Gefion ploughing Zealand from Sweden. (*John Grigsby.*)

Plate 9. Two faces of the goddess: 2. The goddess as taker – a Valkyrie on horseback. Such spirits chose those who were to be slain on the battlefield. (*John Grigsby.*)

Plate 10. The elves dancing, from an English chapbook. The elves were derived from the fertility gods of the pagan English, and like them could be both helpful and malevolent. (*John Grigsby.*)

Plate 11. The Broddenbjerg Freyr. Freyr was a dying and rising fertility god akin to the Greek Dionysos. Did the sacrificial victims of pagan Denmark die embodying this god? (*National Museum of Denmark, Copenhagen.*)

Plate 12. The "drowning" scene from the Gundestrup Cauldron – depicting either ritual sacrifice or an initiation rite. (*National Museum of Denmark, Copenhagen.*)

Plate 13. Ritual burial monuments at Lejre – once the centre of the Goddess cult in Denmark, and later the dwelling place of the Scylding dynasty, whose tragic history is recounted in *Beowulf* and other Northern sagas. (*John Grigsby.*)

Plate 14. The Viking hall at Lejre, possibly built on the site of *Heorot*, the feasting hall terrorized by Grendel and his mother in *Beowulf*. (*John Grigsby*.)

Plate 15. Plan of the Viking halls at Lejre. (*John Grigsby; based on plans by Tom Christensen*.)

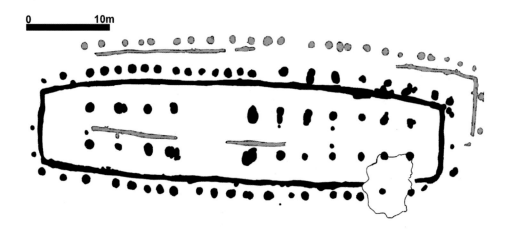

0   10m

Plate 16. The rays of the sun entering Newgrange on midwinter's morning. Do the tales of the midwinter deaths of kings in both Germanic and Celtic myth have their roots in ancient sacrificial ceremonies? (*Martin Byrne; www.carrowkeel.com*)

Plate 17. Odin as depicted on a Viking helmet. Does the usurpation of the old sacrificial fertility cult by the worship of Odin in 5th-century Denmark lie behind the deeds of Beowulf? (*John Grigsby.*)

Plate 18. Odin rides his eight-legged horse Sleipnir, with a cup of mead in hand, from the Gotland stone. Odin's mythical theft of the mead of knowledge offers clues to the events depicted in *Beowulf*. (*John Grigsby.*)

Plate 19. The helmet of Raedwald, the Wuffinga king buried at Sutton Hoo. Might the *Beowulf* poem have been composed for the Wuffinga dynasty? (*Trustees of the British Museum.*)

term 'nightmare' in its original sense. Hag-riding was (and is) the sensation of waking up paralyzed, unable to breathe, with a weight on the chest – in the half awake state it is imagined that this is a demon (known as a succubus if female, or incubus if male – beings whose visitations were usually sexual in nature).[12] The word 'haggard' is derived from this, being the description of the victim's appearance after being 'hag-ridden'. An early Swedish king of the *Yngling* line is reported to have been trampled to death by a 'nightmare' – a Volva in the form of a horse. 'Riding' men to death in such a manner was often an accusation made against 'witches' practising *seithr*. Robert Kirk says a similar thing of the British fairy women:

> There may be many fair Ladies of the aerial order, which do often tryst with lascivious young men, in the quality of Succubi, or lightsome paramours or strumpets, called Leannain Sith, or familiar spirits: so do many ... as if in a strangling by the Night MARE, pressed with a fearful dream, or rather possessed by one of our aerial Neighbours, rise up fierce in the night.[13]

Importantly, here he is linking the orgiastic fairy-lover and the nightmare into one image (*see* page xxx), bringing to mind the maenads who are at first sexually voracious, then cannibalistic. It is as if the carrion-goddess, the night-mare, killed her mate after their union, strangling him after their tryst, a mode of death that brings the bog victims of Nerthus to mind.

It may be that one of the roles of the Vanir priestesses, as the embodiment of the carrion-goddess, the nightmare, was to kill the representative of the god while they straddled him, just as Grendel's Mother is described in the poem as straddling Beowulf:

Ofsæt þā þone selegyst, ond hyre seax getēah

She then bestrode the hall-guest [Beowulf] and drew her dagger

Even if the *Beowulf* poem had not survived, it would have been apparent that Nerthus, as a fertility goddess akin to Demeter, would have had a nightmare side and that she might appear in a monstrous form. And *Beowulf* seems to describe such a creature, in the right location, at the right time – even down to the ritual position that the nightmare should take – astride her victim. Grendel's mother is no invention or interpolation of a folktale motif into a tale of warring tribes. Her part in *Beowulf* is, as Tolkien said, as central as that fertility god Sheaf who begins the poem.

The Christian author of *Beowulf* may not have recognized in this hideous water-hag her original divinity, turning this Vanir goddess into 'just' a monster, a water-hag – a Grindylow (*Grendelow*?). In either case, his hero performed an amazing feat when he dived into her waters and emerged unscathed – unlike the bog victims such as Tollund and Grauballe man who, drunk with the god's sacred-brew, went to their doom '*elfig*', '*gidig*' – possessed by the god, indeed gods themselves – fully believing in the rebirth that would follow.

These men were enacting the death of the wagon-borne fertility god Freyr, Ing, Njorthr, Sheaf or Dionysos – whatever names they knew him by – who died in the winter to be reborn in the spring; he was represented in other lands by a wooden image, cast into the waters, but in Denmark plainly by flesh and blood mortals.

It is possible that these individuals who willingly went to their deaths were priests, but there is another likelihood hinted at in the surviving stories. And this may tell us why Hrothgar feared these monsters, and why his people removed the name of Sheaf from their family tree, as if trying to distance themselves from the old Vanir religion and its dying god: at certain times the person to be killed was the king himself.

Part III

TO KILL A KING

CHAPTER ELEVEN

·

ROYAL OBLIGATIONS

F OR THE 12 YEARS that Grendel haunts Heorot he sits at night on Hrothgar's throne like the shadow of the king, the lord of an empty hall. Hrothgar is powerless to prevent the desecration of this symbol of his kingship. There is a sense that Grendel's appearance somehow reflects on Hrothgar's rule. To what does Hrothgar owe the presence of this uninvited guest? The truth of the matter, however, lies not so much in what Hrothgar has done rather than what he has *not* done. For the clues in the poem indicate that Grendel's appearance has to do with a lapse in kingly function – an obligation tied in with the seasonal wagon tour of the elf-god Freyr and his mate the dark goddess.

Many myths of the wagon-god Freyr were derived, in part, from the seasonal peregrination of a man who it was thought was either possessed by, or embodied, this spirit of fertility. The most likely candidate for such a role was one thought suitably dignified or holy to act as a vessel for the divine presence: he would have been either a priest or the king himself.[1]

A suggestion that he may have been the latter is found in an account concerning Childeric III, the last Merovingian king (deposed in 751) in the *Vita Carolini* (*c.* 829–36) of the Frankish chronicler Einhard. Childeric is described as being borne on a cattle-led wagon:[2]

Whenever he needed to travel, he went in a cart which was drawn in country style by yoked oxen, with a cowherd to drive them. In this fashion, he would go to the palace and to the general assembly of his people, which was held each year to settle the affairs of the kingdom, and in this fashion he would return home again.

It is possible that this was the last vestige of the seasonal peregrination of the fertility god. The Merovingians (whose kings were famed for their long hair, which many contemporaries spurned as 'effeminate' – like the priests of Attis who aped the appearance of their god) were descendants of the Frankish tribes of the Low Countries, who originally may have been counted amongst the Ingaevones. The Merovingians claimed Messianic descent and the wearing of long hair was said to be in imitation of Christ, but this was likely a later Christianized form of the original regal imitation of another 'Lord': Freyr/Ing.

While no historical records survive, there are examples from myth and legend to suggest that it was the king himself who was involved in enacting the fertility god's progress. The Danish sources, for example, tell of many kings who bore the title Frothi (wise/fruitful)[3] – the origin of Tolkien's name Frodo[4] – who were clearly conceived as embodiments of Freyr, for Snorri tells us that *'inn froddi'* (the fruitful) was one of Freyr's names. Of the many kings who bore this name, the son of Skjold in the Danish genealogy (who takes the place held by Beow in the Anglo-Saxon genealogies) was especially famed. This King Frothi was said to have reigned around the time of Christ and during his lifetime there was great peace, known as *'Frótha-frith'* (the peace of Frothi). Such peace was a feature of Freyr's worship, for he allowed no weapons in his temples or blood spilled on his lands. King Frothi's death is illuminating: he was killed by a sorceress in the guise of a *sea-cow* – very reminiscent of the Volva night-mare (*see* page 119). As with Freyr, when King Frothi died it is said the truth was kept from the people and they continued to worship him as a king, though he was dead:

For this reason they would carry his lifeless body about, not, so it seemed, in a hearse, but a *royal carriage*, pretending that this was a service due from his soldiers to a feeble old monarch not in full possession of his strength. Such was the pomp accorded to their ruler by his friends even after his decease. [My italics.]

Both the wagon-borne figures of Childeric and the *Frothi* kings of Denmark suggest that in pagan Germania kings themselves were conceived of as embodiments of the fertility god Freyr. But this sacred enactment did not consist solely of riding in the wagon. They were thought of as 'husbands' of the fertility goddess and part of their rites included a ritual sacred marriage between themselves and an individual enacting the role of the Earth-mother. This was the same act that had been depicted on rock carvings from Scandinavia since the Bronze Age and that formed the basis of the myth of Freyr's wooing of Gerthr.

The Mare of Sovereignty

Perhaps the best example of the enactment of the sacred marriage of a monarch and the land is found in the sagas relating to Olaf Trygvasson, which tell of the many 'liaisons' of Earl Hakon. Hakon was the man who seized power in Norway and tried to reintroduce paganism to a people falling under the spell of Christianity, while the future King Olaf was in Britain (*see* page 93).

Hakon is recorded as spending the majority of his reign travelling around his kingdom and bedding other men's wives, sisters and daughters. While these acts can be seen simply as a powerful man abusing his authority, it may be that he was enacting a type of ritual *droit du seigneur*[5] based on the marriage of Freyr with Gerthr. He is said to have sent his servants to find suitable girls and this may have been consciously based on the deployment of Skírnir by Freyr to woo Gerthr. His bedding of these girls may have been a ritual act to fructify his kingdom; one of these girls seems to have borne a symbolic name associating her with Gerthr, who is first seen with arms blazing like the sun, and who sleeps with Freyr in the grove of Barri (Barley) – she was named Gudrun *lundasol* (sun of the groves).

The goddess represented the earth, the land itself, and in the act of sexual union with her, the king was 'marrying' himself to his kingdom. There is evidence for this in Ireland in a rite called the 'feis' in which the king was wed to the goddess of sovereignty of the land. While no specific evidence exists for an equivalent to the feis in Germanic kingship, there is equivalent symbolism in many other Indo-European societies, which suggests that it may have been widespread in the ancient world. In most of these cases there is connected to such rites the symbolism of the horse – a symbol of kingship and sovereignty.

The horse was inexorably linked to land ownership in ancient Indo-European society. Such a connection is suggestive of a time when new territory was taken or land disputes were settled by the releasing of horses onto the land – the area circumnavigated by the horse belonged to its owner.[6] For instance, it is safe to view the chalk carved image of the Uffington White Horse (c. 1200–800 BC) as a sacred glyph that acted as a permanent territorial marker to the tribes of prehistoric Berkshire.[7] This symbolism also suggests that the names 'Hengist' ('stallion') and 'Horsa' ('horse') were ritual titles taken by the Jutish princes signifying that they were performing the ancient act of taking of new territory (England) under the guidance of the sacred horse of sovereignty. Even today, the place of their arrival, Kent, bears the totemic badge of the horse as its county symbol. Such ritual acts of land acquisition also help explain why in Irish Gaelic the word for invasion (gabala) stems from that of horse (gabal).

Above all, the preoccupation with the horse as an embodiment of the land and sovereignty helps explain the presence of horse symbolism in the many accounts of the sacred union of the king with the Earth-goddess where either he or she takes on a horse form. It is possible that such an image lies behind the bizarre incident in 12th-century Donegal, related by Gerald of Wales, in which an Irish king has intercourse with a mare and then (after it is slaughtered) bathes in a broth of its flesh.[8] Although such a rite may have been thought of by Gerald as an amusing anecdote lampooning the primitive Irish, it closely parallels a kingship ceremony from India known as the Asva-Medha (Horse-Feast).

In the Asva-Medha it was the queen and not the king, however, who symbolically mated with a slain stallion that had previously been allowed to wander over the king's lands for a year, thus confirming the extent of his kingdom. During the Asva-Medha rite, the horse was suffocated and following its mock-intercourse with one of the king's four queens, was cut into three pieces and then burned.

Killing the King

The stallion in the Asva-Medha, who as mate of the queen is representing the king, is clearly perceived of as being 'ridden' (in a sexual sense) and strangled, bringing to mind the Volva who 'trampled' the early Swedish king to death in the *Ynglingatal* (*see* page 119). What these rites reveal is that the sacred marriage between the goddess of sovereignty and the king was also fundamentally linked with a sacred death, in which the goddess, sometimes in the form of the horse-Keres (*see* page 118), took his life. This dual aspect of sovereignty is reflected in Irish tales where her embodiment is usually depicted as both a hideous hag and a beautiful young maid. The true king, worthy to marry her, is one who sees through her ugliness and does not spurn her advances, evidence that they are willing to embrace death itself as part of their kingship.

The king took on grave responsibility in assuming the kingship for he was taking upon himself the very health of the land. As an embodiment of Freyr, the fertility spirit, and by marrying himself to the land, the king's health and that of the land became symbiotically entwined. In Irish myth, a king of the *Tuatha De Danann* named Nuada is forced to abdicate because of the loss of an arm in battle, which suggests that kings were required to be without injury or illness.[9] Twinned with this concept would be the idea that kings should also be young and virile – the human vessel in which the kingship resided would need continual renewal for the land to stay *inn froddi* – fruitful.

There is a story from Snorri's *Ynglingatal* that links the sacrifice of a king with fertility. This is the tale of the Swedish King Domaldi of the Yngling line who is cursed by his stepmother with '*ósgæssa*' (bad luck). Domaldi is ritually killed during a famine to ensure a good harvest. His people did not kill him without trying all other alternatives. First, they offered oxen to the gods, and then, when this did not have the desired outcome, human victims; finally, when the famine had still not abated, it was decided that it was the king's turn to die:

> The sword-bearing men reddened the earth with the blood of their lord, when eager for harvest the Swedes killed the enemy of the Jutes.

The word used in this passage for the act of sacrifice is actually 'sowing', clearly linking him with the cereal gods whose death he was presumably aping. In the anonymous 12th-century *Historia Norvegiae* ('*History of Norway*') based on an earlier (and lost) history of the Ynglings by a 9th–10th-century poet, Tjodolf of Hvin, Domaldi is reported to have been hung to Ceres, the corn mother, 'for the fertility of the crops'.[10]

That such regicide seems to have been most widespread among the Dark Age Swedish monarchs, the Ynglings – the 'sons of Yngvi-Freyr' – is no surprise. Nor is the fact that its occurrence in Denmark seems to parallel the *floruit* of the Ingaevones – the 'friends of Ing'.

Archaeologists have dated the numerous bog bodies found in Denmark and have discovered that the practice of placing humans into the bogs, which began in earnest around 900 BC (although there are earlier Neolithic examples) seems to have come to an end around AD 300. Although based on only a handful of samples, the pattern shows that ritual drowning was most common in the time of Tacitus, but by a later period, the age of migration, the ritual seems to have been in decline.[11] Since no systematic study of the bogs has been undertaken – the 500 or so bodies found so far are all accidental discoveries, and there may be very many more –the pattern of bog deposits seems to match what we know of the political upheavals going on in Denmark at the time. The demise in the bog rite seems to coincide with the assumed date of the establishment of the Danish tribes, the royal house of the Scyldings, the tribe who appear to have removed Sheaf from their genealogy and annexed the Ingaevones.

As the killing of the king had become mostly obsolete in Scandinavia (save for the Swedish kingdom of the Ynglings) by the 5th century, it is unlikely that when Earl Hakon attempted to re-establish paganism in Norway in the 10th century, he would have decided to re-introduce this element of Freyr's cult. It is ironic, then, that he met his death through an attempted 'liaison'.

After Hakon had sent a servant to 'woo' Gudrun *lundasol*, she, like her mythological counterpart Gerthr, initially refused. But Hakon did not have the persuasiveness or the charisma of Freyr. When his messenger asked her again, she and her kin killed him and then set out to lynch Hakon who was forced to hide in a pig sty with one of his slaves. When Olaf Trygvasson heard of this (having newly arrived back in Norway), he offered a reward for Hakon's head. Hakon rightly believed that his own slave who had hidden with him would try to claim the reward, so for two days Hakon fought to stay awake. Eventually, Hakon collapsed with exhaustion and his slave beheaded him[12] – an apt end for one who would be Freyr, husband of *Syr* ('sow' – an epithet of Freyja's) to die as the midwinter boar, beheaded in the pig sty.

The Noose and the Neck-Ring

One aspect of the accounts of ritual regicide found in the *Ynglingatal* and elsewhere that connects them with the bog men of Denmark is the use of strangulation as the means of death. The demise of the Yngling King Agni is a case in point. Agni's wife Skjálf ('*ski-elf* – a name linked to *Skathi*, the winter-wife of Njorthr) strangles the king with his golden neck-ring. When he is asleep in his tent in the shade of the forest, she ties a thick rope to the neck-ring; her followers pull down the tent and hoist the rope over a branch of a tree and hang the king. They then burn the body and flee by boat into the night. What connects his death to the fertility god at the hands of the winter carrion-goddess is the mention of the neck-ring.

Glob was the first to suggest a link between the neck-rings found deposited in bogs in Denmark, the images of dancing goddesses wearing neck-rings common in Scandinavia from the late Bronze Age onwards, and the bog men who had been strangled to death.[13] But why should the goddess be linked with the sinister image of the rope and cord and with the act of strangulation? One suggestion is that in the weapon-less temples of Freyr, the victim could not be beheaded with a sword or stabbed with a blade, and that strangulation (and drowning, too) not only offered a weapon-free mode of death, but also ensured blood was not spilled in the temple.

Another possible explanation is suggested by the imagery used in a medieval Welsh poem, *The Spoils of the Abyss*. Here, a prisoner named Gweir lies bound in the underworld by a heavy blue cord or chain. It has been convincingly argued that Gweir is Pryderi, the son of the horse-goddess Rhiannon, under his childhood name of Gwri Gwallt Euryn (golden-haired hay), whom she is accused of having eaten. Some take the image of the blue chain to be a metaphor for the ocean, but if the child in the underworld is being used as a metaphor for the grain awaiting rebirth in the pregnant earth, the blue cord that holds him in the Earth-mother's womb is plainly the umbilical cord.

The connection between the umbilical cord and strangulation would have been obvious to the ancients: in the days before modern medicine it was more common than now for babies to be strangled by their own umbilicus during birth. It can only be imagined how the birth of such a child would have struck primitive man: the mother was both giver and taker, and when she took life, she did so with the strangling cord, the twisted 'blue chain'. It is hard to conceive that the deaths of the strangled bog men, placed in their watery graves, were not in any way influenced by this image. The symbolism was clear – they were returning to the amniotic fluid of the Mother's womb for rebirth as they had first emerged from it – attached by a twisted cord.

The Love-Death

It has already been mentioned that strangulation or asphyxiation were associated with the visits of the night-mare – or Volva in horse form. A possible alternative origin to the word *seithr*, usually thought to derive from 'seated' (*see* page 109), is that it comes from an Indo-

European root meaning 'to bind with a cord/bond/magical force'.[14] The image of the night-mare also contained an erotic content suggesting that the death of the god was both an act of love and death (*see* Robert Kirk regarding the 'Ladies of the aerial order', page 119). And it may be significant that the act of hanging or strangulation can produce intense sexual excitement (as the practice of auto-erotic asphyxiation has demonstrated) leading to ejaculation.

Bizarre as it may seem, in the ancient rites of the fertility god and goddess, the strangulation of the victim may have been as much sexual as murderous in nature. Its purpose was to promote sexual excitement so that at the moment of the victim's death he would ejaculate, and the 'seed' of the fertility god would leave his body and enter that of the goddess ready for rebirth. This is why the priestess playing the part of the goddess mounted the male. A man being strangled would not be able to bear his own weight; instead, he would have played the passive role. He would be strangled while lying on the floor (or seated, assuming the position of the Rällinge Freyr or the torc-wearing horned god on the Gundestrup cauldron, *see* below and page 90) – hence the image of the goddess or night-mare riding him, as Grendel's mother does in *Beowulf*.

The statuette of Freyr from Rällinge.

Horned figure from Gundestrup Cauldron.

It is of interest that Gefion's myth contains an identical image linking the neck-ring with lovemaking. Norse myth records how she obtained her necklace: like Freyja, who slept with four dwarves, who offered her the Brisingamen necklace in return, Gefion was said to have obtained hers in exchange for an act of love with a youth in which she is described as having her 'thigh over his' – in other words, she was riding him.[15] The connection between the act of love and the neck-ring sheds new light on Wealtheow's gift of the neck-ring to Beowulf on the eve of his confrontation with Grendel's mother (*see* page 10).

'Ornate gold was presented in trophy: two arm-wreaths, with rings and robes also, and the richest collar I have ever heard of in all the world. Never under heaven have I heard of a finer prize among heroes – since Hama carried off the Brising necklace to his bright city, that gold-cased jewel' (*Beowulf*, 1193–200)

The gift seems to 'dedicate' Beowulf to the goddess, marking him out as Freyr/Ing, and in all probability he was wearing this neck-ring when the water-witch straddled him. Certainly it can be linked with watery deaths: Beowulf's lord, Hygelac, dies on the shoreline of Frisia while wearing it (*see* page 11) and a 3rd–4th-century neck-ring found in a hoard at Pietroasa in Gothic Romania demonstrates the connection to Ing: it is inscribed with Gothic runes that read 'sacred to *Ingwa* of the Goths'.[16]

Beowulf is underwater – '*in Gefion's ground*' when the water-hag bestrides him, and in Egyptian tradition the body of Osiris is taken to the Nile marshes where Isis *mounts the corpse* and conceives the god Horus on him. Celtic sources also show this ritual of love-death occurring near or in water.

In one Irish story, CúRoí Mac Daírí, king of Munster, is killed on the banks of the river that runs through his fort in Sleevemish by his wife and her new lover CúChulainn. She is clearly in bed with him at the time, as she binds his hair to the bedpost, pours milk into the stream as a sign to her lover who is waiting outside that her husband is vulnerable, and CúChulainn rushes in and beheads him.

In another tale, one Lugaid kills his foster-brother Fergus Mac Roich while the latter 'sports' in the waters of a lake with Queen Medb of Connacht. She is described as being 'on the breast of Fergus' at the time and has her legs 'entwined about him' (again, she is riding him), when he is killed. The key point here is that Lugaid, like Hodr, who kills Balder in Norse myth, is the brother of the slain man and is also described as *blind*. King Ailill has to aim Lugaid's throw, as Loki guides Hodr. It may be that such an act occurred in the rites described by Tacitus. In the Nerthus myth, Tacitus mentions that a secret rite took place at the end of the wagon-tour that, he seems to suggest, was so sacred that the 'slaves' who observed it were killed:

> After that, the chariot, the vestments, and (believe it if you will) the goddess herself, are cleansed in a secluded lake. This service is performed by slaves who are immediately afterwards drowned in the lake. Thus mystery begets terror and a pious reluctance to ask what that sight can be which is seen only by men doomed to die.

It seems unlikely the 'slaves' were killed because they had seen the goddess naked – like Actaeon killed by his own hounds for seeing Diana bathing. Since Tacitus implies in the text that there is a reluctance to ask what the sight is, it must presumably be more than the bathing itself: something that is so secret that Tacitus's source did not, or could not, record it. But what could be more sacred than the conjoining of the king and the land in a ritual love-death? The hidden rite seen only by 'men doomed to die' was the sacred marriage during which the king was killed. He was strangled, presumably, and then drowned, after which the goddess was washed just as Cybele was in the Almo followed the death and resurrection of Attis, and as Demeter bathed in the Ladon following her rape by Poseidon.

The Brother's Bane

The motif of the washing of the goddess after the killing of the god-king that is mentioned in these sources is also suggested in the myth of Gerthr and Freyr, where it appears in parallel with another motif: the murder of the brother. In *Skírnismál*, Gerthr is referred to as having shining arms, reflecting light as they are wet. When Skírnir arrives to woo her, she initially balks at letting him in, but eventually consents:

> Though I am afraid it may be my brother's killer outside.

This seems a strange thing to say, were it not for the myth of Idunn, the goddess who owns the apples of immortality – and is arguably the same figure as Gerthr. Idunn is described as placing her 'splendidly-washed arms around her brother's killer'.[17] What these tales seem to suggest is that the goddess's 'brother' is killed after which she washes and then embraces her brother's killer. But who is her brother and why is she so duplicitous?

In many versions of the tale, the goddess does not do the deed alone – she has an accomplice. In Welsh myth, the hero Lleu is killed while half-standing in a river, by a man named Gronw 'Pebr' ('the fiery') after being betrayed by his wife Blodeuwedd. The Greek Agamemnon was killed in the bath by his wife and her lover Aegisthus. But in other accounts the relationship between the killer and the killed is made quite clear: Osiris is slain by his *brother*, Seth; Balder by his *brother* Hodr and Fergus by his *foster-brother* Lugaid. In the Bible, Joseph's brothers throw him into a well after he tells them of a dream in which they bow down to him as a sheaf of corn. In the Grail myth we find the warring *brothers* Balin and Balan, who stem from two antagonistic Celtic deities, the brothers Bran and Beli.

The fact is that all these examples rest on the original idea that the god is the twin brother of the goddess. Osiris is the brother of Isis, Freyr of Freyja and thus, by extension, the king is the brother of sovereignty. Whoever becomes king after the demise of the old becomes, by his 'marriage', the brother of the goddess and so the brother of the old king – although, as the spirit of the crops, in essence he is the same being, albeit in a new body. The tales of Gerthr and Idunn reveal that the goddess embraces the new embodiment of fertility after the death of the old. Perhaps she has just been ritually washed in the waters of the grove, having consented to ending her spouse's life – washing the blood of her husband from her arms, washing his bloody clothes, as did the 'washer in the ford' in Irish lore.

This cyclical regicide appears in Saxo Grammaticus's version of the Balder myth, in which he depicts the fight of the brothers Balderus (who was wont to travel the land in a wagon) and Hotherus over the nymph Nanna. Hotherus kills his brother, and places him in a burial mound, but is in turn slain by another brother named Bous – and so the yearly cycle continued.[18]

This sounds very close to the ritual pattern observed at the 'little woodland lake of Nemi' where 'stood the sacred grove and sanctuary of Diana Nemorensis, or Diana of the Wood' recorded by JG Frazer in *The Golden Bough*:

> In this sacred grove there grew a certain tree round which at any time of the day, and probably far into the night, a grim figure might be seen to prowl. In his hand he carried a drawn sword, and he kept peering warily about him as if at every instant he expected to be set upon by an enemy. He was a priest and a murderer; and the man for whom he looked was sooner or later to murder him and hold the priesthood in his stead. Such was the rule of the sanctuary. A candidate for the priesthood could only succeed to office by slaying the priest, and having slain him, he retained office till he was himself slain by [one] stronger or a craftier ...
>
> Within the sanctuary at Nemi grew a certain tree of which no branch might be broken. Only a runaway slave was allowed to break off, if he could, one of its boughs. Success in the attempt entitled him to fight the priest in single combat, and if he slew him he reigned in his stead with the title of King of the Wood (*Rex Nemorensis*).[19]

Accordingly the drowned bog men of Denmark may have been killed at the hands of the embodiment of the goddess and her new 'lover', the next year's king, who would have known that he would in turn suffer the same fate the following midwinter.

Frazer's description of the 'King of the Wood' – 'far into the night, a grim figure might be seen to prowl' – brings to mind the appearance of Grendel at Heorot. The monster stalks the mead-benches, yet he remains unchallenged by Hrothgar for 12 years until one man, Beowulf, is brave enough to slay him and suffer the consequences – a tryst with the lake goddess. The monstrous Grendel does have a direct link to the brother-slaying myth:

> 'Grendel's mother herself, a monstrous ogress ... had been doomed to dwell in dread waters, in the chilling currents, *because of that blow whereby Cain became the killer of his brother.*' (*Beowulf*, 1258–65; My italics.)

Grendel and his mother were the kin of the 'brother-slayer' (*see* page 102). Their very evil stemmed from their connection to this heinous deed that the later poet ingeniously connected to the act of the biblical Cain. But the ultimate origin of this image was the ancient regicidal cycle: the Vanir cycle of sacrificial kingship that the Danes sought to end, in which king killed king, brother killed brother – until Hrothgar's failure in ancient royal obligations brought the cycle to a halt.

In this chapter, after examining many mythical motifs, there seems to be a reasonable consensus on certain points:

1. In Denmark, the king representing the god Freyr enacted a ritual marriage with a priestess embodying the land itself.

2. At the end of the king's reign, he was ritually killed (presumably at midwinter) during a sacred marriage to the priestess by strangulation, after which the goddess was washed and, if the myths are to be believed, took the new king's 'brother' as a lover.

3. The night-marish Grendel's mother, who mounts Beowulf underwater, is a memory of the carrion-goddess of winter, whose lovers' lives were usually ended, strangled in peat bogs following a meal of ergotized porridge.

4. The Danes may have been in the process of establishing a hereditary kingship, rather than the earlier rule by the strongest, thus
   ending the practice of ritual regicide and establishing a dynasty
   known as the Skjoldungs (Scyldings in *Beowulf*).

If the arrival of the 'brother-slayer' Grendel at Heorot is to be seen as
a Germanic form of the 'King of the Wood', then one would expect his
appearance to be intimately connected to midwinter and the sacrificial rites of that time of year. *Beowulf* does not provide any such
information but there are a number of other existing variants of the
Scylding saga in Norse sources that help shed light on this aspect of
the Old English poem.

•

CHAPTER TWELVE

THE HALL TURNED TO ASHES

Boldly the hall reared its arched gables; unkindled the torch-flame that turned it to ashes. The time was not yet when the blood-feud should bring out again sword-hatred in sworn kindred.

BEOWULF, 81–5

THROUGHOUT *Beowulf*, the great hall of Heorot remains standing, yet there are many clues in the poem pointing to its eventual fiery destruction, a result, so the poet tells us, of blood feuds. However, other surviving Norse sagas reveal more of the nature of this destruction, and at the same time show that the events that led to Hrothgar's hall being turned to ashes were not just political conflicts but had a religious element tied in with the death of the king at the hands of the winter-goddess.

Hrolf's Saga

The prose saga of King Hrolf 'Kraki' ('the lean/tall', a name given to him because his face was 'thin and angular, like a ladder carved from a pole') was written in 14th-century Iceland and tells of the deeds of the man who appears in *Beowulf* as King Hrothgar's nephew Hrothulf. Hrolf (**Hro**thu**lf**) nephew of Hroar (**Hro**thg**ar**), with his 12 compan-ions, was a popular figure in Icelandic lore, where he appears as a

Danish Arthur or Charlemagne figure. Though late (and based on a collection of earlier sagas), the saga deals with many of the same figures and events that appear, or are alluded to, in *Beowulf*, though not to such an extent as to suggest that it was based on the English poem. Rather, the close relation between the two tales suggests the existence of an earlier version or versions of the tale (that for convenience will be referred to as the proto-*Beowulf*), existing most probably in Scandinavia, from which both were independently drawn. From the very start, *Hrolf's Saga* illuminates much that is unclear or only hinted at in *Beowulf*.

The first important fact that the non-English sagas offer is the location of Hrothgar's Heorot. All that is gained from the English poem is that the hall stands somewhere in the territory of the Danes, and close to the sea. The Icelandic and Danish sources are adamant that Hrolf's capital was at a place named *Hleidargard* – that is, modern Lejre on Zealand – the place of the nine-yearly ritual sacrifice mentioned by Thietmar of Merseburg and the centre of Nerthus/Gefion's cult (*see* page 54). Lejre would be the capital of the Danish kingdom during the Viking age and it is reasonable to suppose that the site of Hrothgar's Heorot was also at the same location. The large numbers of prehistoric burial mounds and ritual monuments surrounding Lejre suggest that it was a cult centre from very early times, and archaeologists have discovered great feasting halls built here from the 7th century onwards. However, the clues from the tales seem to suggest, perhaps bizarrely, that Heorot belonged more to the former class of monuments rather than the latter.

In the saga, Hrolf gathers around him a band of champions, and heroes from all over the North flock to Hleidargard to join his company. One such is the son of Bera and Bjorn – a hero named *Bodvar Bjarki* (Battle-Bear cub), who will become the greatest champion of Hrolf's retinue.

As with many heroes, Bodvar's birth is far from ordinary. His father Bjorn (Bear) is transformed by witchcraft into a bear when he rejects his stepmother Queen Hvit's advances. The queen calls for the bear to be hunted, but he manages to spend his last night on Earth with his lover Bera (She-Bear) and from the doomed union of this couple are born the three brothers Bodvar Bjarki, Elk-Frodi and Thorir-Hound's Foot. Like Hygelac, in time Thorir will become king of the Geats.

While pregnant with Bjorn's children, Bera is forced by Queen Hvit to eat the flesh of her slain lover, an act that accounts for the odd nature of her children – Elk-Frodi is elk from the waist down, and Thorir Hound-Foot's name speaks for itself. Bodvar's first act as a man is to slay Queen Hvit and so avenge his father. This done, he draws a sword from a stone left for him by his father in a cave, and heads off to see his brother Elk-Frodi. Frodi cuts his calf and allows Bodvar to drink his blood, an act that makes him more powerful. It is Elk-Frodi who suggests that he journeys to the court of King Hrolf.

Bodvar arrives in Hleidargard and immediately defends a man named Hott, whom Hrolf's retainers have taunted and ridiculed, throwing bones at him during their feasts. Bodvar seats Hott beside him, and when the heroes start throwing bones again, Bodvar seizes one and throws it back, killing the man who launched it. News of this deed travels to Hrolf in his fortress, who only then discovers how his retainers have been treating Hott. He asks Bodvar to join his warriors, but he asks that only Hott and he be allowed to sit nearer the king in the hall.

Yule approaches and Bodvar notices that Hrolf's warriors are becoming increasingly gloomy. Hott informs him why:

Hott told him that a huge, monstrous beast had come there the past two winters ... causing much damage. No weapon can bite into it, and the king's champions, even the best among them, do not return home.

The creature seems to be a large dragon-like winged creature that Hott describes as not an animal but 'rather it is the greatest of trolls' (the word troll, in this era, being an all-encompassing term for supernatural creatures).

That Yule, Bodvar and a reluctant Hott confront the beast on the moor outside the hall. Bodvar's sword becomes stuck in his scabbard, but he is eventually able to release it and he kills the creature. Bodvar cuts out the beast's heart and makes Hott eat it, whereon he becomes filled with its courage.

They then decide to trick Hrolf and his warriors, who have not witnessed the deed. They prop the beast up and early next morning cry out that the hall is under attack again; the warriors fear to go forward, save Hott, who rushes forward and appears to kill the beast, thus earning the respect of the warriors. Hrolf, however, sees through the trick, but nevertheless sees a change in Hott and grants him the name Hjalti ('hilt'), after the golden hilt of the sword with which he did his 'brave' deed. Bodvar becomes the best of Hrolf's warriors, and marries his daughter Drifa.

It is Bodvar who suggests to Hrolf that they journey to Sweden and claim his father's stolen treasure from King Adils. King Adils had killed Hrolf's father Helgi, and married his mother Yrsa – seizing his wealth in the process. The Danes leave for Sweden, where they enter the hall of King Adils, king Hrolf disguised as a normal warrior. Adils lights a massive fire within the hall, attempting to burn Hrolf to death, knowing that the Danish King has promised to flee 'neither fire nor iron'. He hopes to flush Hrolf out, as he is unsure which of the many armoured warriors is the king. But, as the flames leap higher, Bodvar and the warriors spring into action, throwing those making the fire into the flames and then rushing to burn Adils too; but he hides in a hollow tree at the centre of the hall and survives the conflagration.

Adils flees outside the hall and sends against the Danes 'a troll ... in the likeness of a boar' that cannot be harmed by swords. The beast bursts into the hall, where Hrolf's dog Gram tears its ears off and the beast flees. But outside, Adils and his men are setting light to the hall. Hrolf's warriors push against its wooden planked sides and manage to free themselves. There is a great battle, during which Adils flees, and the victorious Hrolf returns to the hall and receives his father's treasure from Yrsa, his mother. On the way back to the coast, they are ambushed by Adils, but Hrolf casts a ring given to him by his mother to the floor; when Adils bends to scoop it up, Hrolf slices off his buttocks – and the ambushers are routed. The war party returns to Denmark.

But Hrolf is soon to meet his fate. Hrolf has a sister named Skuld – a half-elvish woman, who was the wife of one King Hjorvard, who was once tricked by Hrolf into sending him a yearly tribute. Skuld, however, incites Hjorvard to stop paying tribute to her brother, calling him a weakling for being subservient. Skuld, a sorceress, has a plan. She tells Hrolf she will pay three years tribute in one go, and arranges to bring it to the hall at Yule. She then secretly amasses an army consisting of 'Norns, elves and countless other vile creatures'. Yule arrives and the army gathers outside Hleidargard. The alarm is raised by Hjalti who realizes the violent intentions of the gathered crowd.

The warriors go to battle – all save Bodvar – but a great bear leads the troops, killing many of Skuld's retinue. Hrolf's men have the upper hand, and victory seems assured but Hjalti realizes Bodvar is not present in the fray and rushes to find him. When Hjalti enters the king's chamber, he discovers Bodvar seated 'idle', and berates him. The roused Bodvar rebukes Hjalti for this ill-deed: the bear, it seems, was Bodvar in spirit form. He had been sitting in a trance using his magic against the queen, but now the magical bear has gone and Queen Skuld is better able to use her dark powers: looking down on the battle from her witch's platform, she casts spells that bring her slain warriors back to life. Her magic means that her army is invincible, as Bodvar knows:

> 'Deep are the ranks of Skuld's army. I suspect that the dead are wandering about. They rise up again to fight against us, and it becomes difficult to fight with ghosts.'

Skuld now joins her army of zombies in the battle – and a storm of enchantments sweeps over the champions, who are defeated to a man. Thus perish Hrolf Kraki and Bodvar Bjarki. Skuld seizes the kingdom, but Bodvar's brothers, assisted by Queen Yrsa, manage to drive her from the throne and destroy her. Then great burial mounds are built for the champions and their king.[1]

Grendel and the Yuletide Troll

Though the action has shifted on a generation, the events of the Icelandic saga clearly parallel many of those of the English poem. Both tales tell of the political machinations of the Swedes, Geats and Danes, of family conflict, honour and blood feud. Yet both also present a set of strange supernatural occurrences that at first seem at odds with the historical background. And the nature of this supernatural incursion is almost identical in both tales.

It is apparent from *Hrolf's Saga* is that the royal hall of the Scyldings at Lejre is threatened by a troll-like creature. The monster that enters the site each Yule is clearly the equivalent of Grendel, but it has acquired not only wings and the ability to fly (like the Keres) but also its arrival is not over a period of twelve years but of two successive years at *midwinter*. Like Grendel, the monster is struck twice: in *Beowulf*, the first strike is made without the use of weapons, while in Bodvar's initial inability to draw his sword may be a dim memory of the spells Grendel uses to make himself immune from weapons. (This magical ability seems then to be passed onto the magical boar that Adils sends into his hall.) The second striking of the monster occurs when the foe is already dead – as a propped-up beast in *Hrolf's Saga* and while lying dead on a bed in the underwater cave in *Beowulf*. In both cases, the weapon used to strike for the second time is a 'golden-hilted' sword, the object Beowulf first notices when he finds the ancient sword in Grendel's underwater cavern.[2]

Obviously, the two accounts have much in common, excepting the date of the attack. It seems as though the Yuletide attack, integral to the argument that Grendel's arrival was part of the regicidal cycle, was omitted by the English *Beowulf* poet in order to suggest that Grendel's threat was a constant evil spanning a number of years rather than something that had happened twice on one specific calendrical date – thus increasing the sense of menace and drama for the audience (*see* page 8).

Beowulf and Bodvar

The most obvious parallel between the tales is the nature and deeds of the heroes, Beowulf and Bodvar – especially given the usual etymology of Beowulf from 'Bee-wolf', a kenning for bear (to which an alternative will be offered in Part IV). Both heroes have a close kin relationship with the king of the Geats – (in Bodvar's case brother, in Beowulf's nephew). Both journey to Denmark and liberate the hall of one of the Scylding clan from a supernatural foe and are then instrumental in wars in Sweden revolving around the figure of King Adils. But while King Adils is the villain of the Icelandic saga, Beowulf is depicted as helping Adils (Eadgils) seize the throne of Sweden from his uncle Onela, the slayer of Hygelac's son Heardred. There is a seeming 'rootless-ness' of the Beowulf/Bodvar figure: unlike the other characters in the tales, the hero is the only one who seems to be able to jump a generation and his allegiance to the Swedish monarch; he is associated with a certain period of Danish history, but not firmly located at a set point. It is to him that the monster-fight belongs, not to Hrolf or Hrothgar, and so when he appears in *Hrolf's Saga* so does the monster.

Although offering parallel views of the same events, the sagas differ in other important respects, showing clearly that one was not derived from the other. The Icelandic saga is rife with the motif of the killing of the king; twice there is an attempt to *burn the king to death in a hall* before he finally succumbs to the machinations of his half-elvish sister Skuld, whose attack on Heorot has something ritualistic about it. In fact it is a magical attack. She herself is a practitioner of *seithr*, and casts her spells while seated on her witch's platform. Hrolf's 'sister', who bears the same name as the Norn who cuts men's life-threads, is none other than a Vanir priestess playing the role of the carrion-goddess, the 'chooser of the slain'– the grim-reaper of this harvest king to whom, one imagines, she had once been wed. And like that of Grendel's mother, her attack on the hall comes after the first attack of the twice-slain 'troll'. And yet, vitally, in *Hrolf's Saga*, unlike *Beowulf*, it is made plain that the appearance of this nightmarish woman is closely connected with the wars over the Danish throne. Her arrival in the story, rather than being an aside, is integral to the theme of the killing of the king.

Something Rotten in the State

Hrolf's Saga deals with the deeds of the Scyldings the generation fol-lowing the death of Hrothgar/Hroar, the king who is the builder of

Heorot and who appears in *Beowulf*. In this saga, a number of characters only hinted at in *Beowulf* play a major role, not least that of Hrothulf/Hrolf himself. But clues in the Old English poem suggest that there is 'something rotten in the state of Denmark' as there is another side to King Hrolf that the later saga glosses over: he becomes king by killing Hrothgar's heir.

On the night that Grendel has been slain, Beowulf is sitting among the youths with Hrothgar's young sons, Hrethric and Hrothmund, when their mother, Wealtheow, speaks these words to their father, concerning their cousin Hrothulf/Hrolf, the son of the king's dead brother Halga:

> 'I hear it is your wish to hold this warrior [Beowulf] henceforward as your son. Heorot is cleansed, the ring-hall bright again: therefore bestow while you may these blessings liberally, and leave to your kinsmen the land and its people when your passing is decreed, your meeting with fate. For may I not count on my gracious Hrothulf to guard honourably our young ones here, if you, my lord, should give over this world earlier than he? I am sure he will show to our children answerable kindness, if he keeps in remembrance all that we have done to indulge and advance him, the honours we bestowed on him when he was still a child.'

Although on the face of it this passage seems straightforward, the Danish and Norse sources prove otherwise. Hrothgar and his nephew Hrothulf appear together in the poem *Widsith*, but here, too, is a hint at future trouble:

> Hroth(w)ulf and Hrothgar *kept peace for a very long time*, uncle and nephew, when they had driven away the race of the Vikings and overcome the array of Ingeld, destroyed at Heorot the host of the Heathobards. [My italics.]

The poet's use of the words 'for a very long time' suggests an eventual falling out, for it becomes clear that Hrothulf/Hrolf did not 'guard honourably' his young cousins. The actual sequence of events is unclear, but it would seem that after Hrothgar's demise, Hrothulf kills his son Hrethric, though what happened to Hrothmund, who does not appear in any other source but Beowulf, is not known. One theory states he may have fled to England.

Hrolf Kraki, who is depicted in Icelandic saga as an ideal and heroic king, achieved his elevated position by murdering his cousin(s) and defying his uncle's and aunt's wishes. But this is not the only intrigue in the Scylding court concerning a nephew of Hrothgar's. In *Beowulf*, Beowulf is not only granted the title of 'son' by Hrothgar, but he is also given the armour due to Heoroweard, Hrothgar's other nephew, the son of his late brother Heorogar (*see* chart, page 233). It is not known why the nephew was shunned. It would seem that Heoroweard's father, Heorogar, was king before Hrothgar, but had died young, and his son was not old enough to reign effectively. If this was the case, then it was poetic justice that Hrothgar, who had seized the throne in place of his nephew Heoroweard, should eventually lose his own offspring at the hands of his other nephew, Hrothulf/Hrolf.

Hrothgar shuns both his brothers' sons so that his own will inherit the kingdom after his demise. Both nephews, Heoroweard and Hrothulf, are fully-grown men; both would no doubt have been able fighters and good leaders, but Hrothgar seems more interested in establishing a hereditary line. To this end, he gives away Heoroweard's birthright to Beowulf, and forces his other nephew Hrothulf to be 'baby-sitter' to the future monarch. In this light, the old king's death was bound to result in bloodshed. Hrothulf will murder his cousin(s?) and seize the throne, and Hrothgar's other wronged nephew, Heoroweard (the King Hjorvard of *Hrolf's Saga*, the husband of the Valkyrie Skuld) will eventually attack and kill King Hrothulf and his men at Yule.

The Scylding/Skjoldung saga is an epic of inter-family feuds, of cousin against cousin, all seemingly based on the machinations of Hrothgar to make his sons king after him, and his brothers' sons determination that this will not to happen. But there seems more to this than the squabbles of a dysfunctional family.

Behind these machinations, it is possible to glimpse the religious conflicts of the age, and the struggles for the establishment of a hereditary kingship over the sacral kingship of the brother-killers, based on rule by the strongest, that was the norm in Germania during the Iron Age.

Political Wars and Ritual Murders

The brother-slaying motif is pronounced in the figure of Hjorvard.[3] In *Beowulf*, Hrothulf/Hrolf and Heoroweard/Hjorvard are cousins, both sharing a grandfather in Healfdene, but their family link is forgotten in *Hrolf's Saga*, where they are brothers-in-law through the marriage of Hjorvard to Skuld, Hrolf's half-sister, fathered on an elf-woman by Halga/Helgi. This elf-woman was said to have appeared as an ugly beggar, but when Helgi allows her into his bed through kindness, she turns into a beautiful maid, like the figure of sovereignty in Irish myth. Skuld, therefore, is no human relation, but like her elf-mother she is the sovereignty of the land – or at least a priestess playing that role.

Hjorvard, as should be expected in the tradition of ritual regicide, marries the 'sister' of the king (ie, the goddess), thus becoming the king's 'brother' – and then slays him at midwinter, accompanied by Skuld, a very clear portrayal of the winter carrion-goddess. What Hrolf Kraki's death overtly demonstrates is that the old ways were still practised in Beowulf's day. It also shows that any previous idea that *Beowulf* was merely a tale concerning the political machinations of a Danish royal house onto which an incongruous monster story had been laid are a fallacy. The political 'historical' family saga itself is rife with the symbols of the ritual killing of the king in which the 'monsters' are integral (as Tolkien had suggested).

Just as the later Icelandic saga of Hrolf recalls that the troll Grendel's arrival was at midwinter, so too it preserves the connection between the arrival of the goddess and the rites of kingship better than the English *Beowulf* poem, where Grendel's mother is depicted as a purely supernatural entity, divorced from her role as king-slayer and mate of the young pretender. Skuld is remembered as sovereignty, and when she came to Heorot, she brought a new king with her.

At this point, it might be thought that too much is being read into the Scylding story – that the attacking and burning of Heorot by Hjorvard and Skuld only coincidentally parallels the events of the brother-battle and the rites of sacred kingship. But one has only to look a little further into the Scylding drama to discover proof. In *Widsith*, Heorot is threatened by a Heathobard named *Ingeld* and Hrothgar and Hroth(w)ulf repel the attack. Ingeld was a son of a king named Froda, who apparently had killed Healfdene, Hrothgar's father.[4] In retaliation, so the Icelandic sagas relate, Hroar/Hrothgar and Helgi/Halga *burn Froda to death in his hall*! In *Beowulf*, Hrothgar attempts to mend the feud by marrying his daughter Freawaru to Ingeld, Froda's son. And though the success of this venture is not mentioned in *Beowulf*, the Old English audience would have known its unfortunate outcome, at which Beowulf himself seems to hint, as if gifted with foresight. On his return to Geatland, he says of Freawaru to his lord Hygelac:

'She is betrothed to Ingeld, this girl attired in gold, to the gracious son of Froda. The Protector of the Danes has determined this and accounts in wisdom, the keeper of the land, thus to end all the feud and fatal wars by means of the lady. Yet when a lord is dead it is seldom the slaying-spear sleeps for long – seldom indeed – dear though the bride may be.'

Ingeld indeed tries hard to keep peace for the sake of his wife, but in the end the family feud overwhelms him and he takes his revenge. In *Widsith*, it is stated that the Scyldings repulsed his attack, but in Saxo's account the attack is successful. The true nature of Ingeld's threat, however, is apparent – he is the son of a Danish *Frothi*-king, a fertility god-king of the Ingaevones. For who are Froda, Ingeld and his wife Freawaru other than Freyr, Ing and Freyja?

In *Beowulf*, Froda and Ingeld are described as Heathobards – neighbours to the Danes – yet in the non-English sources they are integrated into the Scylding clan. Froda is seen as Healfdene's *brother*. This would make the latter's attack on the former a kind of brother-battle over kingship. Given this alternative family connection it is tempting to see the Heathobard Ingeld as a title of Heoroweard, as in Saxo Grammaticus's *Danish History,* where Ingeld, like Hjorvard, is successful in attacking and destroying Heorot. Perhaps these characters were once identical, only to become split into two characters in later tradition. Both Ingeld and Heoroweard are the cousins of Hrolf by marriage with a daughter of one of the sons of Healfdene: Freawaru, who does not appear in the Danish or Norse sources, in the case of Ingeld; and Skuld, who does not appear in *Beowulf,* in the case of Heoroweard. Both women were linked to Freyja, the first by name, the second by her deeds and her ability to resuscitate the dead on the battlefield.

Whether or not Ingeld and Heoroweard were originally the same person, the killing of kings in burning buildings by brothers wed to Freyja-wives is suggestive of a lot more than blood feuds. Chapter 13 examines a Celtic tale that makes this kingship 'cycle' of the Ingaevones much clearer. Not only is another man bearing the name 'Ing-' involved in the killing of a pagan king within a *feasting hall*, but there is evidence that the burning of such 'halls' was not an act of war, but an act of a winter ritual once celebrated throughout north-west Europe.

CHAPTER THIRTEEN

.

THE WANDERING INGUZ

THE CLEAREST EXAMPLE in Celtic lore of a ritual death associated with the winter feast and a feasting hall is a tale called *The Destruction of Da Derga's Hostel*.[1] It is set at the feast of *Samhain*, the precursor of Halloween, on which night the veil between the worlds was thin and there could be intercourse, malign and otherwise, between the mortal world and the otherworld. Samhain was seen as the start of the Celtic year and its symbolism was identical to that of the Germanic midwinter. On this night, the fairy folk had great influence over mankind, and there was a resurgence of a state of chaos. It seems that it was on this night that the king was killed.

The tale tells of the ritual death of an historical king named Conaire Mor. As with all Celtic kings and heroes, his life is bounded by a strict sense of taboos, or *geassa*, which, if broken will bring about his doom. (This is akin to the Norse concept of *osgeassa* (bad luck) that Domaldi's stepmother places on him, resulting in his sacrifice for the health of the crops).

The Destruction of Da Derga's Hostel begins with King Conaire settling a dispute between two of his servants, which is one of his *geassa*. By the end of the day, Conaire has broken them all, through being placed in situations that leave him no choice but to break one *geassa* or another. The day seems engineered to end with the king's death in such a fashion that he himself causes it through his limited choices.

As the disastrous day draws to its close, Conaire and his men seek shelter within a feasting hall, a 'hostel' owned by an elusive figure named Da Derga (Red God). But from the start we see that there is something odd about this hostelry. Three horsemen dressed in red, the Celtic colour of death, precede the entourage – breaking another *geassa*. They tell Conaire they are men of the *sídhe* (fairy folk). 'Though we are alive we are dead', they say, chillingly. Their appearance parallels the 'elves, norns and vile creatures' who are present in Skuld's army.

Conaire's party then witnesses to the arrival of two hideous figures. The man's name is Fer Caille (Man of the Wood), and his wife's Cichuil. Fer Caille is described as a hideous black giant with spiked hair, a single eye, foot and arm, and brandishing a club. His wife is similarly immense and ugly:

> A huge, black, gloomy, big-mouthed, ill-favoured woman; if her snout were thrown against a branch, the branch would support it, while her lower lip extended to her knee.

Conaire knows they spell his doom and he begs them not to visit him in the hostel that night. They do not relent.

Fer Caille has been linked by generations of Celtic scholars to a figure known as the 'Wild Herdsman', a one-eyed shamanic figure who appears in a number of tales as a master of animals – an equivalent to the horned god depicted on the Gundestrup cauldron surrounded by beasts (*see* pages 90 and 131).[2] This monstrous couple are usually accepted as forms of the Dagda and his mate the Mórríghan (*see* page 104), the Celtic Freyr and Freyja, but the pair are reminiscent of nothing more than Grendel and his mother. But there is another link between them and these Vanir gods. Fer Caille is carrying on his shoulder a 'singed, black-bristled pig' – not only a symbol of the Vanir gods, but also of the god slain by the boar.

Conaire's reign has been good – the crops have grown – but by entering the hostel he has sealed his fate:

> 'May God not bring that man here tonight. It is grievous. It is a pig that falls before acorns. It is a child who is aged. It is grievous his shortness of life.'

So says Fer Rogain, Conaire's *foster-brother,* who is amongst an army approaching the hall with the intention of destroying it. That evening, as the hosts of Conaire enter the hall, Fer Caille arrives with his pig. Then a lone woman appears at the door. It is not stated that she is Fer Caille's wife Cichuil, but as he arrives alone and she immediately after, she is conceivably the same creature. Her beard reaches her knees, her mouth was on one side of her head, and she leans on the doorpost and asks Conaire for entry, thus asking him to break another geassa. She is asked for a name, and gives him many including 'Samhain' (Summer's end) and 'Badb' (Battle crow), variant names of the Mórríghan. As with the appearance of the Vanir demons Grendel and Skuld in the halls of Denmark, they presage the death of the King.

Conaire is now doomed. The hall is attacked by a massive army of plunderers – led by his foster-brother and a *one-eyed* warrior named *Ingcel* who is described as a raider from the sea. Da Derga's hall is set alight and extinguished three times. The attacker's druids cause Conaire to thirst, and he sends his most loyal warrior, Mac Cecht, to fetch water, but the rivers of Ireland dry up before him. When he does manage to find water he returns to find his lord is being beheaded – but he gives water to the head *and the head thanks him for it.* Mac Cecht is then killed by a wolf.

A Winter's Tale

The links between this ancient Irish tale and the tales surrounding the Scylding dynasty are striking. In both cases, we see the arrival of a monstrous 'man' and 'woman' (in that order) at a winter festival who threaten the person of the king. Then the hall is burned down – in the Irish tale by *Ingcel* and in the Scylding saga by Hjorvard and *Ingeld.*

The proximity of these names – Ingcel and Ingeld – suggests that the parallel motifs in these tales go beyond pure coincidence. However, the possibility that one is a direct borrowing of the other seems to be ruled out by the fact that too many themes in each are paralleled in their native traditions; both seem firmly rooted in their own cultures.

A similar story appears in the Welsh *Mabinogion* – the tale of the death of Bran the Blessed, king of Britain.[3] Bran, a giant, crosses the Irish channel to rescue his sister Branwen, who is enslaved by her husband, the Irish king. Like the Dagda, Bran is the owner of a magical cauldron received from a pair of figures who are identical to Fer Caille and his wife – only they are described as dwelling *beneath a lake*, exactly like Grendel and his dam. They are portrayed as having *melyngoch* ('yellow-red') hair, the same fiery orange hair as found on the bog people.[4] In this source, there is a link between the bog people and the fertility gods whom they were imitating in death.

Because Bran is so large, he is housed in a specially designed 'hall' which is subsequently destroyed around him when the forces of the Irish king Matholwch (Bran's *brother-in-law*) attack. A fire is lit and the Irish king's son is thrown upon it by his uncle Efnissien. Battle ensues and the Irish dead, like the dead warriors of Skuld, are able to regenerate by being placed in Bran's magical cauldron of rebirth, which has fallen into the hands of the Irish, until Efnissien enters and destroys it, forfeiting his life. Bran is killed (*wounded in the thigh*) and beheaded, but his head continues to entertain his men after his death.

There are many close parallels between this Welsh tale and that of the demise of both Conaire and Hrolf. Bran is killed in a feasting hall by an attacking army led by his sister's husband (like in *Hrolf's Saga*), and his enemies have a method of regenerating their dead (originating from a pair of monstrous lake-dwellers), as has Skuld with her *seithr* magic. Bran's severed head, like that of Conaire, speaks after his death, and Bran's name means 'raven', comparable with that of Hrolf in Saxo Grammaticus's *Danish History*, where Kraki is said to mean 'crow', not 'lean/tall'.

The existence of this Welsh variant of the regicidal myth, containing elements of both the Irish and Danish tales yet not necessarily derived from either, further suggests that these are not borrowed tales but ancient shared myths. These Celtic parallels show that far from being an anomaly, the killing of Hrolf by Skuld and Ingeld/Hjorvard and the arrival of Grendel and his ugly mother in Heorot all fit a pattern of events surrounding the ritual death of a monarch common in both the Germanic and Celtic worlds. These are therefore most likely derived from a shared tradition – that of the midwinter rites of the Neolithic fertility religions.

Although the Celts seem to have had no midwinter festival (or, at least, none that left any traces in their myths), and any knowledge of a midwinter feast may have been forgotten or obliterated with the adoption of Christmas, their Neolithic ancestors certainly did. We know this from the orientation of many of their megalithic structures, the most obvious of these being Newgrange – the home of the Dagda – which was built so that on the morning of the winter solstice the rising sun would penetrate the 'sun window' above the doorway and enter the back chambers (*see* page 104).

To ancient man, winter was truly a time of hardship. What was most anticipated in this dark season was the return of light and warmth and the first sign of this was midwinter's day: it was the day of the death of the old year's sun and its rebirth as the sun of the new year. And what better day to kill the old king, the old year, the old sun and instate the new than the day the heavens were doing the same?

Macc Oc

There is a connection between the Dagda and the New Year, aside from the architecture of his home, that explains the presence of *Ing* in these tales. The Irish story *The Wooing of Etain* relates how the Dagda took a fancy to Boand (White Cow), the goddess of the river Boyne, who was the wife of Elcmar, the resident of Brugh na Boinne (Newgrange) before the Dagda (though some argue that Elcmar and the Dagda are one and the same). The Dagda bewitches Elcmar so that he is unable to perceive the passing of time: consequently, the nine months he stays away from Newgrange seem to be but *one day*. During this time, the Dagda impregnates Boand, who gives birth to a son she names Macc Oc (Young Son), 'for young is the son', his mother said, 'conceived and born within one day!'

When the youth is grown, he asks his foster-father, Midir, to tell him the identity of his real parents. When he discovers he is the

Dagda's son, he asks his father to recognize him and grant him land. The Dagda tells him that he is destined to rule in Newgrange, and that he must therefore confront Elcmar, its present occupier. The Dagda tells him that he must:

> 'Go into the Brugh at Samhain,[5] for that is a day of peace and friend-ship among the men of Eriu [*Ireland*], and no one will be at odds with his fellow. Elcmar will be in ... the Brugh with no weapon but a fork of white hazel in his hand.'

Macc Oc must then:

> 'Go to Elcmar and threaten to kill him.'

But, he is told, it will not be necessary to kill him if Elcmar agrees to his request – that Macc Oc be allowed to be king of Newgrange for one night and day. This all goes to plan, but when Elcmar comes to reclaim his kingdom, Macc Oc tells him that as time is made up of nights and days, Elcmar has effectively given him the Brugh in perpetuity. When Elcmar complains to the Dagda, the chief of the *Tuatha* says:

> 'He [Macc Oc] hewed at you menacingly on a day of peace and friend-ship, and since your life was dearer to you than your land, you surrendered the land in return for being spared.'

Elcmar is given a new home and Macc Oc receives Newgrange. For a while there continues to be tension between Elcmar and Macc Oc, and in trying to broker peace, Midir, Macc Oc's *foster-father*, loses an eye, which Macc Oc is able to heal with the help of Diancecht, the *Tuatha* physician.[6]

The usurpation of Elcmar by the 'Young Son' at Newgrange is clearly related to the usurpation of the old king at the winter feast. As with the 'peace' of Freyr in Germania and the weapon-free wagon ride of Nerthus, this rite occurred within a time of 'peace and friendship'.

At this time, the old king gives up his land and his kingship for the young pretender, who comes threatening to end his life. He is the New Year Freyr, come to oust the old.

But there are other clues in this story that such identification is not without substance. For one thing, like Freyr, Macc Oc is a god of love and liaisons. He looks after the two lovers Diarmuid and Grainne, whose tale is a retelling of the death of the god. Diarmuid runs off with Fionn MacCumhal's wife Grainne ('Sun'), but Diarmuid is killed by a *boar* who is his *brother* under enchantment.[7] And, in a parallel to the myth of Frothi, when Diarmuid is killed he is taken to Newgrange *on a wagon*. Macc Oc is able, when he so wishes, to send a spirit into his body and make him talk, just as the heads of Bran and Conaire Mor can speak after their deaths, and Odin is able to converse with the severed head of Mimir when the former offers him his *eye*.

If this connection between Macc Oc and Freyr was not enough, the principal myth concerning Macc Oc is about his dreaming of, and pursuit of, a maiden named Caer Ibormeith, a myth which bears many similarities to the wooing of Gerthr by Freyr.[8] This was the subject of a poem by WB Yeats, whose title contains the Young Son's other name: *The Dream of the Wondering Angus*. The name may be written Oenghus, Aengus or plain Angus. Whichever way, it is clear that, given his pedigree and mythos, his name is a Celtic equivalent of 'Ing', derived from the Indo-European root *Inguz* and recorded in Gothic as *Enguz*. The Inguz/Angus name parallel is not just coincidental. The name 'Macc' found in 'Macc Oc' is the Celtic patronymic, meaning 'the son', the *exact* Celtic equivalent of 'Ing'.

The wealth of imagery concerning day, night and birth suggest that the 'Young Son' Ing/Macc Oc, conceived and born in a day, is the 'New Year' sun that achieves victory over the old on midwinter's morning. The one-eyed Ingcel of the Da Derga myth is the solar disc itself, the great unblinking eye that is the sign of the victory over winter glimpsed through the roof box at Newgrange on midwinter's morning, the appearance of which signifies that the old year, the old king, the old sun is defeated.[9] The death of the old king takes place on midwinter's night after the sun has sunk into the sea in the west.

Thus the god dies in the water – he drowns – but the next morning the new sun arises, coming from out of the sea in the east like a child from the amniotic fluid.

The blaze of the new sun illuminates the names of the god-killers of myth: Beli (Brightness) kills Bran; Lleu (Light) is killed by Goronw Pebr (the Fiery), and, at the end of time at Ragnarok, Freyr, wielding his antler weapon (having lost his sword 'Belisbani' – Beli's bane), is overcome by Surt, a fire giant, who burns the cosmos and destroys the hall of the gods. And Balder is killed by the 'blind' Hodr, while Fergus Mac Roich is killed 'sporting in the water' by the blind Lugaid (Light). Perhaps these 'blind' gods were originally one-eyed.

This is why Hrolf Kraki is attacked by Ingeld (if Saxo Grammaticus is correct); Hrolf is attacked by Hjorvard and Skuld and his hall destroyed (in *Hrolf's Saga*); Conaire Mor is killed at Samhain by Ingcel, the one-eyed raider from the sea; and why Macc Oc achieves victory over Elcmar at Samhain though conceived and born in but a day. In a practice rooted in the megalithic age, the kings of the ancient North enacted the midwinter demise and rebirth of the sun.

The Hall with Seven Doors

One change that does at first seem to have taken place is the location of the winter rites. In Neolithic Ireland, the victory of the Young Son took place within megalithic passage graves – and in Denmark at the passage graves such as Øm (just a few kilometres from Lejre) as well as the horseshoe temples at Turlstrup and Ferslev, which were oriented to the midwinter sunset (*see* pages 30–31). The horseshoe temples, like the feasting halls of the sagas, were destroyed by fire after an unknown ritual (perhaps concerning the rebirth of the dead). Initially, these seem at odds with the 'secular' banqueting halls of Celtic and Germanic myth, but this is illusory. There is good evidence that what were described by later Christian writers as halls were, in reality, ritual structures.

Da Derga's hall is described as having seven doors and seven apartments and a road running through it – clearly an uncomfortable place to stay the night! The house of CúRoí Mac Daíré, the man betrayed by his wife Blathnat and her lover CúChulainn, had a river running through it and was said to revolve like a millwheel. These structures appear to be more like open-air temples. The main hall of the men of Ulster at Emhain Macha was said to have twelve apartments, designed by thirty seers, and the pillars were erected by seven men. These numbers clearly have a calendrical significance, suggestive of specifically designed ritual sites rather than banqueting halls. In fact, archaeologists seeking to uncover evidence of the feasting halls mentioned in Irish literature, such as Emhain Macha and Dun Ailinne in Leinster, have so far been unsuccessful. Instead, on the very sites mentioned in the sagas, they have uncovered wooden ritual enclosures consisting of rings of posts suggestive of Neolithic sites such as Woodhenge near Stonehenge, where many concentric posts formed 'doorways' through which calendrical observations could be made.[10] These doorways were the descendants of the sun window of Newgrange. Woodhenge, like Stonehenge, was oriented to the midwinter sunset, and at the centre of the site archaeologists found a child with his head cleft in two by an axe: a midwinter sacrifice.[11]

Conaire, it must be concluded, met his death at a ritual site – perhaps a wooden grove of posts constructed, like Bran's hall in the Welsh myth, to be burned down. And not only at Turstrup and Ferslev is there evidence for such ritual conflagrations, for Emhain Macha and Dun Ailinne were also deliberately burned to the ground, in an act not of violence or war, but of ritual.

The motif of the burning of the king in his hall, found in both Germanic and Celtic myth, is an ancient ritual process – and not an uncommon one, as can be gathered by reading the chapter headings of Snorri's *Ynglingatal*:

King Visbur's sons burn him in his hall;
Solvi burns King Eistyn in his hall;
King Ingjald burns six district kings in his hall;
King Ingjald burns King Granmar and King Hjorvarth in their hall;
King Ingjald and his daughter burn themselves in their hall.

A similar list of deaths can be compiled from Celtic sources – including a king who is burned in his hall *and* drowned in a vat of mead. King Diarmuid, son of Fergus, is attacked in the hall of Banban; he hides in a vat of ale and is drowned when the hall is set alight and the ridgepole crashes onto his head.[12] Muirchertac dies in the same way – hiding in a vat of wine while the hall is destroyed by the sons of *the one-eyed* Cormac.

A similar mode of death is suggested in the *Ynglingatal*, where Fyolnir, son of Yngvi-Freyr, who is king at Uppsala, drowns in a vat of mead in the house of his friend, the peace-loving King Frothi of Lejre.[13] The drowning of Freyr's son at the future site of Heorot, indeed within the hall itself, shows that the deaths in feasting halls can be connected to the drowning in the sacred lakes of Nerthus. It was not necessary for the king to go to the lake – the lake could go to the king.

While the original drowning rite may have taken place in a 'temple of Nerthus' consisting of a ring of posts (which were subsequently burned) beside or over a stream, or on an island in a lake, perhaps the vat was used when a lake was not available – a portable drowning device. Such deaths are depicted on the Gundestrup cauldron, where a female figure is shown, accompanied by a wolf, plunging a man head first into a vat (*see* plate 12). This act of killing, however, seems to have been magical, for the warriors portrayed lining up to be 'drowned' seem to spring up again, mounted on horseback. It is a scene of ritual regeneration, reminiscent of the Irish warriors in the tale of Bran, who enter the cauldron for rebirth – like the cut corn they will spring up anew. Thus, through drowning, the old king lives on as an elf in the burial mound, or like King Frodi on the wagon, touring the land as a corpse awaiting rebirth once more.

The clues given in the sagas suggest that Heorot was a ritual site, but while archaeologists excavating Lejre have uncovered massive feasting halls on the site, the earliest found so far dates to some 150 years after the events described in *Beowulf*. Was there once a hall similar to the massive 43.3-m long and 11.5-m wide 9th-century Viking hall that stood on this spot,[14] or were the later poets projecting their own knowledge of such sites on an oral tradition involving 'feasts' and 'killings' and 'burnings' that actually took place at ritual enclosures? On balance, the evidence points to Heorot originally having been a ritual structure – a structure within which the appearance of hideous Vanir spirits might not seem so out of place when they arrived on the longest night; the kind of structure that would be easy to build and easy to burn. If the image of a ritual structure, potentially on a sacred island, which is yearly rebuilt with accompanying human sacrifice, sounds fanciful, one has only to read Strabo's account of a rite carried out by Gallic priestesses:

> In the ocean, he [Poseidonios] says, there is a small island, not very far out to sea, situated off the outlet of the Liger river; and the island is inhabited by the women of the Samnitae, and they are possessed by Dionysus and make this god propitious by appeasing him with mystic initiations as well as other sacred performances; and no man sets foot on the island, although the women themselves, sailing from it, have intercourse with men and then return again. And, he says, it is a custom of theirs once a year to unroof the temple and roof it again on the same day before sunset, each woman bringing her load to add to the roof; but the woman whose load falls out of her arms is rent to pieces by the rest, and they carry the pieces round the temple with the cry of 'Ev-ah', and do not cease until their frenzy ceases; and it is always the case, he says, that someone jostles the woman who is to suffer this fate.[15]

These women 'possessed by Dionysos' are evocative of the priestesses of the Vanir, the Volva. It could be that Nerthus's shrine near or at Lejre would have been similar to this.

The Worst of Winters

The midwinter rite not only helps elucidate the killing of the kings and the burning of their 'halls', but also suggests an origin for that most famous of Norse myths, Ragnarok – the doom of the gods, the final battle at the end of time in which the Aesir are defeated. Not only would Ragnarok occur in *winter*, it would be *fimbulvetr* – 'the worst of winters'. From the underworld, the giant wolf Fenrir would burst his chains and swallow Odin whole (though his son Vidar would tear the wolf apart in recompense). Thor would kill the world serpent but die of his venom, Freyr would be slain by the fire giant Surt, and Valhalla would be burned to the ground by him; the cosmos itself would be destroyed and renewed, rising from the primal ocean as a green mound on which the world tree Yggdrasil still stood. Balder would be reborn from Hel, and two humans, Lif and Lifthrasir, who survived Ragnarok by hiding within Yggdrasil, would repopulate the world (much as the wily King Adils hides in the central pillar of his burning hall in *Hrolf's Saga*, and by doing so survives its burning).[16]

While later Norse myth makes it clear that this event will occur at the end of time, the rituals reveal that this renewal of the cosmos was once a yearly event. Each year saw the 'time of the wolf' and the killing of the king. The message was clear to the king – your sacrifice by the one-eyed one at midwinter will mean rebirth in some future spring.

The figures of Grendel's mother, Skuld and the Mórríghan are the representatives of sovereignty come to claim the life of the old king, who will be killed in his 'hall' by the embodiment of the one-eyed sun god. And Grendel, too, not only his Valkyrie-mother, fits into this pattern.

It was suggested earlier that Grendel's arrival at Heorot (reminiscent of the arrival of Fer Caille in Conaire's myth, and linked through *Hrolf's Saga* to the midwinter festival) could be tied in with the figure of the 'King of the Wood' who, as sovereignty's old champion, waits for a successor to challenge his kingship at Yule – a challenge that Hrothgar, but not Beowulf, fails to take up. This suggestion finds support in another English poem concerning a midwinter feast, interrupted by an apparition as hideous as that which faced the men of Heorot in the days of Hrothgar: *Sir Gawain and the Green Knight*.

·

CHAPTER FOURTEEN

A MIDWINTER GAME

IT IS THE FEAST OF New Year at Camelot – and into King Arthur's hall bursts a giant figure, green in colour, bearing an axe in one hand and a holly branch in the other. He challenges Arthur's knights to a 'Christmas game'– that he will receive a blow to the neck with his axe if the champion is willing to have the blow returned in a year and a day's time. Gawain, Arthur's nephew, accepts on the king's behalf. He takes up the axe and cuts off the head of the Green Knight, thinking that would be the end of the matter, but the Green Knight takes up his severed head and asks Gawain to journey to the 'chapel green' in a year and a day's time.

Just under a year later, Gawain sets off to meet his doom. He travels north to the Wirral and is in the wilds on Christmas Eve when a castle appears magically and its owner, Sir Bertilak, welcomes him. He asks Gawain to spend Christmas with him before he journeys to the chapel green, which is only a few miles away. Gawain feasts with Bertilak, noticing two ladies – Bertilak's beautiful young wife and an ugly old hag.

Bertilak goes out to hunt each day and he sets Gawain another Christmas game – each will give to the other whatever he receives that day. Gawain soon finds this uncomfortable as he is being seduced by Bertilak's wife, and each night he has to give his host the numerous kisses he has received from the temptress.

On the last day before his departure, Gawain nearly succumbs to the lady's advances, but his piety and morality win over. When Bertilak returns with a paltry fox's skin from his hunt, Gawain still only has welcoming kisses in return – but he has hidden from his host one thing. Lady Bertilak has given him a green silk girdle that she says will protect him from the axe of the Green Knight.

The next day Gawain comes to the chapel green, a cave or barrow beside a stream, and he hears the sharpening of an axe – it is the Green Knight. Heroically, he offers his neck, but flinches and is berated by the Green Knight. Once more, the giant moves to strike, and seeing Gawain is ready he swings his axe down a third time. This time he grazes the skin – no more – and Gawain jumps up, having fulfilled his promise.

Then the truth comes out. The Green Knight is Sir Bertilak under enchantment. The whole thing has been a test by the ugly hag – in fact, Arthur's sister Morgan le Fay – who has sought to bring dishonour to Camelot, and thus has been foiled. Gawain has passed the test, save for failing to mention the green girdle – hence the chiding nick on the neck he receives.[1]

This 14th-century poem contains many of the elements of the midwinter rite.[2] The Green Knight, coloured an appropriately vegetal hue, arrives at a feasting hall at New Year and, though beheaded by Sir Gawain, like the Vanir deities he is able to be reborn through the magic of Morgan le Fay (the Mórríghan) – as were the warriors of Skuld in *Hrolf's Saga*. Gawain, like the 'Young Son', kills the fertility god, only to undergo (albeit symbolically) a ritual killing himself a year later. Not only is this a myth based on the yearly cycle, there are also striking similarities to the *Beowulf* story:

1. The monstrous Green Knight, like Grendel, enters the hall of the king at Yule (deduced from *Hrolf's Saga*; *see* page 143).

2. Like Grendel, the Green Knight is magically impervious to weapons. Although his head is cut off with his axe, he is unhurt.

3. The Green Knight is beheaded by the king's champion, just as Grendel is injured in the hall by Beowulf; and just as Grendel flees,

so the Green Knight lives to fight another day, riding out of the hall with his head in his hand.

4. While awaiting the journey to the monster's lake(-side) home, both Beowulf and Gawain are guests in the hall of a ruler and receive from each ruler's wife a gift. Lady Bertilak gives Gawain a garter that offers him the magical ability to survive the beheading and Beowulf is given a neck-ring by Wealhtheow, Hrothgar's wife (*see* page 132). The neck-ring is the mode of death of the sacral king, but to wear the neck-ring dedicated the victim to the goddess and, presumably, secured him a place as a god in the otherworld, as Freyr in the burial mound. This might also be the origin of the magical properties of the 'girdle' in the Gawain poem.

5. Like Beowulf, Gawain follows the 'fiend' to his lair – a 'cave'. In *Sir Gawain and the Green Knight*, this is a burial mound, in a craggy ravine associated with nearby water that 'bubbles as if boiling', and in *Beowulf* a cave in the depths of 'swirling waters' 'turbid with blood' below 'hoary rocks' and 'dark cliffs'.

6. Both Gawain and Beowulf survive the life-threatening attack at the lake.

7. Both Gawain and Beowulf overcome the attempts of a hag to bring about disaster.

These are the similarities, but there are also discrepancies. Firstly, Grendel's beheading, unlike that of the Green Knight, occurs at the lake rather than in the feasting hall; and secondly, the role of the 'goddess Morgan' in *Gawain* is downplayed and much more passive than that of Grendel's mother in *Beowulf*. It may be that these differences can be attributed to the fact that the *Gawain* poem is a composite crafted from two Irish tales.

The first of these is *Fled Bricrend* (*Bricriu's Feast*), which tells of the attempts of three Ulster warriors, CúChulainn, Leoghaire Baudach and Conall Cernach, to decide which of them should receive the prime cut of boar at the feast, the right of Ulster's 'champion'. The three undergo a series of tests to determine who should be champion, including two versions of the 'Christmas game' previously proposed by the Green Knight. Two figures (this seems to be the same incident multiplied by the storyteller for effect) offer their heads for the heroes to strike. The first is Uath Mac Imoman (Fear, Son of Terror), who *emerges from a lake* and whose challenge only CúChulainn accepts – on the following night the axe blade that is brought down on the hero's neck magically turns away, leaving CúChulainn unharmed. The second figure is a Bachlach (Churl), a huge ugly figure with a tree in one hand and an axe in the other. When CúChulainn wins the contest for the second time, the Bachlach reveals himself as CúRoí Mac Daírí.[3]

Sir Bertilak (or Bercilak in some translations) is evidently a name derived from the Irish Bachlach, and his entrance to Camelot parallels the arrival of CúRoí at Bricriu's feast holding an axe in one hand and a tree in the other. Like CúChulainn, Sir Gawain survives the beheading attempt, though his recompense comes a year and a day, not a single day, after the supernatural foe has been struck.

The second tale that the *Gawain* poet has used is *The Death of CúRoí* (*see* page 132), a midwinter king-killing myth, in which CúChulainn and Blathnat, CúRoí's wife, conspire to behead the Munster king in his own hall, bound to his own bed, beside the stream.

The combination of the two tales allows the poet to extend the time scale of the 'Christmas game' and to add in the motif of seduction by the host's wife. Gawain, a good Christian, unlike the pagan CúChulainn, is not seduced, and so the Green Knight is not murdered by the young upstart as would have ritually been the norm. Instead, it is Sir Gawain who has to undergo his part of the bargain by the lake.

These Irish tales are close enough in terms of characterization and plot lines to suggest that they were originally versions of the same myth in which the spirit of fertility itself was killed and reborn each midwinter (in the person of the king). Anyone bold enough to strike the head from the old king would have to be sufficiently brave to face the same fate the following year – although safe in the knowledge that as husband of the goddess, he would become a god after death. The 'beheading game', it transpires, is shorthand for the fertility cycle.

Grendel's Challenge

It is evident that the Green Knight is a form of Fer Caille, 'Man of the Wood', who journeys to the 'feasting hall' at midwinter in order to be slain by the new representative of the god, the future husband and champion of sovereignty. The Green Knight is the old vessel of the fertility spirit, the *Rex Nemorensis*, and like the 'King of the Wood' bears a weapon in one hand and a branch in the other, the 'Golden Bough' in Frazer's version (*see* page 135), the holly branch in the English poem. As the one-eyed Bachlach he represents the weak sun of the old year, declining in strength, black as the winter earth. Grendel is such a figure – his abode, like that of Uath Mac Imoman, a lake – who visits Heorot every Yule until a suitable champion can better him. This champion is Beowulf, who like Gawain acts in place of the king, wrestles with the monster (as Gunnar Helming did with the image of Freyr in the wagon; *see* page 94), thus injuring Grendel – rendering him, like the armless Irish King Nuada (*see* page 127), unsuitable to rule. He then wears, like Gawain, a magical talisman '*sacred to Inguz of the Goths*' that guarantees immortality, yet – finally bringing the regicidal cycle to an end – he kills the lake-mother and does not die himself.[4]

Both *Beowulf* and *Gawain* offer a version of a pagan myth that is skewed to present a whole new image. The *Gawain* poet under the influence of his Christian morality had his hero resist the temptations engineered by the goddess Morgan and, similarly, Beowulf does not become the goddess's husband and victim. But this skewing of the myth was not due to Christian influences, but those of another cult. And this was the same cult that led to the wiping of Sheaf from the Danish genealogy – the cult of Odin.

New Cults

Something had happened at Heorot during the age of migration that made the poets take note and tell, and retell, the events of these times. In 5th–6th-century Denmark, after years of pressure on the land, encroaching sea and political strife, a strong people called the Danes emerged into history. It may be that one factor enabling the Danes to become a military and political force from amongst the other Iron Age Ingaevones was that they had developed a concept of hereditary kingship. Unlike previous tribes, whose kings were potentially sacrificed each year or reigned for a limited span of time, the Danes established a royal dynasty – the Scyldings. A social system based on regicide or on elected kings where there is no land ownership (as described by Caesar; *see* page 22) can be neither stable nor strong, particularly when pitched against invading or warring tribes. Only in hereditary kingship is there the accumulation of wealth and land needed to build a loyal aristocracy and a strong warrior elite tied to a particular geography, not liable to flee in the face of opposition.

The tale of Hrothgar suggests that the political upheavals of his reign lie in his attempt, through nepotism or from concern for his people, to guarantee the rule of his children. But while the ruling family and the warrior aristocracy might have rejected an older set of beliefs based on fertility rites and replaced them with the worship of the warrior deities, the Aesir, the average Ingaevonian farmer would no doubt have continued with his ancient beliefs.

The tales of *Beowulf* and Hrolf Kraki might refer to a crisis point in this 'conversion' when the old cults were being overtaken by the new. In troubled times, the priests of the Vanir may have wanted Hrothgar to make the ultimate sacrifice – believing that for twelve (or two) years the land had needed such a sacrifice, as had always been required. Perhaps Hrothgar had not celebrated the ritual marriage with the land and the priests of the Vanir were applying pressure on him, and the people themselves were demanding the ultimate offering. It might have been that other scions of the Scylding dynasty were not as willing as Hrothgar for the kingship to become hereditary – perhaps they were willing to become a sacral king in the old fashion; after all, Hrolf (Hrothulf), Hrothgar's nephew, was to become a victim of the old regicidal system, being killed as his hall burned, wed to the sovereignty of the land as embodied by Skuld.

In Hrothgar's time, it seems that the Danes were in trade contact with the Geats, who were the enemies of the Ynglings of Sweden. It is not known why the Geats and Ynglings were enemies, but it could have been religious. If the Geats worshipped the Aesir and had given up the ritual regicide of the Vanir cult that still persisted amongst the Ynglings, perhaps this was why it was the Geats who answered the cry for help that went out from Demark. In this case, the coming of 'Beowulf the Geat' may not have been so much military in nature as religious.

And if Beowulf the 'Geat', the hero from over the sea, was not a mortal warrior as portrayed in *Beowulf,* this would explain why he exists in no genealogy, why his name does not alliterate with the other members of the Geatish family tree, why he can shift from one generation to another, and why folktale elements gather around him. What if Beowulf was not a man at all, but a god?

Part IV

BARLEY WOLF

CHAPTER FIFTEEN

·

THE DEMON'S HEAD

The Geat champion did not choose to take any treasures from
that hall, from the heaps he saw there, other than that richly
ornamented hilt and the head of Grendel ... The carrying of
the head from the cliff by the mere was no easy task for any of
them, brave as they were. They bore it up, four of them, on a
spear, and transported back Grendel's head to the gold-giving
hall...Then was the head of Grendel held up by its locks.

BEOWULF, 1612–15, 1635–9, 1647

WHEN BEOWULF HAS at last defeated Grendel's mother and
struck her head from her body, he searches her underwater lair
until he finds the remains of Grendel, who has died of his wounds,
beheads him, and takes the severed head to Heorot. While such behaviour can be credited to primitive 'trophy taking' appropriate to the
ancient world, it would be unwise in light of the many-layered nature
of this poem to be dismissive of this act: for the beheading of a
demonic opponent forms a major part in the hero-deeds of many
Indo-European gods, a fact that leads to questioning whether
Beowulf was really a human hero at all.

War of the Gods

While Sir Gawain's victory over the scheming goddess Morgan was
credited to his Christian faith, we know that Beowulf the Geat lived
and died a pagan in the darkest years of the Dark Ages. In seeking a

motivation for Beowulf to seek to end the tyranny of the dark goddess and her hideous son, it is the actions of Odin, the chief god of the Aesir, whose victory over the Vanir was well known throughout the North, that provide the prototype for the heroic deeds of Beowulf in vanquishing the power of these nightmares.

Snorri is our main source for this conflict. In *Ynglingatal* he relates how Odin was a great warrior chief who had come from the lands east of the Don river (in other words Asia – an attempt by Snorri to demythologize the name 'Aesir'), the capital of which was Asgard.[1] Odin had conquered many peoples and was always victorious in battle, and when he turned his face to the lands to the west of the Don, Vana-land, he came into conflict with its rulers, the Vanir.[2]

In other versions, the war between the gods is precipitated when the 'witch' Gullveig ('lust for gold' or 'gold-brew'), also known as Heid ('shining one'), enters Asgard.[3] Gullveig, so most scholars agree, was the Vanir goddess Freyr, associated in many tales with gold and with dark magic. Perhaps because of her lust for gold, or more likely, because of her magical powers, she is hoisted on a spear by the Aesir and burned three times on a fire in the hall. But the witch, adept in powerful Vanir magic, steps out of the fire reborn each time. The conflict begins between the two families of gods the moment Odin casts his spear amongst the Vanir.

Eventually, after both Asgard and Vanaheim are wrecked by the war and neither side is victorious, offers of truce are made and hostages are sent from both camps to ensure peace. Kvasir, a Vanir god, accompanies Njorthr and his twin children, Freyr and Freyja, to Asgard, and gods named Hoenir and Mimir go to Vanaheim. (Snorri states that Kvasir was not a Vanir god but was created from the spittle of the two families of gods who spat into a bowl – *kvas* means strong beer.) Also, as part of the truce, the Aesir take some of the Vanir goddesses as wives. Hoenir does not turn out to be a great hostage – seemingly wise, but only when under instruction from Mimir – so the Vanir behead Mimir and send his head back to the Aesir, where Odin preserves it in spices and oil, places it in Mimir's Well, and later consults it as an oracle.

This and similar myths were once thought to symbolize the vanquishing of the old local farming gods by the warrior gods of incoming 'Indo-European' tribes, who it was believed had blazed a trail throughout Europe from the Russian steppes at the beginning of the Bronze Age, slaughtering and taking over non-Indo-European cultures as they did so. But while the idea of a nomadic warrior way of life did indeed filter out from the steppes at this time, it is more likely that the Indo-European languages and their accompanying myths had arrived much earlier with the practice of farming (*see* page 28).[4] In fact, what these myths seem to portray is not the arrival of a new people and language, but a fundamental shift in the makeup of society.

In earlier times, the main gods had been those associated with farming rites and food production. But when tribes became more mobile and under increasing military pressure to defend their land from attack, the importance of the farmer waned in favour of the warrior. And just as the warrior band and the war leader now dominated the tribe, so too the gods themselves followed suit and became ruled by a warrior god.

Such changes required a massive shift in the outlook of the tribes, and the myths of the warring families of gods not only helped explain the changes but also clarified the new divine 'pecking order'. Such myths were no doubt crafted by the priests of the warrior gods, and so it is no surprise to find the once supreme farming gods depicted as inferior to their replacements. The 'losers' are demonized and downgraded as they lose their potency.

This is not to say that the old cults were totally eradicated. In classical Greece many of the old rites coexisted side by side with those of the Olympians; the mysteries of Dionysos, though mistrusted by the state, were allowed to continue, as were those of the barley-mother Demeter at Eleusis. It is likely that this was also the case in barbarian Europe, though remote enclaves of Vanir-dominated tribes – of which Denmark was presumably one – would have remained relatively untouched by the Aesir cults, until the age of migration.

This 'divine war' myth helps to explain why the warrior gods, always portrayed as violent and victorious, always seem to form truces with their opponents, and even marry into the family of the old gods. This is not a myth of total annihilation of old traditions, merely a jostling for position and, in some cases, the adoption by the new ruling classes of many of the elements of the previous regime. Despite a change in the dominant function of society, everyday farming rites would have continued much as before amongst the rural population, although perhaps overseen by the new pantheon. The old traditions were not so much cast out as adapted to suit the new cult.[5] And perhaps the major example of this was the adoption of the ritual intoxicant of the fertility religion by the warrior gods, as is made clear in Norse mythology.

The Demon Drink

The god Kvasir, created from the saliva of the gods, was said to have contained all the combined wisdom of the gods in his being, but this power was coveted by two dwarves, the brothers Fjalar and Galar. The brothers invite him to a feast and murder him, letting his blood (and the wisdom it contained) flow into three vessels, where it mixes with honey and ferments into the 'mead of wisdom' or 'mead of inspiration'. The brothers later give the mead to a giant named Suttung in recompense for having killed his parents. He takes it to Jutenheim (giant-home), where he hides it in the mountain of Hnitbjorg, where it is guarded by his daughter Gunnlod. Odin hears of this and, disguised as a man named Bolverk, secretly slays the farm labourers of Suttung's brother Baugi, and then bargains with Baugi that he will do their work in the fields for the harvest if in return he is offered a draught from Suttung's mead.

Baugi is unable to get a draught from his brother, but he bores a hole in the mountain into which Bolverk slips in the form of a serpent. Once inside the mountain, Odin resumes his normal form and woos the maiden Gunnlod, the mead's keeper, so that after three days she allows him to drink from it. Once he has the mead in his mouth, he escapes back to Asgard as an eagle, spitting the mead into a vessel just in time before Suttung, in the form of a bird, is able to catch him. Thus Odin won the mead of inspiration from the gods.[6]

The meaning of the cunning theft of the magical drink is not really explained in the Norse sources, but in the light of other European myths the tale fits within a pattern that could be called 'the stealing of the magical drink' in which a hero, usually aided by a warrior god, steals the drink of immortality from the 'demons'. There are different versions of this myth, but the one that fits closest with the Norse story of the truce of the Vanir and the creation of Kvasir is found in the Hindu Indian *Mahabaratha*.

In this tale, the gods and demons are involved in a struggle, but the struggle is depicted as a giant tug-of-war using a serpent as a rope and a mountain as a pivot that turns in the ocean. As the ocean (described as the 'milky' ocean) is churned, a magical butter called *soma* is produced that has the property of giving the gods immortality.[7] Rahu, a demon, seizes it and drinks it, but Vishnu, king of the gods, decapitates him with a discus, and takes the soma from the throat of the severed head. Another god, Nara, fires his bow into the crowd of demons and they flee into the underworld.

The Hindu myth contains many of the same images that are seen in the Aesir-Vanir war: Odin flinging his spear into the Vanir host mirrors the firing of Nara's bow; the combined effort to make a drink of immortality by the two warring families of gods, in one myth using saliva, in the other through a tug-of-war; and perhaps it is possible to add to these the drilling of a hole into the mountain, into which a serpent is able to crawl in the myth of Suttung.

The Soma Theft

Other myths suggest that this idea of co-operation may be mere 'spin' by the ruling warrior class, for they portray the gaining of the magical drink as out and out theft. Early Hindu tales depict the soma as a 'well of immortality' in which dead warriors could be revived, like those revived by Skuld on the field of battle, or those thrown into the cauldron of Bran, who emerge alive, though devoid of the power of speech.

In these myths, the gods send an envoy who, like Odin, woos the demon king's daughter, and she betrays the secret of immortality. In one version, the king of the gods, Indra, sends a girl named Sarama to obtain the soma (described as the milk of three magical cows) – she steals it by swallowing it, and then, like Odin in his eagle form, vomits it back up when she returns to the land of the gods.

In the Irish tale of the battle between the Tuatha De Danann and an evil demonic race, the Fomhoire, the Tuatha possess a revivifying well, but a Fomhoire named Ruadhan discovers and destroys it. In another version, the Fomhoire are said to have owned the well; the Dagda, disguised as Ruadh Rhoffessa, steals into the camp and is forced by the Fomhoire to eat a vast amount of porridge from a hole in the ground. He returns to his land and vomits it up. This tale of over-indulgence makes no sense when viewed alone, but in light of Sarama and Odin's theft of the soma its meaning becomes apparent.[8]

Interestingly, the same motif appears in the story of CúRoí Mac Daírí's death. When CúChulainn woos Blathnat and beheads CúRoí, part of his quest is to obtain from CúRoí a magical cauldron and three magical cows that produce vast quantities of milk. This makes no sense on its own, but a reading of the tale of Sarama explains that the three magical cows produce soma. It appears the theft of the mead is tied in with the killing of the king.

But what exactly is soma? In Hindu myth, it is a kind of powerful intoxicant, known as *haoma* in Iranian sources. A number of different theories have been put forward as to its exact identity, indluding *amanita muscaria* (fly agaric), Syrian rue, ephedra, cannabis, opium and a simple fermented alcoholic drink. In the early Indian poem, the *Rig Veda*, soma is confusingly described as both the juice of a leafy plant and also as something resembling a kind of fungus or mushroom; seemingly the term soma was applicable to a variety of different species.[9] Archaeological excavations in Turkmenistan, for instance, have uncovered evidence for the ritual use of ephedra (an amphetamine) mixed with cannabis in some areas and opium in others. In the damper climes of Europe, ergot fungus was used, as it was at Eleusis, where those taking the hallucinogenic barley drink were granted a sense of personal immortality through the visions it induced.

There is a strong link between such a ritual drink and the meads of knowledge/immortality that throng Indo-European myth. The revivifying cauldrons that populate these tales are likely to be ritual vessels that offered immortality through religious experience. If this is so, these vessels should be interpreted as offering the followers of a vegetal cult a belief in immortality. Such an interpretation is suggested in the tale of Bran, in which the Irish dead emerging from the cauldron are unable to speak. When viewed in the light of the mysteries of Eleusis (*see* page 81), where the celebrants were not allowed to tell any non-initiate of their experiences, this silence can be viewed as a ritual stance. After all, the word 'mysteries' derives from the Greek word *muein,* meaning to keep the mouth closed. It seems that rebirth from the cauldron was a symbol of being initiated into the vegetal mysteries, and it was this sacred drug and its accompanying experience that was 'stolen' by the warrior gods, so that it would become their attribute alone. Hence, Freyja comes to Asgard and teaches her regenerative knowledge to the wily Odin, giving him the power to bring the dead to life, and fill his hall Valhalla with the souls of slain heroes who will fight beside him at Ragnarok.

What the gods are stealing is not a potion per se but the *vegetal power of regeneration*, the power that enables Odin to die and be reborn on the world tree Yggdrasil; the power of the Green Knight, the spirit of fertility, to regenerate itself after death: *the power possessed by the corn and all green things*.

This theft of the potion was adapted from existing motifs that played a vital part in the old cyclical myth – the transferral of sovereignty from the old monarch to the new. This is demonstrated by the role of the 'demon's daughter', a role enacted by Blathnat, the wife of CúRoí Mac Daírí, in Irish myth and Gunnlod, the daughter of the giant Suttung, in Norse myth. These figures are enacting the ancient role of the duplicitous goddess of sovereignty who passes her favours on to her lover, the new king, and helps him defeat her old champion.

Talking Heads

There is an Indian myth that tells how the warrior god Indra won the secret of soma. The secret was possessed by a sage named Dadhyanc, but he refused to part with it so Indra cut off his head. The head fell into a lake and then floated to the surface whereon it finally uttered to Indra the secret.[10] In this tale, we learn that as with the decapitated head of the demon Rahu, the soma is seen to reside in the head (or throat) of the beheaded monster; in a similar way, in Norse myth, Odin is shown obtaining knowledge from the pickled head of Mimir in its well. Might the head of Grendel dragged from out of the waters of the lake have been a similar object?

The Greek hero Orpheus provides us with one clue as to how a severed head could give knowledge and its connection with the theft of soma – his head is severed by the maenads and floats to the isle of Lesbos, where it becomes an oracle.[11] For the Celts, the head was the seat of the soul and the motif of a talking head frequently occurs in their myths as demonstrated in the myths of Bran and Conaire (*see* pages 152 and 153). Certain druidic rites referred to in the myths suggest that severed heads could be used for oracular purposes. The origins of this concept are to be found, once again, in the imagery of the vegetal world.

The one constant recurring theme in the myths discussed here is the passing on of fertility, the reproductive urge of nature, from one season to the next. This 'force' is present in the new seed that is reaped from the parent plant, hence the imagery of the seed in the winnowing-basket as a symbol for the reborn god. But a parallel image to the emasculization of the god is his decapitation, which the act of striking the ear of corn from the sheaf resembles; in this way, the new growth will sprout from the *head* of the dead plant.

If soma is this essence, the 'force' that regenerates yearly in the corn, then it is present in the harvested ear – the head. This head is either 'buried' (sown) so that the next year's crop can grow from it, or the grain is 'burned' and 'drowned' (malted and soaked) to produce an alcoholic drink. This is the imagery we see used in the folk song *John Barleycorn*:

They filled up a darksome pit
With water to the brim,
They heaved in John Barleycorn,
There let him sink or swim.

They wasted, o'er a scorching flame,
The marrow of his bones;
But a Miller us'd him worst of all,
For he crush'd him between two stones.

If one brings to mind the kings placed in vats of mead, crushed by falling pillars and burned in their halls, an image arises as to how their deaths are linked to the vegetal cycle. When the body of the god is crushed, burned and drowned, the 'spirit' then enters the drink itself. In Indian myth, soma is personified as Agni, the sacrificial fire which burns in the water. The modern term 'fire-water' for alcoholic beverages demonstrates how ancient man may have interpreted the 'kick' of liquor as the vegetal spirit (a term we still use today) that induces ecstasy. In this way, the spirit of the god can be passed on by imbibing the ritual drink in which the head of the god is preserved. And by this means it is possible to acquire the characteristics of the deity, just as the eating of the flesh of the Yuletide troll gives Hjalti strength, and the blood of the dragon supped by Sigurd in the Norse myth gives him superhuman abilities. Again, as we hear in *John Barleycorn*:

And they hae taen his very heart's blood,
And drank it round and round;
And still the more and more they drank,
Their joy did more abound.

John Barleycorn was a hero bold,
Of noble enterprise,
For if you do but taste his blood,
'Twill make your courage rise.

It is easy to see how the image of the fermented 'head' of corn can become the image of a 'talking' head, passing on the occult knowledge of soma and rebirth – the fertility 'force' flowing out of the god's severed head to the drinker. And it is on this image that the rites of the transferral of kingship were based, as well as the taking of the head of Grendel beneath the water.

The spirit resident in the 'head' or body of the dead king would be transferred to the new king through ceremonial actions, hence the importance of the preservation of the body of the dead king on which the rites were to take place. The 'spirit' was still seen as residing in the body of the dead god until it could be magically transferred. In Egypt, this was done in an elaborate rite called the 'opening of mouth' ceremony; the new pharaoh, playing the role of Osiris's son Horus, had to open the mouth of the mummy of the deceased pharaoh, an act that was seen both to transfer kingship magically to the successor and also to bring back fertility of the land. The opening of the mouth transferred fertility into a new, more virile vessel and the land blossomed in accord. What is of major importance is that to perform this rite the Horus king had to present the mummy *with his eye* (albeit symbolically).[12] There can be little doubt that this ceremony was almost identical to the image preserved in Norse myth in which Odin presents his eye to the preserved head of Mimir. In each case, this action turns them into the one-eyed solar god who takes on the mantle of fertility deity from the dead king. Thus Odin becomes known as *Baleygr* (Furnace-eye) – he becomes the New Year sun.[13] It is reasonable to speculate that similar rites took place in ancient Germania on the preserved bodies of the bog people. Indeed, maybe they were placed in peat bogs *because of* their known preservative properties. Such an occurrence would explain the honour shown to the bodies of the deceased after death: the honour still paid to the corpse of Frothi as he is paraded on his chariot; the respect shown to the dead Freyr in his burial mound. Like the head of Mimir, the bog bodies had a part to play in the kingship rites even after their deaths.

The theft of the 'mead of inspiration' or soma from the decapitated demon was a reinterpretation of the transferral of kingship in the old farming cult. By utilizing this myth, it was possible to introduce into the emerging cult the ritual drink of the farming gods. Odin, therefore, became the ultimate incarnation of Ing – the one-eyed god who kills off the old king – but with no intention of being killed in turn the following year by another upstart.

The 'war of the functions' myth sought an end to the ritual cycle itself by inordinately lengthening the reign of the god. The god would be slain, the cosmos burned, but only at the end of time. For now, the victory over the demons was complete. The warrior gods had the upper hand – had acquired the power once ascribed to the Vanir and their priestesses. Odin now has the power to reanimate the dead. The giants and demons were slain. But even though the gods knew this was not for good, the king reigning in the present could rest assured there would be no challenge to his hereditary, not sacral, kingship.

Killing Grendel

It was not the winter alone that turned the hideous pair that threatened Heorot from fertility gods to dark, negative creatures. The ruling gods of the emerging military aristocracy had furthered the process – demonizing the old gods until they were little more than monsters. Grendel was just such a creation. He was a god turned monster. In origin, he was the fertility spirit to be murdered, beheaded in the water so that the new god could steal his soma, his revivifying draught of vegetal immortality. But Grendel had become a nightmare, a bogey, haunting Heorot until a man worthy of such a foe would face him.

In killing Grendel, Beowulf does not act out of turn; he beheads the lake terror, as the kings of old had done to become king in their turn, and he bears the severed head back to Heorot. But he also commits an act hitherto unseen in Denmark. When the lake-witch sits astride him, knife in hand, instead of yielding his life for the good of the crops, he strikes her foul head from her shoulders. He kills the mother-goddess of the ancient Ingaevones in her own sacred lake.

Unlike the preserved remains of the bog bodies of antiquity, this one man was able to sink below the surface of Nerthus's sacred lake and emerge unscathed. The slaying of Grendel's mother is a northern European equivalent of the Greek myth of the slaying of the hideous gorgon Medusa by Perseus. The poet Robert Graves suggested that the Perseus myth symbolized the violent ending of the older Earth-goddess cult by incoming warrior tribes, and there is reason to presume that something similar was happening here.

It is an act worthy of the Aesir god Odin, who casts his spear amid the Vanir and overcomes them – a deed whose imagery was used in the charm against a sudden pain, in which the victim casts a spear back at the Vanir spirits who plague him (*see* page 107). It is the act of a god.

The stomach contents of Nerthus's victims reveal that sacrificed kings imbibed the sacred drink before their deaths in order to pass its secret on to the new king in necromantic rites, just as the demon Rahu swallowed the soma prior to his beheading by Indra. But when the soma was passed on to the Aesir gods, to what use did they put it? When Beowulf killed Grendel, what use did he make of the fertility spirit? A clue is given in the myths of the revivifying cauldron that is coveted by the warrior gods – it is a weapon of war. Indo-European myth is quite open as to the use to which the Neolithic vegetal sacrament was put in later times. And it is a use that finally unravels one of the most intriguing questions posed to us by the Anglo-Saxon Beowulf: the true meaning of his name.

CHAPTER SIXTEEN

•

THE BRIMWYLF

AROUND THE TIME of the Beowulf story, a great religious change was taking place in Denmark which formed a background to the dynastic feuds and struggles recorded in the sagas. It was as a result of this conflict that the Scylding clan struck Sheaf from their ancestral lineage to distance themselves from the sacrificial demands of the old religion and instead placed the warrior god Odin at the head of their family tree in his place (*see* page 73). That Sheaf appears in English lore suggests this usurpation occurred after the English had left the continent (around AD 410–500), which places the deposition of 'Sheaf' and elevation of Odin around the late 5th–early 6th centuries – again, the date ascribed to the events in *Beowulf*.

It is evident that in many respects the tale of *Beowulf* depicts a mythological event, and it is exactly the kind of myth we would expect to have arisen in Denmark in this time of crisis. Had the *Beowulf* manuscript not survived, it still might have been possible to deduce that the ending of the Nerthus religion and its replacement by the Odin religion would have accrued the motifs of the Aesir-Vanir war: a warrior who slays magical demons, defeats the monstrous fertility deities, perhaps by beheading them, acquiring from them the secret of immortality. All this seems to fit in with the version of events described in *Beowulf* save the last point, for though he takes Grendel's head it is not expressly linked with the stealing of the barley-intoxicant of the Vanir religion. At least not on the surface.

Dutch Courage

In Indo-European myth, after the soma is stolen it becomes an intoxicant used to give martial valour in battle. Indra drinks it before he kills the serpent Vritra, the demonic god of the older worship. The *Rig Veda* describes the feeling of imbibing it:

> We have drunk the soma; we have become immortal; we have gone to the light; we have found the gods. What can hatred and the malice of a mortal do to us now, O immortal one? Inflame me like a fire kindled by friction ... Weaknesses and diseases have gone; the forces of darkness have fled in terror.[1]

It gave courage and strength, and a sense of immortality that enabled one to be fierce in battle, unafraid of death. Again, this theme is reflected in *John Barleycorn*.

> John Barleycorn was a hero bold,
> Of noble enterprise,
> For if you do but taste his blood,
> 'Twill make your courage rise.

The folk song is referring to alcoholic drink and the majority of warriors would have had to rely on everyday ale to put fire in their blood. Ancient peoples would have not joined in the horror of battle sober; it was often the case that men became drunk before a conflict. In one notable case, that of the battle of Catterick in North Yorkshire, between a northern Celtic tribe, the Votadini, and the newly established Anglo-Saxon kingdom of Deira and Bernicia, the Celts got so drunk before the battle they were almost annihilated, as their poet Aneurin, the only survivor, recounts bitterly:

> *Glasfedd a hancwyn, a gwenwyn fu*

> Pale mead was their drink, but it was poison.

But the warrior aristocracy seemed to have had more than ale in their horns. There is convincing evidence for the use of ritual intoxicants not only to induce a sense of invulnerability, but also a kind of martial fury in battle, all related strangely to the imagery of the warriors *becoming* wild animals – especially the boar, the bear and the wolf.

Bear Shirts and Wolf Heads

In Iranian lore, this 'fury' is called aēšma where it is associated with the boar. The warrior is seen as 'a wild, aggressive, male boar with sharp fangs and sharp tusks, a boar that kills at one blow'.[2] It is possible that Vanir warriors once went into battle in a similar fashion: The boar was one of the cult animals of Freyr and Freyja, and Tacitus mentions in the *Germania* that boars were sacred to the Baltic Æestii tribe, who like the Anglii and their neighbours were worshippers of the mother-goddess. The Æestii were reported as wearing the boar symbol as a talisman against harm, possibly in the form of a mask. This was a custom that was likely the origin of the many depictions of this animal that appear on armour and weapons, especially helmets such as the boar-crested helmet from Benty Grange, Derbyshire. 'Boar shapes' are mentioned as appearing on the helmets of the Geats in *Beowulf*, where they are said to protect the warriors.[3]

> Boar shapes shone above the cheek-guards, adorned with gold, bright and fire-hardened, kept guard over life

Boar-helmed warrior from Viking Torslunda helmet.

Plutarch mentions masks of 'hideous animal heads' being worn by the Cimbri and Teutones, though what animals he does not say. The best known such magical transformation was that of the Norse *berserkr* (bear shirts), warriors of Odin who transformed themselves into bears in battle, an ability used by Bodvar Bjarki.[4] But it was the wolf, above all other creatures, that typified this fury to the ancient north-west Europeans. In Celtic tradition, the hero CúChulainn undergoes a magical transformation in battle, where he becomes physically distorted into a monstrous killing machine. This is known as his 'fury' or *fearg* and is related to the Germanic *vargr* (wolf), a word Tolkien used in *The Hobbit* and *The Lord of the Rings* in its Anglicized form *warg* to denote a huge wolf.[5] Similarly, in Homeric tradition the martial fury that possessed the warriors on the plains of Troy was called *lyssa* (wolfish rage) derived from the Greek *lycos*.[6] And in Scythian tradition, *haumavarga* (haoma/soma wolves) were warriors who took soma so that they would become wolves in battle. With regard to Odin, Snorri begins the *Heimskringla* with a description of this god:

> It is said with truth that when Asa-Odin came to the northlands, and the *diar* [gods] with him, they introduced and taught the skills practised by men long afterwards ... He knew the arts by which he could shift appearance of the body any way he wished ... Odin was able to cause his enemies, ... swords to cut no better than wands. His own men went to battle without coats of mail and acted like mad dogs or wolves. They bit their shields and were as strong as bears or bulls.

Odin's special abilities – his imperviousness to blades, and his transformations into carrion animals in battle – are clearly Vanir attributes taught him by Freyja. But most importantly to our theme, as Snorri states, Odin's warriors could also appear in the shape of wolves. The Norse word for these warriors was *ulfhednar* (wolf heads).

In *Volsung's Saga*, two warriors, Sigmund and his son Sinfjotli, are depicted as becoming wolves by wearing wolf skins, much in the same way as berserkers became transformed by wearing their 'bear shirts'. Sigmund and his son enter a house where they see two men asleep with wolf skins hung over them:

> Sigmund and Sinfjotli put the skins on and could not get them off. And the weird power was there as before: they howled like wolves, both understanding the sounds.[7]

They go on a killing spree in the forest until such a time as the wolf skins could be removed, whereon they burn them in the fire. And it is possible to extend this 'wolfish' connection to the barley brew of the Danish bog men, for the ergot fungus which was the active ingredient of this ritual porridge was also known colloquially as the 'wolf's tooth'.

Wolf-warrior from Vendel helmet.

Wolf motif from Sutton Hoo purse-clasp.

The Wolf's Tooth

There is a suggestion of wolf–ergot association in the Germanic folk-lore figure of the *roggenwolf* (rye wolf), a lycanthropic spirit of the cornfield that was said to inhabit the last sheaf of corn and strangle its victims.[8] This evil spirit seems to have been a personification of ergot, which when consumed could cause convulsions and wryneck, in which the neck would be violently twisted to one side, leading to the feeling of being strangled. The reason for depicting the roggenwolf as a wolf is suggested by other of the physical sensations experienced after taking ergot – burning, thirst, massive appetite, delusions, itching and the sense of becoming an animal – all suggestive of lycanthropy. If warriors had once drunk ergotized beer before battle it explains why they may have thought they were literally becoming wolves. This is made more intriguing by the fact that the words *vargr*[9] and 'ergot' are thought to be derived from the same Indo-European root word *wergez* meaning 'to strangle'.[10] If the roggenwolf was ergot portrayed in the form of beast, then its description as both a wolf and a strangler follows logically. In 17th-century England, ergot poisoning was known as the 'strangulation of the mother', suggestive of the bog victims who had indeed been strangled by the Earth-mother's representative after eating the contaminated grains. In this way, the ergot fungus provides a direct link between the strangled bog men and the wolfish warrior cults – the 'wolf's tooth' was the ritual drink of both.

The use of the 'wolf's tooth' in the ritual drink might help explain the presence of the wolf on the Gundestrup cauldron shown as accompanying the goddess plunging warriors into her vessel of rebirth. Similarly, it is likely that the burning sensation the ergot caused was associated with the initiatory fire of the mysteries in which the child Demophoön is placed by Demeter to give him immortality (*see* page 81). Such an origin can also be postulated for the triple burning of the Vanir witch Heid/Gullveig in Asgard. The burning does not harm her but is demonstrative of her immortality and invincibility. Perhaps ergot was seen as creating the same 'inner fire' that is part of many shamanic experiences.

No wonder ergot was so sacred. Its imbiber was 'burned' and 'strangled', was effectively reborn, just like the sacral king himself. In taking ergot, an initiate of the Vanir vegetal cult would become one with the deity and, undergoing a powerfully transformative experience of identity with the 'lord', would become *ylfig, gidig* (*see* page 108).

Interestingly, in the killing of the king rites the burning motif is often connected to the symbolism of the wolf. Ragnarok was said to begin with the unchaining of the giant wolf Fenris, whereon Surt the fire-giant would burn the cosmos. The binding of Fenris in Hel must be seen as part of the Aesir-Vanir war. It has a counterpart in Greek myth, where the immortal Zeus overcomes the Titans by binding his father Cronos in the underworld. Cronos, like Fenris, will be released at the end of time whereon a Golden Age will ensue.

A sign that Fenris may represent the Vanir gods and their brew is that when binding him, the god Tyr loses his hand, bitten off by the *teeth of the wolf*. Taken in excess, ergot had a massively damaging effect on the nerve endings, causing gangrene, loss of limbs and, in large enough doses, death. The myth of Tyr might have been a cautionary tale about the danger of the Vanir cult drink.[11]

If the ritual drink of the Vanir had been 'stolen' and used by the Aesir warrior bands, this would help explain the similarity between the carrion-spirits of the Vanir, the Valkyries, and the animal transformations the latter used in their states of martial fury. It may have been that such warriors were seen as embodying the death-Keres of the Vanir, bringing death to their opponents.

The *ulfhednar* of Odin, then, mimicked the wolfish carrion spirits of the Vanir, though quite how much of these wolfish attributes were derived from the ergot fungus and how much from the carrion animal itself is impossible to determine. Whatever the ultimate origin of the lupine imagery, the *Beowulf* poet shows Grendel and his mother belonged to this same symbolism. Repeatedly, the poet describes them in terms suggestive of lupine characteristics: *brimwylf* (water-wolf), *grundwyrgenne* (ground-wolf) and *heorowearh* (sword-wolf).[12] These words are commonly translated in a manner that loses the wolf symbolism, but this is misleading because the poet was describing these monsters as what would now be known, for want of a better term, as 'werewolves'.

The Haelfhundingas

This is where the inclusion of the *Beowulf* poem within a 'book of monsters' (*see* page 13) becomes important.[13] Three of the four other texts within Cotton Vitellius A.xv mention similar creatures: *The Letters of Alexander to Aristotle* and *The Wonders of the East* both mention a strange breed of men known as the *haelfhundingas* ('the half-hound people'), described as being men with dog's heads. And the *Life of St Christopher* can be connected to these people, as in the Old English tradition he is described thus:

> He had the head of a hound, and his locks were extremely long, and his eyes shone as bright as the morning star, and his teeth were as sharp as a boar's tusks.

His shining eyes link him with Grendel, as does his long hair, by which the *Beowulf*-poet describes Grendel's severed head being held. But why is this saint depicted in such a fashion? One feasible answer is that because St Christopher is usually seen as carrying the Christ Child over a river, this Christian image somehow fused with a native Old English tradition of a dog or wolf-headed psychopomp who carried the dead over the 'river of death' into the underworld, a memory of which is preserved in the lore of the shining-eyed coal-black phantom hounds said to haunt pathways and graveyards in England (in East Anglia going by the name of *Black Shuck,* derived from the Old English *scucca* (demon), used in *Beowulf* to describe Grendel).[14]

St Christopher seems to have picked up some of the symbolism of the death-bringing wolfish spirits of paganism, becoming in the process a wolf-Valkyrie such as Grendel and his mother. When *Beowulf* was placed within a folio with three other texts containing lycanthropic imagery this was not a coincidence. Cotton Vitellius A.xv is not just a book about monsters, but monsters of a specific type – werewolves.

The Gelding

If any doubt were remaining that Odin's theft of the 'mead of inspiration' was in reality his acquisition of the ceremonial ergot drink of the Vanir, there remains one last piece of evidence – his practice of *seithr* magic[15] – that can be unmistakably linked to ergot.

When Freyja teaches Odin *seithr* magic, Snorri tells us it was thought 'shameful' for a man to practice it, and he uses a specific term for this practice: '*ergi*'. This term can be translated as meaning the passive partner in homosexual sex, but its use here probably had a wider symbolic meaning.[16] The practice of shamanism is often associated with cross-dressing or transexualism, and Odin, who bears many shamanistic traits, is known as 'the gelding' in the *Edda*, linking him to the castrated effeminate priests of Attis. In the *Germania*, Tacitus mentions the Naharvali tribe, whose ancient grove was presided over by a priest who dressed as a woman. This cross-dressing had the symbolic value of representing either the shaman as 'superhuman' – neither male nor female but both – or someone 'different' to whom the normal laws of society did not apply. Such people were known in Native American tradition as 'contraries'; they rode their horses backwards, slept in the day and dressed as women, but they were powerful medicine men. The unmanly 'mimes' at Uppsala, the effeminate nature of Dionysos and the priests of Attis all seem to fit into this symbolism.

As the term *ergi* was only applicable to the *passive* partner in homosexuality it does not seem to refer to the sexuality of the person, but their role. The passive man in homosexual sex is the equivalent of the 'female' in heterosexual sex, and therefore *ergi* suggests the passive role played by the sacrificed king in his love-death: the king is mounted by the woman, is subservient to her. As the term *ergi*, like *vargr*, is derived from *wergez* we find ourselves in possession of another clue that Odin had stolen the ergot-drink of the old religion, and by doing so had acquired the shamanic secrets of its effeminate priests. Odin was no mindless destroyer, he takes and adapts the old religion to his own designs. In this respect, Caesar's equating him with

Mercury (*see* page 49) becomes obvious, for Mercury was the god of thieves and trickery. Odin steals every useable aspect of the older cult (or rather, the priests of the Aesir retain everything useable from the Vanir cult) while adapting the kingship rite towards a hereditary kingship rather than a sacrificial one. The old magical practices do not die out; Odin becomes the divine magician *par excellence*. He hangs on the world tree Yggdrasil for nine nights and days, a spear thrust in his side, a regenerating self-sacrifice in the Vanir mould that allows him to learn the magic of the runes. Odin, as warrior and shaman, bridges the gap between the two cults.

Odin is a god of many names and disguises. He is Grimr (Hooded one); Gelding; Long-beard; High One; Glad of War; Spear-Thruster; Bolverk; Gondlir (Wand-bearer); Wanderer; Ygg (Terrible One).[17] But this list is far from comprehensive. And another name can be added to it.

In the East, where soma/haoma was the ritual drink of the warrior cults, the wolf warriors went by the name of *haumavarga*, soma wolves. The equivalent title in regions where the sacred 'soma' was the ergotized barley drink would be an *ergot wolf* (warg) *rye wolf* (roggenwolf) or *barley wolf*. And what is the Old English translation of 'barley wolf'? It is *Beowulf*.

In the very name Beowulf, we witness the theft of the magical potion of the Vanir, a theft not explicit in the poem, though suggested in the decapitation of the wolfish Grendel. In this Old English poem, we see the tale of the ancient victory of an Aesir 'barley wolf' over Vanir wolf-demons and the ending of an age-old practice. This 'barley wolf' was Odin/Woden, who also bore among his many titles *Geat*, meaning 'the Goth'.[18] Beowulf the Geat was no man, he was the god of the Aesir.

Does this mean that the tale was wholly legendary and 'Beowulf' was a kenning for Odin, suggestive of his victory over the demonic forces of an old and abhorrent tradition? If so, he was later euphemized into a warrior from Geatland by the *Beowulf* poet or his immediate predecessors in much the same way as Snorri tried to make Odin a mortal chieftain from Asia. But this is not the whole story.

The Hooded Man

In England, the Angles of Northumbria were converted from paganism to Christianity in 627. This moment of conversion is described by Bede, who relates the destruction of a heathen shrine at Goodmanham by Coifi, the pagan priest of Edwin of Northumbria:

> So he formally renounced his pagan superstitions and asked the king to give him arms and a stallion – for hitherto it had not been lawful for the Chief Priest to carry arms or to ride anything but a mare – and, thus equipped, he set out to destroy the idols. Girded with a sword and with a spear in his hand, he mounted the king's stallion and rode up to the idols. When the crowd saw him, they thought he had gone mad; but without hesitation, as soon as he reached the shrine, he cast into it the spear he carried and thus profaned it. Then, full of joy at his knowledge of the true God, he told his companions to set fire to the shrine and its enclosures and destroy them.

Learning this from a good 'historical' source, this seems to be a straightforward conversion. But Coifi means 'hooded one' – a common epithet of Odin/Woden – and if this story had come down to us in another form, it would probably have been believed that it was a myth based on Odin/Woden's war against the Vanir.

That Coifi was unable to bear weapons hints that he was a priest of Freyr, who allowed no weapons in his temple. Nor was he allowed to ride – again, because the stallion was sacred to Freyr. But when he converts and is able to bear arms and ride a stallion, the image is totally incongruous with that of a Christian priest, but not of a priest of Odin. When Coifi profanes the Vanir shrine, he does so in a manner suggestive of the victory of Odin: he throws his spear and burns the temple. In reality, this event was either a conversion to Wodenism misinterpreted by Bede as a Christian conversion, or a strange Christian rite employing the native symbolism of the Aesir-Vanir war to its own ends – something not to be dismissed, given Pope Gregory's advice to

Mellitus to make the most of pagan shrines and festivals to get the Christian message across (*see* page 46).[19]

The tale of Coifi shows that a deed that on the surface could be interpreted as purely mythological may still have been acted out in physical reality. In a similar fashion, were the deeds of Beowulf entirely mythical or did priests or warriors from an Aesir-dominated land (possibly Geatland in Sweden) come to Denmark at Hrothgar's request to help impose a new cult in place of the old one, acting out in the historical plane an event from the timeless world of myth? If Bede's record of events in Northumbria is accurate, then it is proba- ble that the same mechanism was at work in Denmark: warriors or priests journeyed to the lake shrine of the strangling mother and there ended her cult.

The war between the Aesir and Vanir cults may have continued for a few generations until Odinism took hold, but when it was eventu- ally complete, the old fertility god, the sheaf that was cut down at winter, was removed from the Danish family tree for good, the old family 'head' struck from the genealogy by the sword of Beowulf. In place of the Sheaf came Skjold son of Odin, a shield-bearing warrior who kills a bear as a child, in whose myth there is no mention of sea journeys or vegetal symbolism. In time, it is said, Skjold becomes the husband of Gefion (having been exorcised of her dark side), making a dutiful wife of the goddess of sovereignty. In bedding her, he justifies his taking of the land, as is always the way with such victors.

Whatever events did occur in Hrothgar's Denmark can now only be glimpsed through an old, misunderstood poem. But like the Trojan War, the Minotaur in the labyrinth and the legends of Arthur, the strange tale of the monster-slaying Beowulf was, at root, histori- cal. *Something* happened in migration-age Denmark that inspired generations of poets. And that something was a forceful ending to a megalithic-aged fertility cult practised by the ancestors of the English people.

Finally, the idea of a human hero need not be discarded either. If, as at Goodmanham, the cult-war was physically enacted with the destruction of the old Vanir temples or groves, then somewhere beneath the myth of Odin's victory stands a historic man who may, like Coifi, have played the role of this god in an act dictated by mythology, but who nevertheless entered the lakeside shrine of Nerthus and profaned it, perhaps with bloodshed. The deeds of that man, whatever his real name or status, was the germ-seed around which the tale of Beowulf was to grow.

★　　★　　★

In trying to determine what the *Beowulf* poem is about, the majority of scholars have worked backwards from the flowering glory of the *Beowulf* poem itself, seeking roots in the dark soil of folktale and romance. But this book has sought to work the other way, starting with the ancient megalithic cult of the fertility god and the Earth-goddess, through its continued practice in Iron Age Denmark, until the final ending of this regicidal cult by Odin-worshippers during the era in which *Beowulf* was set.

To argue that the deeds of *Beowulf* are just borrowings from popular folk story (such as the 'bear's son', *see* page 15) is to ignore what we know actually occurred. The fact is the regicidal lake-mother cult *was* superseded in Denmark during the age of migration. If we had not already heard the tale of *Beowulf*, it would have been reasonable to suppose such a ritual conflict could have generated a 'legend' concerning the victory over a lake-dwelling hag by a heroic warrior. That such a motif forms the backbone to *Beowulf* confirms this theory.

In time, however, some folkloric motives did become accrued to the tale (*see* page 139) so that in *Hrolf's Saga* the hero becomes the 'bear's son': the berserker Bodvar Bjarki, son of Bjorn and Bera. But in the earliest extant version – the Old English *Beowulf* – he remains the *barley wolf*.

EPILOGUE
People of the Wolf

WHILE THE WARS of kingship and religion were raging in the old country, the 'new' England was gradually being settled by the descendants of the Ingaevones, who had not forgotten the divine Scef nor his gifts to humankind. In the act of sailing to a new land by boat, the English unconsciously imitated the epiphany of their god, for they would have brought sheaves of corn with them across the ocean, just as his myth had always portrayed. Accompanying the barley seed were tales of Sheaf and Beow, and also a calendar rich in the cycles of sun and moon, sowing and harvesting, that told of the Mothers' night, of the ancient affiliation to the forces of nature. Some of the warriors may have been followers of the new cult – although the shrines to Woden in England may be late arrivals – but most would have been Vanir worshippers, sons and daughters of the Earth-mother, the people of Ing.

They were led, legend tells us, by Hengist and Horsa, Stallion and Horse, thus claiming the new land in the name of the mare of sovereignty and the stallion of kingship. Such twin horsemen, gods of the Vanir, appear in Norse tradition as the Haddingjar – meaning 'long/womanly-hair'[1] and it may have been these who brought Ing with them, as the old rune poem says:

Ing waes aerest mid Est-Denum
Gesewen secgum, oth he siddan est

Ofer waeg gewat; waen aefter ran;
Thus heardingas thone haele nemdun'

Ing was first seen among men among the East Danes
till he later departed [east or back?]
over the sea the wagon ran after;
thus the heardingas/Haddingjar [?] named the hero.

To these people the old gods were not the vicious night-mares the later religions conceived them to be: they accepted their dual nature as one accepts that night follows day and winter follows summer, so the gods of life also brought death, and through this death the promise of rebirth. To them, the news of the death of the lake-mother and her kin would have been an extreme shock, but how did news of this event reach them?

Many suggestions have been aired over the date and location of composition of *Beowulf* (*see* page 14). Some have suggested it was written as an elegy to King Offa of Mercia in the 10th century, others that it was composed in Wessex under Alfred the Great in the 9th century. However, the most likely is that it was written in East Anglia in the 7th century. Firstly, the pro-Danish stance of the poem suggests that it was either written at a date prior to the Viking raids on England (from the 8th century onwards), or it was written in Danish-occupied England (the Danelaw) after this date. As the forms of the names used do not bear any traces of Viking influence, it must be assumed that *Beowulf* was not a tale written by or for Vikings, and so a date before the 8th century is indicated. Also, the names are Saxon and the genealogies and family trees match those found in the early poem *Widsith* and other dateable early sources. Secondly, the name of Grendel begins to appear in English place names usually associated with pits or bodies of water from the 700s onwards (for instance it is recorded that in 739, one Aethelheard of the West Saxons granted land to the Bishop of Sherbourne, 'from Dodda's ridge to Grendel's pit'.)[2] The appearance of this name means one of two things – that Grendel was a well-known name for a water demon in Old English (a theory not borne out by linguistic evidence) or the story of *Beowulf* was already known by then.

If the composition of *Beowulf* does date to the late 7th–early 8th century, then, based on the literary sophistication needed to produce the poem, there are two possibilities as to its source. The first is Northumbria, a centre of great learning before the rise of Vikings, and the second is East Anglia, a region once discounted until the discovery of the ship burial at Sutton Hoo.

The Wuffingas

The modern story of Sutton Hoo begins in 1926, when Colonel William Pretty bought land near Woodbridge, Suffolk, that included several large burial mounds within its limits. After his death, his widow turned to spiritualism, and after reportedly seeing the ghost of a man on horseback and other strange figures amongst the mounds, she asked local archaeologist Basil Brown to excavate them. His excavations began in 1938 and a year later he had uncovered a ship burial in 'mound 1'. In fact, what Brown uncovered was not a ship as such but a 90-ft long 'shadow' in the sand, complete with rusty rivets, where a ship had once lain before decomposing. In all, over 250 precious artefacts were found but not the body of the king: this, like his vessel, had dissolved into the earth.[3]

It is now thought that the Sutton Hoo ship burial was the grave of King Raedwald[4] of East Anglia, who ascended the throne in 599 and died some 25 years later, and whom Bede records as one of the early *Bretwaldas* ('wide rulers') – what might now be termed an 'over-king' of all the Anglian tribes in England south of the Humber. Raedwald had a very colourful history: on a visit to the court of the Kentish King Ethelbert (Hengist's great-great-grandson), he was converted to Christianity by St Augustine, but when he returned home he continued to honour both Christ and the pagan gods, side by side in his temples. Although a pair of baptismal spoons were found in the ship burial, the whole pagan burial site suggests that Raedwald was not setting sail for a Christian heaven.

The contents found within the ship revealed that Raedwald's people were in trade contact with the peoples of the Continent. Buried with him were a host of objects including a silver dish from Byzantium (stamped with the mark of Anastasius I, who reigned from 491–518); three cauldrons, two drinking horns, a six-stringed harp; nine spears, a wave-patterned sword worthy of a noble warrior, a large shield decorated with a dragon and birds; an imposing helmet crested with a serpent and with a face-guard formed from a stylized bird with protective boar-heads at the tip of each wing (*see* plate 19); a whetstone sceptre with a stag mounting and eight ancestral faces staring out from its sides, and an elaborately jewelled 'purse' containing 37 Merovingian coins and 3 blanks – money to pay the 40-strong spectral crew who would have rowed Raedwald over the river of death to the land where the sun sleeps at night.

Raedwald's grave offers us a window into the world described in *Beowulf*. Many of the objects described above match those described in the poem, and as many seem to have been family heirlooms, they may even have dated from Beowulf's day. There were only a few generations separating Raedwald from the characters mentioned in Beowulf. Before Raedwald had come Tyttla (d. 599), and before him Wuffa (d. 577) – after whom the East Anglian dynasty were named the *Wuffingas* – and then before him Wehha, who would have been king of the East Angles when 'Beowulf' was supposedly king of the Geats.[5] As it is only in East Anglia that the rite of ship burial is found at this time, this in itself suggests that the poet who originally composed *Beowulf* – and included in it a ship burial for Scyld – had either known of, or was in some way connected to, the East Anglian court and its funerary tradition

The court of the Wuffingas, a people still entwined through trade to the tribes of the Continent and practising the rite of ship burial, might have offered a fertile source of inspiration for the *Beowulf* poet. Further supporting this theory is that the grave goods at Sutton Hoo suggest a strong connection between the East Anglian ruling house and the land of Beowulf himself – Sweden.[6]

When archaeologists uncovered the ship burial and its goods, they were struck by the similarity to a number of finds associated with the burial mounds of the Scylfing kings at Uppsala in Sweden. Not only did these ancient mounds, thought to belong to the very kings that appear in *Beowulf* and *Hrolf's Saga* (Onela and Eadgils/Adils), contain ship burials, but the armour contained within them, especially the helmets, were almost identical, even down to the use of the same basic 'fallen warrior' and 'dancing warrior with spears' motifs found on them. Originally, archaeologists believed the Sutton Hoo helmet was from Sweden, but it is now seen as a native piece of craftsmanship, based on Swedish models.[7] This shared burial rite and material tradition suggests there was a great affinity between these two peoples on opposite shores of the North Sea at this time. Whether or not this indicates a Swedish origin for the Wuffingas, or just a shared cultural link, possibly through trade, it does provide a reasonable basis from which to suggest an Anglian origin for *Beowulf*, concerned as it is with Swedish dynasties and Scandinavian bloodlines.

Dynastic Connections

A number of attempts have been made to determine whether the Wuffingas might have been related to any of the dynasties mentioned in the poem.[8] One of the first ideas put forward was that Wiglaf the Waymunding, who defends Beowulf from the dragon, was related to the Wuffingas through his father Weohstan – who some suggested lay behind the 'Wehha' of the Wuffinga family tree. While this is not impossible, it seems more likely that the Wuffinga family tree before Tyttla was mostly mythical, like that of Wessex, and that Wuffa and Wehha may be mythological entities rather than flesh and blood ancestors.

A further school of thought sought to identify the *Wuffingas* with a tribe named the *Wulfings*, who are mentioned in *Beowulf* as neighbours of the Geats in south-west Sweden. This is not a spurious connection, for the name Wulfings (people of the wolf), is also the meaning attributed to the Wuffingas – for the name Wuffa, probably that of a mythical ancestor of the Anglian royal line, is a diminutive of Wulf (wolf) and can be interpreted as meaning 'little wolf'.

The Wulfings of *Beowulf* seem to be important, but are not really mentioned in detail, as if it was assumed that the audience was already acquainted with them. According to the poem *Widsith*, the Wulfings were ruled by an ancestral figure called Helm, but little more is said of them. It has been suggested that Beowulf's father Egdetheow may have fought the Wulfings as a young man, but that Hrothgar had intervened and made peace between the neighbouring tribes, in recompense for which Beowulf came to the aid of Hrothgar. But it is also possible that the Wulfings were directly related to the Danish Scyldings through marriage.

In the non-English versions, it is Hrolf who is the main protagonist of the Skjoldung saga, yet in *Beowulf* the action concentrates on the earlier generation and has the monstrous incursion of Grendel occurring under Hrothgar. Was this because the royal family for whom *Beowulf* was arguably composed had a reason to celebrate a possible dynastic connection with Hrothgar but not Hrolf? A clue to this possibility is to be found in the Wuffinga genealogy.

The name Hrothmund appears in the genealogy of the Wuffinga King Aelfwald (713–49) three generations above Wehha. This name only occurs once elsewhere in Germanic literature: in *Beowulf*. This other Hrothmund is the son of Hrothgar who disappears when his brother Hrethric is killed by Hrothulf/Hrolf Kraki (*see* page 146). If the Wuffingas were the descendants of Hrothgar's and Wealtheow's son Hrothmund, then there is good reason to see why Hrolf (Hrothulf) should be seen as alluded to in *Beowulf* as a potential villain.[9]

This connection between the two Hrothmunds might be seen as coincidental, were it not for a further connection between Hrothgar and the Angles in *Hrolf's Saga*, where he is called the king of Northumbria. While such a title is clearly impossible, in some respects it can be explained as a misunderstanding on behalf of the Icelandic author (writing 500 years after the events he describes), if it was once well known that Hrothgar's son was related to the Anglian scions of the Wulfings, the Wuffingas. The reason why he may have fled to the Wuffingas, it seems, is because his mother, Wealtheow, was a Wulfing, for in *Beowulf* she is called a *Helming* – an epithet that may be derived from *Helm*, the ancestor of the Wulfings according to *Widsith*.

Wealhtheow's name is interesting; it is formed from two words: *wealh* (foreigner) means someone who speaks a non-Germanic language, and *theow* (slave). Thus it could be that she was a foreigner married to cement a dynastic alliance. Perhaps she was English but of Wulfing/Wuffing descent, a queen from the new Anglia, one of the early Anglian settlers who intermingled with the Celtic population. If Wealhtheow was British/English and had married the king of the Danes to cement the Wuffing/Scylding alliance, this could explain why her son might flee to the royal house of the East Angles.

These genealogical conundrums suggest that there may once have been a connection between the Wulfings and Wuffingas – even if that connection was one of wishful thinking or poetic licence. For all we know, Raedwald and his kin might have been the descendants of simple pirates from Old Anglia who struck it lucky, warriors chiefs or federates who struggled their way to power, but who allied themselves through trade with Swedish tribes and invented a connection with them to establish a sense of nobility and royalty. Or maybe the Wuffingas were a Swedish royal house, kin to the Wulfings, who sailed from Scandinavia to England and dominated the newly arrived Anglian tribes. Whatever was the case, maybe the name 'Wuffinga' had nothing to do with a mortal ancestor named Wuffa but with a mythical wolf god, perhaps even the 'barley wolf' himself, Odin/Woden – the god who in heathen times headed the Wuffinga family tree.

There are clues on the artefacts excavated at Sutton Hoo that the wolf was more than a nickname for Raedwald's supposed grandfather. On the sceptre found next to where the king's body once lay there was a gold-foil wolf halfway up the shaft, and on the lid of the purse containing the payment for the ghostly oarsmen appears a fantastical image of a man standing between two wolves. The presence of these wolfish symbols on the regalia of people who called themselves the 'people of the wolf' suggests that *Beowulf* was a 'family myth' of the Woden-descended Wuffingas and that it is in their royal court at

Rendlesham that the tale of the barley wolf's victory over the wolf demons of the old religion was first recorded.

A Dark Age Parable

But why was *Beowulf* written? Although it may have been a simple tale to while away the long, dark winter evenings, the very nature of the poem suggests a hidden agenda. It is clear that the Vanir cult existed in England, but if the tale of *Beowulf* was that of a Woden cult, and perhaps the cult myth of the Wuffingas, then presumably at some point the Wuffingas in East Anglia were faced with a similar position to the one that Hrothgar faced in Denmark. They were a warrior aristocracy ruling over a people who still worshipped the old religion. In such a case, it is possible that *Beowulf* was propaganda for this new regime. The tale could have been seen to legitimize the overthrowing of the old paganism and the installation of the new cult of Odin/Woden – a poetical allegory to legitimize this Swedish royal house and justify its eradication of the older native faith.

Before long an even newer cult, Christianity, arrived, but as it was essentially a tale of religious conversion the sentiment behind *Beowulf* remained potent. On this evidence, it is possible that the poem as we know it – Christianized and effectively purged of anything overtly pagan – was composed shortly after the demise of (the, albeit nominally, converted) King Raedwald from a lost pagan original or originals. In many ways, Raedwald offered a parallel to the mythical hero. Like Beowulf he was essentially a non-native, a Swede who had ended the pagan cults of the local *Anglii*. Both men were buried in a mound stacked high with the heirlooms of the old religion.

The Last of the Wuffingas

It is more than likely that Raedwald knew the tale of the god-man Beowulf, his wolfish ancestor, who overcame the dark *wargs* of the ancient religion– the dread mother of the lake and her dark winter son – with their too heavy demands on the person of the king.

Perhaps he also knew that when he died, the old faith of the barley wolf would die with him, its pagan treasures vanishing from the world of men to accompany him to the *great deep*.

But the wolf god continued to protect its own, even when his own religion had changed and been taken over. According to the *Anglo-Saxon Chronicle*, the last of the line of the Wuffingas, King Edmund, died by Viking hands in the year 869:

> In this year the [Danish] host rode across Mercia into East Anglia and took winter quarters in Thetford and the same year King Edmund fought against them and the Danes had the victory, and they slew the king and overran the entire kingdom.

The king was buried in the town that still bears his name – Bury St Edmunds. Although he is a celebrated Christian martyr, there is something about his death that recalls the ancient cult-war and the heroic deeds of Edmund's ancestors, and the ultimate ancestor, the wolf-god Beowulf. When he was killed by Vikings (he was tied to a tree and shot full of arrows, reminiscent of Balder), his head was struck from his shoulders and hidden in a wood.

> There was eke a great wonder, that a wolf was sent,
> by God's direction, to guard the head
> against the other animals by day and night.
> They went on seeking and always crying out,
> as is often the wont of those who go through woods;
> 'Where art thou now, comrade?' And the head answered them,
> 'Here, here, here.' And so it cried out continually,
> answering them all, as oft as any of them cried,
> until they all came to it by means of those cries.
> There lay the grey wolf who guarded the head,
> and with his two feet had embraced the head,
> Greedy and hungry, and for God's care durst not
> taste the head, but kept it guarded against [other] animals.
> Then they were astonished at the wolf's guardianship,

and carried the holy head home with them,
thanking the Almighty for all His wonders;
but the wolf followed forth with the head
until they came to the town, as if he were tame,
and then turned back again unto the wood.[10]

These motifs of the killing of the king, the severing of his head, its
ability to speak although severed and the connection with the wolf do
not arise in this legend by sheer chance. In addition, when the head is
reunited with the body it miraculously joins back onto it, like that of
the Green Knight, leaving just a small scar. We know this as in Abbo
of Fleury's *The Life of St Edmund*, written in 985, it is related how he saw
the body, and that it was supple as if embalmed and bore no trace of
wounds save for a scarlet 'thread' about the neck. It has been suggested that the body of St Edmund discovered in the fens was in fact
a prehistoric bog body, and that in trying to find their murdered king,
his people had uncovered the remains of a sacred king of the old religion still bearing the marks of his ritual strangulation.[11]

Like a king of the old religion the preserved body of the saint, like
that of King Frothi (*see* page 124) was deemed holy, and offered mira-
cles of healing to his worshippers. And so by some strange irony, the
last of the Wuffingas, the People of the Wolf, was given the kind of
honour formerly only known by the god-kings of old, all the while in
place of the martyr's body lay an interloper, a husband of the lake-
mother, an ancient king freed from the mother's embrace after a
thousand years.

St Edmund was remembered and revered long after the tale of
Beowulf's victory over the dreaded lake-goddess and her kin, once
sung loudly in mead-halls, was utterly forgotten by the English
people. When at last it did emerge again into the light of day, like the
bog body of 'Edmund', after nearly 1,000 years, the rites and religion
that informed it had been forgotten. Just as the bog body had been
taken for a Christian king, so the tale of Beowulf – a visitor from a lost
age – was taken as a fiction, an amusing tale, but it bore the traces of
an ancient ritual event.

Survivals

Whether or not the wolf and head motifs in the St Edmund story are coincidental, the tale of Edmund, last of the Wuffingas, shows that elements of the old cults may have survived the conversion. The persistence of rites such as the *Aecerbot* (field remedy), which calls on the Earth-mother and is full of pagan sexual imagery concerning the fertilizing seed and plough of the god impregnating the earth, bring to mind the old cults. This is not to say that pockets of pure paganism survived, more that ancient images, superstition and magic were retained and incorporated into the new faith. Harvest queens on wagons, and crying the neck, are the survival of magic and superstition within the framework of a new religion. For the conversion to Christianity warranted no giant conceptual leap. In essence, the myth of Christ was not much different from the Vanir religion of the earlier tradition. Christ the 'Son of Man' was surely the same spirit as 'Ing (Son) son of Mannus' he was the dying and rising god under a new name, whose sacred symbol was still the 'bread of life'. Born on the Night of Mothers, he entered the tomb, like Freyr, until the stone was rolled away and he emerged alive, reborn.[12]

Christianity, however, brought the 'good news' that all men, not just initiates or warriors, could now feast in the hall of the gods. And kings no longer needed to die at the end of the year for their people, as Christ had died for all mankind. Indeed, the conversion from the Vanir cult to Christianity was probably no more traumatic than had been the change from the fertility cults to the militaristic cults of the Aesir. At root, they were both re-imaginings of the same basic myth. Thus, the people of a rural English parish, in celebrating the harvest festivals and the Nativity, observing the farming year, appointing a 'harvest queen', and believing in fairies and other spirits, were not leading radically different lives from those of their Continental ancestors at the time of the Egtved girl (*see* page 34).

The real severance from our ancestral heritage is something that has occurred only in recent times. Sheaf and his elf-gods may have survived the pogroms of Dark Age Denmark, the sword of Beowulf, and the coming of the Christ, only to fall to the ungodly powers of industrialization and urbanization.

Part folktale, part myth, part history, *Beowulf* offers us some consolation for the loss of much of our heritage. The horse and the rider have long vanished from our land; only the deeds of the barley wolf remain with us, a splinter of a lost mythology, a fragment of Dark Age epic from a more heroic age, first heard by kings long ago but miraculously surviving invasion, dissolution and fire to thrill, entertain and educate today.

NOTES

Prologue: Where Now the Horse and Rider?

1. For the ending of native Saxon culture by the Norman conquest but also of possible survivals see Shippey, T, (1992), pp. 35-8.
2. For JRR Tolkien's attempt to create a replacement 'mythology for England' as well as Tolkien's debt to Anglo-Saxon lore in general *see* Shippey, T, (1992), especially p. 268.
3. On the history of the *Beowulf* manuscript, *see* Chambers, RW, and Wyatt, AJ, (1943), pp. ix-xix.
4. For the figure of Arthur as propaganda for the Norman Kings of England, see Fife, G, (1990), pp. 37-9.
5. For information on the *Waldhere* fragments discovered in Copenhagen, see Branston, B, (1993), p. 6, and Herbert, K, (2000), pp. 261-71.
6. Translations of the Old English poems '*Deor*' and '*Widsith*' can be found in Bradley, S (ed.), (1995).
7. Tolkien's poem 'Where now the horse and the rider?' occurs in chapter 6 of Tolkien, JRR, (2002).
8. His essay 'Beowulf: The Monsters and the Critics', is printed in Tolkien, JRR, (1997), along with his essays on translating *Beowulf* and *Sir Gawain and the Green Knight*. The Anglo-Saxon poem from which it is derived – *The Wanderer* – is translated in Bradley, S (ed.), (1995).
9. For the archaeological discovery of the Sutton Hoo ship burial, *see* Carver, M, (1998) pp. 2-24.
10. For the effect of the Sutton Hoo find on Beowulf criticism, see Chambers, RW, (1963), pp. 507-23.

Introduction: The Keenest for Fame

1. Numerous editions of the *Beowulf* poem are available, both in Old English and in translation. For ease of reading and understanding, Seamus Heaney's award-winning prose translation (2002) is perhaps the most accessible, while the translation by Michael Alexander (1986) (used in the quotes found in this book) occupies the middle-ground between a literal translation and one that makes sense to the average reader. Nothing, however, can better the Old English poem itself, and for this the ideal starter is Porter, J (trans.), (2003), which gives the literal translation on the page opposite the vernacular text.

2. On the use of language, dialect and origins of the poem, good introductions are found in Chambers, RW, (1963), and Newton, S, (1999), although the bibliographies found in the former and in Orchard, A, (2003), suggest many further avenues.

3. We know this because when Beowulf recounts his tale to Hygelac on his return to the land of the Geats, it differs in some minor respects to what we have been told earlier in the poem. *See* Alexander, M, (1986), pp. 39–40.

4. For Hygelac as the 'Chochilaicus' mentioned in the chronicles of Gregory of Tours, *see* Chambers, RW, (1963), pp. 2–5, and for the historicity of the Swedish king Eadgils/Adils pp. 6–10.

5. On the early theory that Beowulf was an echo of an earlier pagan sun god, *see* Chambers, RW, (1963), pp. 41–8. Much of this original mythological work was done in early 20th-century Germany and is hard to come by.

6. For a discussion of the 'bear's son' or 'the three princesses', the original appears in Grimm, J and W, (1993), but the main source of debate is Panzer, F, (1910), summarized in Chambers, RW, (1963), pp. 368–70. It was Grimm who suggested that Beowulf originally meant 'bee' in Grimm, W, (1854), p. 342.

Chapter 1: Clans of the Sea Coasts

1. On the silting-up of the Wantsum Channel, *see* Harris, S, (2001), pp. 4–5.

2. For details of the wanderings of the Cimbri and Teutones, *see* Cunliffe, B, (2001), p. 368.

3. The history of Roman attempts to annex Germania, especially the horror that faced Varus, are evocatively retold in Schama, S, (1996), pp. 88–9. Varus's defeat, told by Vellius Paterculus, is translated in Jackson, JS (ed. and trans.), (1889), p. 536.

4. A very readable translation of the *Germania* is Tacitus (trans. Mattingly, H and Handford, S), (1986) – it is from this version that I quote. It is possible that Tacitus's source for the *Germania* was King Masyos of the Semnones tribe, who visited Rome in AD 92 when Tacitus held the office of Praetor, and so his information is to be respected, *see* North, R, (1997), pp. 141, 210.

5. An overview of Iron Age German archaeology can be found in Cunliffe, B (ed.), (1994), chs 10, 12.

6. Although by Tacitus's time there is evidence that land was beginning to be awarded to status individuals, this was possibly through Roman influence.

7. On the term 'German' as a linguistic tag rather than an ethnic one, see Mallory, JP, (1994), pp. 84–7; Hutton, R, (1997), p. 269 mentions the similarities and differences between the Germanic and Celtic cultures and languages.

8. On 'wer-gild' (man-price), *see* Chambers, RW, (1963), p. 77 and Stenton, F, (1986), pp. 261, 303–4.

9. *The Battle of Maldon* is perhaps the second best-known of all Old English poems, *see* Gordon, E (trans.), (1949).

10. On the Langobardi who would in time settle in Italy, giving their name to the region of Lombardy, *see* Collins, R, (1999), pp. 132–3, 196–217.

11. For the Saxons and the Chauci, *see* Myres, J, (1987), pp. 48–54 and pp. 50–5 respectively. While Myres remains a good source for overview of the invasions, a more modern and archaeologically more up-to-date academic view is that found in Dark, K, (2000). Rudgley, R, (2002), provides a simple and entertaining account that does not get bogged down in argument and counter-argument.

Chapter 2: Former Days

1. The Gothic historian Jordanes in his *Getica* (a history of the Gothic peoples written in AD 550) referred to Scandza as *'vagina nationum'* (the womb of nations), see Rudgley, R, (2002), ch 4.
2. The prehistory of Denmark is covered well in Glob, PV, (1971), as well as in its European context in Cunliffe, B (ed.), (1994), over many chapters.
3. On ancient Danish megaliths, *see* Glob, PV, (1971), pp. 53–100. This is not only a good introduction to a rarely covered subject, but is written with the traveller in mind.
4. The link between the 'Great Goddess' and the tombs of the Neolithic is mentioned in Glob, PV, (1971), p. 100, but is questioned in Hutton, R, (1997), pp. 39–44
5. For the use of Neolithic hallucinogens, *see* Sherratt, A, (1996), and Rudgley, R, (1993), pp. 19–33.
6. Details of the Tustrup ritual site can be found in Piggot, S, (1980), p. 116 and Glob, PV, (1971), pp. 95–6.
7. For details of the tomb at Øm – the best book is in Danish – *see* Johansen, BJ, (2003). The site is in excellent condition and is about 40 minutes east of Lejre on foot on the road to Øm.
8. For solsticial fire lighting in Europe, *see* Hutton, R, (1996), pp. 311–21, 366–9.
9. For the introduction and use of corded ware and beaker pottery, *see* Cunliffe, B, (2001), pp. 160–1, 215–19 and 217–21.
10. Glob, PV, (1983), provides a very readable and evocative introduction into the 'golden age' of Danish prehistory, and includes many photographs of the excavations and artefacts. *See* pp. 110, 112 for Glob's interpretation of the Kivik grave carvings.
11. For a good introduction to the age of migration, *see* Cunliffe, B (ed.), (1994), ch 13 and Collins, R, (1999) pp. 47–54.
12. Rudgley, R., (2002) pp. 111–18.
13. My source for the quote from the *Anglo-Saxon Chronicle* (compiled in the 9th century) is Savage, A (trans.), (1986).
14. For the ending of Roman Britain, *see* Dark, K, (2000), which explores this difficult subject and offers an alternative to the long-held idea that the Anglo-Saxon 'invasion' was short, violent and all-encompassing. He is also a good source for early Germanic burials in England, but more detailed evidence is found in Lucy, S, (2000).

Chapter 3: At the Altars of Their Idols

1. Three works provide a good overview of Anglo-Saxon heathenism: Bates, B, (2002), Branston, B, (1993) and Herbert, K, (1994).
2. For the Runic alphabet, *see* Pollington, S, (2002).
3. Pollington, S, (2003), provides translations of the magico-religious manuscripts mentioned here and elsewhere in this book.
4. Bede's calendar is discussed in Herbert, K, (1994), pp. 19–22, while a less forgiving approach appears in Hutton, R, (1997), pp. 271–2.
5. For the Coligny Calendar, *see* Hutton, R, (1997), pp. 143, 178, and Cunliffe, B, (1999), pp. 188–9.
6. For the days of the week, *see* Hutton, R, (1997), pp. 265–7.

7. For place-name evidence, *see* Stenton, F, (1986), pp. 99–100, who also discusses the various types of shrine on pp. 100–2. Although it is possible to find the four gods of the weekdays, it is not known if others existed alongside, since they are not presently recognized as divine. In many books, Watling Street, the Roman road from Richborough to Chester, is recorded as 'the street of the people [*inga*] of a Saxon named Watta or Watla'. But Tolkien postulated that it was named after the mythological Wada, father of the giant Weland, and that 'Watling Street' ('the street of the children of Wade') was originally the name of the Milky Way in Germanic paganism. When the Germanic tribes reached Britain, the name of this road across the heavens was applied to the road across England, the like of which they had not seen before. Perhaps many other gods lie buried in this way. For instance, was Reading really named after the descendants of a man named 'Redda' and not the goddess Rheda mentioned by Bede?

8. For details on Yeavering, *see* Hope-Taylor, B, (1979).

9. Details of the shrines used by later Vikings as a clue to the nature of Anglo-Saxon places of worship, *see* Ellis Davidson, HR, (1988), pp. 31–5.

10. For good introductions to the Norse gods, *see* Ellis Davidson, HR, (1990), though the most entertaining introduction is Crossley-Holland, K, (1980).

11. For background on Snorri Sturluson and his works *see* the very good introduction to Snorri (trans. Hollander, L), (2002), pp. ix–xv.

12. For the range and development of the Celtic gods, *see* Green, M, (1986) and (1989), p. 1.

13. For Odin's possible origin as a Gallic Mercury, *see* Helm, K, (1946), pp. 60–71, discussed in North, R, (1997), p. 305.

14. The Vanir gods and goddesses are discussed in best detail by Ellis Davidson, HR, (1990).

15. The Matronae are best illustrated in Green, M, (1986), pp. 72–102

Chapter 4: In Dread Waters

1. For the best introduction to human sacrifice in Pagan Europe, including a possible proof for the famous Celtic 'wicker man', *see* Green, M, (2001), pp. 68–9.

2. The reports of Adam of Bremen and Thietmar of Merseburg are to be found in Ellis Davidson, HR, (1988), pp. 24 and 58–9 respectively.

3. For the Danish bog sacrifices, nothing can beat Glob, PV, (1988). This book is well written and well illustrated – and, above all, haunting.

4. For Iron John, *see* Grimm, J and W, (1993), pp. 612–19, and Grigsby, J, (2002).

5. For Lindow Man, *see* Stead, I, Bourke, J, and Brothwell, D, (1986), and Turner, RC and Scaife, RG (eds.), (1995).

6. For the stomach contents of the bog men, *see* Stead, I, Bourke, J and Brothwell, D, (1986), pp. 99–135, and Turner, RC and Scaife, RG (eds.), (1995). pp. 59–61. For the presence of ergot in the stomachs of the Danish bog men, *see* Green, M, (2001), pp. 84, 194.

7. For effects of eating ergot and its outbreaks, *see* Rudgley, R, (1999), pp. 95–6 and McKenna, T, (1992), pp. 134–6.

8. For the discovery of ritual wagons in Danish bogs, *see* Glob, PV, (1988), pp. 166–71, and discussed in Ellis Davidson, HR, (1990), pp. 93–6, 103, 135.

9. *See* Ellis Davidson, HR, (1990), p. 113.

10. The link between Gefion/Geofon and water is discussed at length in North, R, (1997), pp. 221-6.

Chapter 5: Scyld Scefing

1. The link between Scef and Tennyson's *The Idylls of the King* was suggested in Herbert, K, (1994), p. 16.
2. *See* Herbert, K, (1994), p. 15.
3. The appearance of Scef in Aethelweard's genealogy can be found in Campbell, A (ed.), (1962), p. 33. William of Malmesbury's mention of Sheaf appears in his *Gesta Regum Anglorum* (1989).
4. 'Ing' as the patrynomic is in Herbert, K, (1994), p. 16.
5. On *Widsith* - the best introduction to the poem and all the characters mentioned is Chambers, RW (ed.), (1912).
6. For details of Skjold, *see* Chambers, RW, (1963), p. 77. Skjold's history is told in Saxo Grammaticus (trans. Fisher, P; ed. Davidson, HE), (2002).
7. For harvest customs, *see* Chambers, RW, (1963), pp. 81-3, while the Byggvir and Pekko analogies appear on pp. 297-301.
8. Chambers, RW, (1963), pp. 83-4.
9. The moon god Sin's 'Quffah' boat appears in Hooke, SH, (1963), p. 25.
10. The solar boat of Egypt, so like that of ancient Scandinavia, appears in Rundle-Clark, RT, (1978), pp. 118-9, 235-6.
11. *The Spoils of the Abyss* by 'Taliesin' is translated well in Matthews, C, (1987), pp. 107-8. This is further discussed, along with other mythological poems by 'Taliesin', in Matthews, J, (1991). For the historical poems by the real Taliesin, the historical poet of the north after whose pseudonym the other, later, poet wrote, see Williams, I, (1987).
12. For Tolkien's thoughts on, and use of, the figure of Sheaf, *see* Tolkien, JRR (ed. Tolkien, C), (2002), pp. 85-97.

Chapter 6: The Barley God

1. Tammuz's story appears in Hooke, SH, (1963), pp. 20-3.
2. Adonis is discussed in Graves, R, (1960), (vol. 1), pp. 69-73, and Frazer, JG, (2004), pp. 237-52.
3. *See* Frazer, JG, (2004), pp. 252-7.
4. Osiris's myth is summarized in Rundle-Clark, RT, (1978), pp. 97-180.
5. *See* Rundle-Clark, RT, (1978), pp. 235-6.
6. For Dionysos, *see* Kerenyi, C, (1976), and Harrison, J, (1991).
7. Harrison, J, (1991), pp. 413-25.
8. Kerenyi, C, (1962) offers the best overall discussion of the rites and mysteries practised there.
9. For details of the Eleusinian cult drink, the *kykeon*, and its identification as ergot, *see* Wasson, SK, Hoffman, A, and Ruck, C, (1978); and Wasson, SK, Ott, J, Ruck, C and Doniger O'Flaherty, W, (1986). This theory is further examined in Rudgley, R, (1999), p. 96 and McKenna, T, (1992), pp. 130-37.
10. For the drowning of the fertility god, *see* Rundle-Clark, RT, (1978) p. 104.

Chapter 7: Freyr

1. The 'sex-change' theory of Nerthus/Njorthr is discussed and dismissed in North, R, (1997), pp. 20-2.
2. The similarity of Germanic god and goddess names is argued in Ellis Davidson, HR, (1990), p. 106.
3. The source for Tacitus's role as a head priest of Cybele's cult is North, R, (1997), p. 45.
4. The most comprehensive and concise discussion of Freyr and his attributes is found in Ellis Davidson, HR, (1990), pp. 92-103.
5. For the sacred boar, *see* Ellis Davidson, HR, (1990), p. 98 and (1988), pp. 50, 141, 202.
6. Aldhelm of Sherbourne's letters concerning the 'foul pillar' can be found in North, R, (1997), pp. 51-2.
7. For '*Prija*' as 'beloved', and the use and misuse of the term 'prick', see Herbert, K, (1994), p. 24.
8. On the origins of the Gundestrup cauldron, *see* Cunliffe, B (ed.), (1994), pp. 401-3, and Devereux, P, (2003), pp. 51-2, who offers an exciting explanation of its varied symbolism.
9. For a contemporary description of the effeminate priests of Attis, see Apuleius (trans. Graves, R), (1985), ch. 12.
10. For Freyja and her ability to transform into a falcon, *see* Davidson, HR, (1990), pp. 39, 42, 44.
11. A translation of *Skírnismál* is found in Titchenell, E-B, (1998), pp. 248-54

Chapter 8: The Wagon Ran After

1. The saga of Olaf Tryggvason appears in Snorri Sturluson (trans. Hollander, L), (2002), pp. 144-244.
2. The source for Gunnar's tale is *Flateyarbok* in the *Elder Edda*, written around 1400, *see* Larrington, C, (1999).
3. The reference to Lytir is from *Flateyarbok*, 1, 467 and the 'wooden men' – the wooden idols of Freyr, mentioned in the *Elder Edda* – are discussed in North, R, (1997), pp. 94-5.
4. The field remedy charm, the *Aecerbot*, is quoted with a good commentary in Pollington, S, (2003), pp. 477-8, and Griffiths, B, (2003), pp. 185-90.
5. Ing as an aspect of Freyr is discussed in depth throughout North, R, (1997), and Ellis Davidson, HR, (1990), p. 104.
6. Yngvi-Freyr is mentioned in Snorri Sturluson (trans. Hollander, L), (2002), p. 14.
7. For the word 'rune' meaning 'magic' as a whole, not just letters, *see* Pollington, S, (2002), p. 10, in which the *Old English Rune Poem* is also translated.
8. On the appearance of Ingui in Bernicia, *see* North, R, (1997), pp. 42-3

Chapter 9: The Elves

1. The Norse creation myth appears in *Voluspa* in the *Elder Edda*, translated in Titchenell, E-B, (1998), pp. 91-100, and in Snorri Sturluson (trans. Faulkes, A), (1995), pp. 10-12.
2. For the connection between the elves and Freyr, *see* Ellis Davidson, HR, (1990), pp.

105, 156. General British fairy lore is to be found in Briggs, K, (1977), and in Spence, L, (1948).

3. For the fairy aversion to iron, *see* Spence, L, (1948), pp. 181–2, 257.
4. For the *genii cucullati* as elf-like hooded spirits, see Davidson, HE, (1988), pp. 108–9.
5. The best summaries of Anglo-Saxon beliefs concerning the elves are Pollington, S, (2003), pp. 456–61, and Griffiths, B, (2003), pp. 47–54. These books also deal with the disease-bringing aspects of the elves and the numerous charms used to protect one from them.
6. The Icelandic land-spirits (as non-human nature spirits) are found in Davidson, HE, (1988), pp. 102–8, while she discusses the derivation of the elves from ancestral spirits on pp. 115 and 122.
7. For the Elf of Geirstadt and St Olaf, *see* Davidson, HE, (1988), p. 122.
8. The tradition of leaving food for the fairies is mentioned in Spence, L, (1948), p. 188 and throughout Evans-Wentz, WY, (1988). If any reader knows of the continuation of any such custom or fairy-belief today, the author would very much like to hear about it, via the publisher.
9. *Alfablot* appears in *Cormac's Saga* (written in Icelandic between AD 1250–1300, and based on a lost 12th-century saga); *see* Collingwood, WG, and Stefansson J, (trans.), (1991), ch. 22.
10. The terms *ylfig* and *aelfsiden* are discussed in Pollington, S, (2003), pp. 460–1
11. *Aelfsiden* is discussed in North, R, (1997), pp. 55, 85, 105, 317–8. It may be that the Old English term '*wanseoc*' found in these medical manuscripts may mean 'Vanir-sick': that is, an illness caused by the Vanir (the phrase itself is of major importance as it shows that the Vanir were known in Old England).
12. Tacitus comments on how the Germans valued women as being 'holy' and having prophetic abilities, mentioning Veleda of the Bructeri tribe, who was honoured as a goddess. Her name means simply 'seer' and was probably a title related to the Brythonic Celtic word '*gweled*' (to see) and the Irish druidic title of '*filidh*' (poet), also derived from the verb 'to see'. In the Greenland saga of Erik, there is a description of one who practised her craft around the same time as Olaf Trygvasson was ending the rites of Freyr in Norway. Her name was Thorbiorg – one of an original group of nine, she was summoned to a village to see when a famine would end. Her description is colourfully given in full, even down to her cat-skin gloves and a hood lined with cat skin. She is described as wearing a blue dress with a pouch at the belt containing her magical equipment – stones, feathers, etc – and having a staff mounted with magical stones, with brass ornaments up it. She sits on a specially constructed high-seat (perhaps so she could see). Her 'sitting' follows a meal consisting of animal hearts and goat's milk. A Christian girl named Gudrid sings a special chant, albeit reluctantly, having been taught it as a child, and the seer forecasts an end to the crisis. *See* Bates, B, (2002), ch. 16.

Chapter 10: Choosers of the Slain

1. For the Greek Keres, *see* Harrison, J, (1991), pp. 41–3, 165–217.
2. For the war of Zeus and the Titans and its derivation from Indo-European myth, see Lincoln, B, (1991), pp. 10–12, 39 and Campbell, J, (1964), p. 80.
3. For the many varied names of Valkyries, *see* Davidson, HE, (1988), p. 96 and Crossley-Holland, K, (1980), pp. 156–7

4. For the episode in the *Vita St Gregory* concerning the 'prophetic' crow, *see* North, R, (1997), p. 177.

5. For the Irish Morrighan as a battle-crow/raven, *see* Green, M, (1986), pp. 101, 120.

6. The nature of the Norns are discussed in Crossley-Holland, K, (1980), pp. xxviii–xxiv and Davidson, HE, (1988), pp. 96, 164.

7. For phantom black dogs, see the thought-provoking articles by Trubshaw, B, (1994).

8. Details of the hags of folklore and legend appear in Briggs, K, (1977), pp. 57–60 (Cailleach), 206 (Grindelow), 242 (Jenny Greenteeth). It has long been accepted that behind Black Annis and the other hags that bear the name 'Annis'or 'Annie' lies Danu, mother of the Tuatha De Danann.

9. For Demeter Erinyes, *see* Kerenyi, C, (1962), pp. 31–2. The imagery behind the rape is deciphered as follows: The goddess is the cold winter earth that swallows the grain in the winter so it may emerge reborn in the spring. To do this, the earth must be cut open and the seed inserted, and thus in some myths we have the imagery of the goddess being 'raped'.

10. The sources for the tale of Skathi are Snorri Sturluson (trans. Hollander, L), (2002), p. 12 and Snorri Sturluson (trans. Faulkes, A), (1995), pp. 23–4.

11. The cannibal-mother-mare Leucippe is mentioned by Graves, R, (1960), (vol. 1), pp. 106, 110.

12. Hag-riding is mentioned in Briggs, K, (1977), p. 216 and Simpson, J and Roud, S (eds.), (2003).

13. Robert Kirk's 'Secret Commenwealth of Elves, Fauns and Faires' is available online at http://www.sacred-texts.com/neu/celt/sce/.

Chapter 11: Royal Obligations

1. The main views on regicide and sacral kingship in ancient Scandinavia are McTurk, R, (1974–7) and (1994), who argues against the position and North, R, (1997) who argues in favour pp. 260–66.

2. North, R, (1997), p. 47.

3. Frothi appears in Saxo Grammaticus (trans. Fisher, P; ed. Davisdon, HE,) (2002).

4. *See* Shippey, T, (1992), pp. 185–8.

5. For Hakon's *droit du seigneur* (the right of the feudal lord to sleep the first wedded night with the bride of any of his vassals), *see* North, R, (1997) pp. 262–4.

6. For details on the horse rituals of the Indo-European peoples (including Asva Medha), *see* Mallory, JP, (1994), pp. 135–7.

7. The dating of the Uffington White Horse to the late Bronze Age is found in Castleden, R, (2000), p. 48.

8. The bizarre rite recorded in 12th-century Donegal by Gerald of Wales can be found in *Giraldus Cambrensis* (trans. O'Meara), (1951), p. 93.

9. The tale of the wounded King Nuada is in Rolleston, TW, (1987), pp. 107–8.

10. The more unfortunate kings, Domaldi and Agni, appear in Snorri Sturluson (trans. Hollander, L), (2002), pp. 17–19 and 22–38 respectively.

11. The range of dates for the practice of bog sacrifice in Denmark appears in Turner, RC, and Scaife, RG (eds.), (1995), p. 147.

12. Olaf then beheaded the duplicitous slave.

13. As to their strangulation, Glob mentions the symbolism of the neck-ring in (1988), pp. 163–7.

14. Interestingly, the original name of this goddess has been reconstructed by linguists as *Kolyo* (the coverer), who is seen to drag men to her domain, the underworld, by fetters or bonds. For the connections of this goddess to Seithr, *see* Lincoln, B, (1991), p. 108.

15. Gefion riding her lover is mentioned in the *Lokasenna* poem of the *Elder Edda*, quoted in North, R, (1997), p. 225.

16. North, R, (1997), pp. 140-9.

17. North, R, (1997), pp. 254-5. The ultimate mythic origin of these motifs is found in the characters 'Twin' and 'Man' of Indo-European myth. For details of these beings and their fate, see Lincoln, B, (1991), p. 12. These creation mythologies are also discussed in Stone, A, (1997), pp. 113-16.

18. Saxo's 'Balderus' is discussed in North, R, (1997), p. 128.

19. JG Frazer's much-used quote is found in Frazer, JG, (2004), pp. 2-3. Frazer has been much maligned, but for an overview of the pro- and contra-Frazer stance of scholars since the publication of *The Golden Bough*, *see* Hutton, R, (1997), pp. 325-8.

Chapter 12: The Hall Turned to Ashes

1. For Hrolf Kraki one can do no better than to read the translation by Jesse Byock, (1998). Byock offers great introductory notes that include detailed comparisons with the plot and characters of *Beowulf*.

2. These parallels are also discussed (in more depth) in Chambers, RW, (1963), pp. 15-31.

3. Chambers, RW, (1963), pp. 15-20, 426-9 offer an overview of the character of Hjorvard and pp. 20-5 give a summary of the character of Ingeld.

4. Ingeld is also discussed in Shippey, T, (1992), pp. 186-8.

Chapter 13: The Wandering Inguz

1. From the *Book of the Dun Cow*, a 12th-century manuscript but which may originally date from the first part of the 8th century, the tale of Da Derga can be found in Gantz (trans.), (1986), pp. 60-106. Gantz's translation is prefaced with an excellent introduction that discusses its probable ritual content.

2. The hideous Fer Caille is linked to the Wild Herdsman of Welsh myth in Grigsby, J, (2002), pp. 42-5.

3. Bran's story appears in Gantz, J (trans.), (1985), ch. 2.

4. The link between the red hair of the bog men and the *melyngoch* hair of the cauldron-folk in Bran's tale is suggested in Stead, I, Bourke, J and Brothwell, D, (1986), p. 173.

5. For the Celtic feast of Samhain as the 'hinge in the year' when odd happenings occurred, *see* Rees, A and B, (1990), p. 89.

6. Macc Oc's tale is found in Gantz, J, (trans.), (1986), pp. 37-42.

7. The tragic tale of Diarmuid and Grainne is prefaced in Rolleston, TW, (1987), pp. 297-304.

8. The tale of Caer Imbormeith, so like that of Gerthr, appears in Gantz, J, (trans.), (1986), pp. 107-12.

9. The midwinter alignment of the Newgrange monument is discussed in depth in O'Kelly, M, (1994), pp. 123-5.

10. For the 'feasting halls' of ancient myth as dim memories of ritual sites, *see* Harbison, P, (1988), pp. 156–8.
11. Details of the Woodhenge child sacrifice are to be found in North, J, (1996), pp. 347–58.
12. The source of the tale of Banban the Hospitaller is Rees, A and B, (1990), pp. 333–5.
13. Fyolnir's drowning appears in Snorri's *Ynglingatal* (trans. Hollander, L), (2002), pp. 14–15.
14. For the Viking halls at Lejre, *see* Byock, J, (1998), pp. xviii–xxiii, which includes a plan of the halls. One can visit the site of these halls, arguably the site of Heorot, today. They lie at the tiny hamlet of Gammel Lejre, a half hour's walk north of Leijre train station. The hamlet is surrounded by a massive ritual landscape of barrows and standing stones.
15. Strabo's mention of the destruction and sacrifice of the island priestesses' temple is from *Geographia*, iv, 4, 6 quoted in Green, M, (2001), p. 194.
16. A good summary of all Norse sources of the Ragnarok myth is in Crossley-Holland, K, (1980), pp. 173–6.

Chapter 14: A Midwinter Game

1. Easily available translations of *Sir Gawain and the Green Knight* are Tolkien, JRR, (1979) and Stone, B (trans.), (1986).
2. Tolkien mentions the pagan origins of the tale in Tolkien, JRR, (1997), pp. 72–3.
3. The Irish story of Bricriu's Feast that forms the main backbone of the Middle English poem can be found in Gantz (trans.), (1986), pp. 219–55.
4. A suggested link between the tales of *Sir Gawain* and *Beowulf* to bog ritual is found in Stead, I, Bourke, J, and Brothwell, D, (1986), pp. 172–3.

Chapter 15: The Demon's Head

1. The nature of Odin is discussed by Snorri Sturluson (trans. Hollander, L), (2002), pp. 10–13.
2. Snorri Sturluson (trans. Hollander, L), (2002), pp. 7–8.
3. The appearance of Heid/Gullveig that precipitates the conflict is mentioned in Crossley-Holland, K, (1980), pp. 7, 184.
4. For the theory that the Indo-European languages arrived with farming, *see* Renfrew, C, (1998), followed up by Renfrew, C, and Bellwood, P (eds.), (2002), and linked with genetic models of dispersal in Forster, P, and Toth, A, (2003), and Gray, RD, and Atkinson, QD, (2003).
5. For the 'War of the Functions', *see* Mallory, JP, (1994), p. 139.
6. Kvasir's myth is found in Snorri Sturluson, (2002), pp. 10–13 and his *Edda* (trans. Faulkes, A,), (1995), pp. 61–4.
7. For the Hindu myth of the Churning of the Milky Ocean, *see* Doniger O'Flaherty, W (trans.), (1975), pp. 274–80.
8. The link between *sarama* and the Dagda's porridge is made in Grigsby, J, (2002), pp. 127–8.
9. For the original identity of *soma* (as ephedra and other stimulants), *see* Rudgley, R, (1993), pp. 43–55; (1999), pp. 226–9, and McKenna, T, (1992), p. 101.
10. For the myth of the decapitation of Dadhyanc, *see* Doniger O'Flaherty, W (trans.), (1975), pp. 56–9.

11. For the myth of Orpheus, *see* Harrison, J, (1991), pp. 455–77.
12. For the Opening of the Mouth Ceremony, *see* Rundle-Clark, RT, (1978), p. 122.
13. For the name 'Baleygr' as an epithet of Odin, *see* North, R, (1997), pp. 263, 328.

Chapter 16: The Brimwylf

1. There are many Hindu poems that deal with the taking of soma – *see* Doniger O'Flaherty, W (trans.), (1981), p. 135.
2. The magical-martial tradition of Aesma appears in Lincoln, B, (1991), p 133,
3. For the magical properties of boar helms, *see* Ellis Davidson, HR, (1988), pp. 49–50.
4. Information on the berserkers is found in many sources, especially Eliade, M, (1995), pp. 81–4; Byock, J, (1998), p. xxiv; and Bates, B, (2002), pp. 157–9.
5. For the connections between *vargr*, *warg* and ergot, *see* the excellent essay by Stone, A, (1994), the source of much of this chapter's information on ergot and lupine folklore.
6. For the next best source, especially on 'wolfish rage' as part of an Indo-European martial cult, *see* Lincoln, B, (1991), ch. 10 (*haomawergez* and *ulfhednar* are mentioned on p. 134).
7. The *Volsung Saga* fragment that deals with transformation into a wolf appears in Byock, J, (1999), pp. 44–7.
8. The folklore surrounding the *roggenwolf* is found in Frazer, JG, (2004), pp. 352–6.
9. In time, the term *vargr* (and its English variants *wearg/wearh*) came to mean 'outlaw' – someone who could be hunted down and killed like a wolf, for which the killer would incur no penalty. As the usual method of killing an outlaw was by hanging or strangulation, this suggests that *vargr* had little to do with the crimes committed by later outlaws (which were varied), but rather with the method of execution. This seems to suggest that in later Christian times, taking ergot for military or ritual purposes was seen as a heinous crime and that its practitioners were outlawed; in time *vargr* and its association with strangulation became synonymous with outlawry.
10. The link between ergot and strangulation are made clear in Stone, A, (1994).
11. The burning magical heat of the berserkers is discussed in Eliade, M, (1995), pp. 81–4.
12. Stone, A, (1994).
13. For the idea that the Cotton Vitellius manuscript was meant to be a 'Book of Monsters' based on the inclusion of tales describing '*Haelfhundingas*', *see* Orchard, A, (2003), pp. 24–5.
14. The *scucca* (demon) is mentioned in Griffiths, B, (2003), pp. 55–7 while Newton, S, (1999), pp. 143–4 links this creature with Grendel and the Black Shuck of East Anglian folklore.
15. For Odin's adoption of *seithr*, see Snorri Sturluson, (2002), p. 11.
16. His use of '*ergi*' is found in Stone, A, (1994), and North, R, (1997), p. 85.
17. The various names of Odin quoted here are found in Crossley-Holland, K, (1980), pp. 64, 248.
18. For a discussion of the term 'Geat' as a mythological name rather than a tribal appellation, including the adoption of the term by Odin, *see* North, R, (1997), p. 138.
19. For a discussion of the Northumbrian priest Coifi's relation to the figure of Odin, *see* North, R, (1997), pp. 332–4.

Epilogue: People of the Wolf

1. For the long-haired twin gods, the Haddingjar, that possibly stand behind Hengist and Horsa, see Ellis Davidson, HR, (1990), p. 170.
2. For the occurrence of Grendel place names in Anglo-Saxon England, see Bates, B, (2002), p. 81, and Chambers, RW, (1963), pp. 304-8.
3. For an overview of the discovery and finds at Sutton Hoo, see Carver, M, (1998).
4. For Raedwald, see Carver, M, (1998), pp. 22-3, 34; Rudgley, R, (2002), pp. 168-72 and for a discussion of his pedigree, see Orchard, A, (2003), p. 78.
5. The Wuffinga family tree appears in the thought-provoking Newton, S, (1999).
6. Their connection with Sweden is mentioned in Wood, M, (1987), pp. 74-5.
7. The parallels between the goods buried at Sutton Hoo and those found at Uppsala are discussed in Newton, S, (1999), p. 111.
8. The links between the Wuffingas and the various tribes mentioned in *Beowulf* are discussed in Newton, S, (1999), pp. 106-7, 125-31.
9. The figure of Hrothmund and the Wuffinga genealogy are discussed in Newton, S, (1999), ch. 4.
10. Abbo of Fleury's quote concerning King Edmund's martyrdom can be found online at www.wmich.edu/medieval/research/rawl/edmund/index.html along with other vernacular texts describing these events – in translation.
11. For more on the suggestion that Edmund's miraculously preserved body was that of a prehistoric sacrifice, see Stead, I, Bourke, J, and Brothwell, D, (1986), p. 175.
12. Survivals of Anglo-Saxon paganism after the conversion are mentioned by Herbert, K, (1994), pp. 18-19 and Branston, B, (1993), p. 183.

BIBLIOGRAPHY

Alexander, M, (trans.), *Beowulf*, Penguin, 1986

Apuleius, (trans. Graves, R) *The Golden Ass*, Penguin, 1985

Bates, B, *The Real Middle Earth*, Pan MacMillan, 2002

—— *The Way of Wyrd*, Arrow, 1996

Bede, (trans. Sherley-Price, L), *Ecclesiastical History of the English People*, Penguin, 1990

Blair, J, *The Anglo-Saxon Age*, Oxford, 2000

Bradley, S, (ed.), *Anglo-Saxon Poetry*, Everyman, 1995

Branston, B, *The Lost Gods of England*, Constable, 1993

Briggs, K, *A Dictionary of Fairies*, Penguin, 1977

Byock, J, *The Saga of King Hrolf Kraki*, Penguin, 1998

—— *The Saga of the Volsungs*, Penguin, 1999

Caesar, Julius, (trans. Handford, SA), *The Conquest of Gaul*, Penguin, 1986

Campbell, A, (ed.), *Chronicon Aethelweardi*, Oxford, 1962

Campbell, J, *The Masks of God Volume 3: Occidental Mythology*, Penguin, 1964

Carver, M, *Sutton Hoo: Burial Ground of Kings?*, British Museum Press, 1998

Castleden, R, *Ancient British Hill Figures*, S B Publications, 2000

Chambers, RW, (ed.), *Widsith: A Study in Old English Heroic Legend*, Cambridge, 1912

Chambers, RW, and Wyatt AJ, *Beowulf, with the Finnsburgh fragment*, Cambridge, 1943

Chambers, RW, *Beowulf: An Introduction*, (3rd edition), Cambridge, 1963

Collingwood, WG, and Stefansson, J, (trans.), *The Life and Death of Cormac the Skald:* Being the Icelandic Kormaks Saga, Llanerch, 1991

Collins, R, *Early Medieval Europe 300–1000*, Palgrave, 1999

Cross, TP, and Slover, CH, *Ancient Irish Tales*, Dublin Figgis, 1938

Crossley-Holland, K, *The Penguin Book of Norse Myths: Gods of the Vikings*, Penguin, 1980

Cunliffe, B, (ed.), *The Oxford Illustrated Prehistory of Europe*, Oxford, 1994

—— *The Ancient Celts*, Penguin, 1999

—— *Facing the Ocean*, Oxford, 2001

Dark, K, *Britain and the End of the Roman Empire*, Tempus, 2000

Devereux, P, *Fairy Paths and Spirit Roads*, Vega, 2003

Doniger O'Flaherty, W, (trans.), *Hindu Myths*, Penguin, 1975

—— (trans.), *The Rig Veda*, Penguin, 1981

Eliade, M, *Rites and Symbols of Initiation*, Spring, 1995

Ellis Davidson, HR, *Gods and Myths of Northern Europe*, Penguin, 1990

—— *Myths and Symbols in Pagan Europe*, Syracuse, 1988

Evans-Wentz, WY, *The Fairy Faith in Celtic Countries*, Colin Smythe, 1988

Fife, G, *Arthur the King*, BBC Books, 1990

Forster, P, and Toth, A, 'Toward a phylogenetic chronology of ancient Gaulish, Celtic, and Indo-European', *Proceedings of the National Academy of Science*, vol. 100, no. 15, 22 July, 2003

Frazer, JG, *The Golden Bough*, Canongate Classics, 2004

Gantz, J, (trans.), *The Mabinogion*, Penguin, 1985

—— *Early Irish Myths and Sagas*, Penguin, 1986

Gibson, A, and Simpson, D, (eds.), *Prehistoric Ritual and Religion*, Sutton, 1998

Giraldus Cambrensis, (trans. O'Meara), *Topography of Ireland*, Dundalk, 1951

Glob, PV, *Danish Prehistoric Monuments*, Faber and Faber, 1971

—— *The Bog People*, Faber and Faber, 1988

—— *The Mound People*, Paladin, 1983

Gordon, E, (trans.), *The Battle of Maldon*, Methuen, 1949

Gordon, R, (trans.), *Anglo-Saxon Poetry*, Everyman, 1949

Graves, R, *The Greek Myths*, (2 vols), Pelican, 1960

Gray, RD, and Atkinson, QD, 'Language-tree divergence times support the Anatolian theory of Indo-European origin', in *Nature*, 426, 435–9, 2003

Green, M, *The Gods of the Celts*, Sutton, 1986

—— *Symbol and Image in Celtic Religious Art*, Routledge, 1989

—— *Dying for the Gods*, Tempus, 2001

Griffiths, B, *Aspects of Anglo-Saxon Magic*, Anglo-Saxon Books, 2003

Grigsby, J, *Warriors of the Wasteland*, Watkins, 2002

Grimm, J, *Deutsche Mythologie*, Munich, 1854

Grimm, J and W, *The Complete Grimm's Fairy Tales*, Routledge, 1993

Harbison, P, *Pre-Christian Ireland*, Thames and Hudson, 1988

Harris, S, *Richborough and Reculver*, English Heritage, 2001

Harrison, J, *Prolegomena to the Study of Greek Religion*, Princeton, 1991

Heaney, S, (trans.), *Beowulf*, Faber and Faber, 2002

Helm, K *Wodan*, Giessen, 1946

Herbert, K, *Looking for the Lost Gods of England*, Anglo-Saxon Books, 1994

—— *English Heroic Legends*, Anglo-Saxon Books, 2000

Hight, G, (trans.), *The Saga of Grettir the Strong*, Everyman, 1972

Holmes, G, (ed.), *The Oxford Illustrated History of Medieval Europe*, Oxford, 1990

Hooke, SH, *Middle Eastern Mythology*, Pelican, 1963

Hope-Taylor, B, *Yeavering: An Anglo-British Centre of Early Northumbria*, Stationery Office Books, 1979

Hutton, R, *The Pagan Religions of the Ancient British Isles*, Blackwell, 1997

—— *The Stations of the Sun*, Oxford, 1996

Jackson, JS, (ed., trans.), *Compendium of Roman History*, London, 1889

Jackson, KH, *A Celtic Miscellany*, Penguin, 1986

Johansen, BJ, *Øm Jættestue*, Little Creek Publishing, 2003

Jones, P, and Pennick, N, *A History of Pagan Europe*, Routledge, 2000

Kerenyi, C, *Eleusis*, Princeton, 1962

Kerenyi, C, *Dionysos*, Princeton, 1976

Larrington, C, *The Poetic Edda*, Oxford, 1999

Lincoln, B, *Death, War and Sacrifice*, Chicago, 1991

Lucy, S, *The Anglo-Saxon Way of Death*, Sutton, 2000

Mallory, JP, *In Search of the Indo-Europeans*, Thames and Hudson, 1994

Markale, J, Merlin, *Priest of Nature*, Inner Traditions, 1995

Matthews, C, *Mabon and the Mysteries of Britain*, Arkana, 1987

Matthews, J, *Taliesin*, Aquarian, 1991

McKenna, T, *Food of the Gods*, Rider, 1992

McTurk, R, 'Sacral Kingship in Ancient Scandinavia', *Saga-Book* 19, 1974–7

— 'Sacral Kingship Revisited', *Saga-Book* 24, 1994

Meyer, K, *The Death Tales of the Ulster Heroes*, Dublin Institute for Advanced Studies, 1993

Myres, J, *The English Settlements*, Oxford, 1987

Newton, S, *The Origins of Beowulf and the Pre-Viking Kingdom of East Anglia*, DS Brewer, 1999

North, J, *Stonehenge: Neolithic Man and the Cosmos*, HarperCollins, 1996

North, R, *Heathen Gods in Old English Literature*, Cambridge, 1997

O'Kelly, M, *Newgrange*, Thames and Hudson, 1994

Orchard, A, *A Critical Companion to Beowulf*, DS Brewer, 2003

Panzer, F, *Studien zur germanischen Sagengeschichte*, Munich, 1910

Piggot, S, *Ancient Europe*, Edinburgh, 1980

Pollington, S, *Rudiments of Runelaw*, Anglo-Saxon Books, 2002

Pollington, S, *Leechcraft – Early English Charms and Plantlore*, Anglo-Saxon Books, 2003

Porter, J, (trans.), *Beowulf: Text and Translation*, Anglo-Saxon Books, 2003

Rees, A and B, *Celtic Heritage*, Thames and Hudson, 1990

Renfrew, C, *Archaeology and Language*, Pimlico, 1998

Renfrew, C, and Bellwood, P, (eds.), *Examining the Farming/Language Dispersal Hypothesis*, McDonald Institute for Archaeological Research, 2002

Rolleston, TW, *Myths and Legends of the Celtic Race*, Constable, 1987

— *The Alchemy of Culture*, British Museum press, 1993

— *The Encyclopaedia of Psychoactive Substances*, Abacus, 1999

— *Barbarians: Secrets of the Dark Ages*, Channel 4 Books, 2002

Rundle-Clark, RT, *Myth and Symbol in Ancient Egypt*, Thames and Hudson, 1978

Savage, A, (trans.), *The Anglo-Saxon Chronicles*, Heinemann, 1986

Saxo Grammaticus, (trans. Fisher, P; ed. Davisdon, HE), *History of the Danes*, Brewer, 2002

Schama, S, *Landscape and Memory*, HarperCollins, 1996

Sherratt, A, 'Flying up with the souls of the dead', *British Archaeology*, 15 June 1996

Shippey, T, *The Road to Middle Earth*, HarperCollins, 1992

Simpson, J, and Roud, S, (eds.), *A Dictionary of English Folklore*, Oxford, 2003

Snorri Sturluson, (trans. Faulkes, A), *Edda*, Everyman, 1995

Snorri Sturluson, (trans. Hollander, L), *Heimskringla – History of the Kings of Norway*, Texas, 2002

Spence, L, *The Fairy Tradition in Britain*, Rider, 1948

Stead, I, Bourke, J and Brothwell, D, *Lindow Man – The Body in the Bog*, British Museum Press, 1986

Stenton, F, *Anglo-Saxon England*, Oxford, 1986

Stone, A, 'Hellhounds, Werewolves and the Germanic Underworld', *Mercian Mysteries*, vol. 20

Stone, A, *Ymir's Flesh*, Heart of Albion Press, 1997

Stone, B, (trans.), *Sir Gawain and the Green Knight*, Penguin, 1986

Tacitus, (trans. Mattingly, H and Handford, S), *The Agricola and the Germania*, Penguin, 1986

Titchenell, E-B, *The Masks of Odin*, Theosophical University Press, 1998

Tolkien, JRR, *The Monsters and the Critics and Other Essays*, HarperCollins, 1997

—— (ed. Tolkien, C), *The History of Middle Earth Vol. 5: The Lost Road and Other Writings*, HarperCollins, 2002

—— *The Two Towers*, HarperCollins, 2002

—— *Sir Gawain and the Green Knight, Pearl and Sir Orfeo*, Unwin, 1979

Trubshaw, B, 'Black Dogs in Folklore', *Mercian Mysteries*, vol. 20, 1994

—— 'Black Dogs: Guardians of the Corpse Ways', *Mercian Mysteries*, vol. 20, 1994

Turner, RC, and Scaife, RG, (eds.), *Bog Bodies: New Discoveries and New Perspectives*, British Museum Press, 1995

Wasson, SK, Hoffman, A, and Ruck, C, *The Road to Eleusis*, New York, 1978

Wasson, SK, Ott, J, Ruck, C, and Doniger O'Flaherty, W, *Persephone's Quest: Entheogens and the Origins of Religion*, Yale, 1986

Westwood, J, *Albion: A Guide to Legendary Britain*, Paladin, 1987

William of Malmesbury, *Gesta Regum Anglorum*, Llanerch Press, 1989

Williams, I, *The Poems of Taliesin*, Dublin Institute for Advanced Studies, 1987

Wood, M, *In Search of the Dark Ages*, BBC Books, 1987

APPENDICES

Timeline: 8000 BC–AD 1939

c. 8000 BC   Mesolithic (Middle Stone) Age in northern Europe. Hunter-gatherer groups in river valleys of Scandinavia. First evidence of organized cemeteries at Vedbaek (Zealand) and Skateholm (Sweden).

c. 6000   Arrival of farming and Indo-European languages in south-east Europe from Anatolia.

c. 4200   Neolithic (New Stone) Age begins in northern Europe with the arrival of farming and Indo-European languages. First megaliths built in Scandinavia.

c. 4000   Possible split of Indo-European languages into 'Germanic' and 'Celtic' groups.

c. 3500–3000   Massive building of megalithic monuments throughout Atlantic coastal regions of north-west Europe.

c. 3300–3200   Building of the passage graves at Newgrange, Ireland and Øm, Denmark.

c. 3200   Building of the Tustrup 'necropolis' in Jutland.

c. 3000–2500   Use of 'Corded Ware' pottery and rise of individual burial tradition in Scandinavia.

c. 2500–2000   'Beaker' period in western Europe. Rise of metalworking, but Stone Age continues in Scandinavia.

c. 2000	Start of characteristic 'spiral' style of Scandinavian metalwork.
c. 1500	'Golden age' of Bronze Age Denmark. Tree-trunk burial under round mounds. Era of the cord-skirted Egtved girl.
c. 1300	Trundholm 'sun chariot' constructed.
c. 1200	Bronze Age 'systems collapse'.
c. 900	First evidence of ritual deposition in bogs.
c. 750	Beginning of Celtic 'Iron Age'.
c. 730–540	Rise in warrior elites in Western Europe.
415	Alcibiades steals the cult drink of Eleusis.
c. 291	Sacrificial death of Grauballe man.
c. 200	Death of Tollund Man.
c. 250–100	Building and ritual destruction by fire of massive wooden circular enclosures in Ireland.
120	Cimbri and Teutones begin their migrations south from Denmark.
113	Cimbri and Teutones invade North Italy.
105	Cimbri and Teutones defeated by Roman general Caius Marius.
55 BC	Julius Caesar crosses the Rhine.
AD 9	Defeat of Roman commander Publius Quintilius Varus in the Teutoburg forest.
16	Romans withdraw behind the Rhine.
92	King Maysos of the Semnones tribe visits Rome, perhaps providing Tacitus with information to write his *Germania*.
98	Roman historian Cornelius Tacitus writes *Germania* (*'On the History and Geography of Germany'*).
168–180	Rome attacks the Germans following five years of barbarian incursions.

c. 200	Ritual deposit of wagons at Dejbjerg, Jutland.
c. 250	Appearance of runic script on items from Jutland.
280	'Saxon Shore' forts built on east coast of Britain to defend land from Saxon pirates.
c. 300	Possible emergence of the Danes. Ending of practice of human sacrificial bog offerings.
367	Britannia raided by Picts, Scots and Saxons.
370	Arrival of Huns around the Black Sea. Germanic tribes begin to push west en masse.
396	Alaric the Goth destroys Eleusis, ending 2,000 years of its Mystery cult.
406	Vandals, Alans and Sueves (Suebi) cross the Rhine.
407	Last Roman troops leave Britain with Constantine III.
410	Alaric the Goth sacks Rome.
c. 410–49	Possible Germanic settlement in Britain.
c. 425–59	Reign of Vortigern.
449	Traditional date of arrival of Hengist and Horsa at Ebbsfleet, Kent.
c. 450	Abandonment of Saxon settlement at Feddersen Wierde.
c. 490–500	Battle of Mons Badonicus: English defeated by Britons, possibly under Ambrosius Aurelianus.
c. 500–515	Possible timeframe for Danish events that occur in *Beowulf.*
c. 515–75	Possible timeframe for Swedish events that occur in *Beowulf.*
c. 520–21	Death of Chochilaicus (King Hygelac in *Beowulf*) in territory of the Hetware tribe.
c. 525	Death of King Ohthere of Sweden.
c. 535	Death of King Onela of Sweden.
c. 535–75	Reign of King Eadgils of Sweden.

540	Gregory of Tours writes his *Frankish Chronicle* and Gildas writes his *De Excidio*.
550	Gothic historian Jordanes writes *Getica* ('A History of the Gothic Peoples').
555–616	Reign of King Aethelbert of Kent.
c. 577	Proposed death of Wuffa of East Anglia; succeeded by Tyttla.
597	St Augustine arrives in Kent and converts Aethelbert.
598	Battle of Catreath (Catterick), North Yorkshire: Celts of the Gododdin tribe defeated by a joint army of Angles from Deira and Bernicia.
599	Death of Tyttla of East Anglia; succeeded by Raedwald who becomes *Bretwalda*: ruler of all Anglian kingdoms south of the Humber
c. 7th century	Composition of poem *Widsith*.
601	St Gregory's letter to Mellitus concerning the conversion of pagan shrines into churches.
604	Death of St Augustine.
613	Edwin of Northumbria flees to court of Raedwald at Rendlesham.
617–33	Reign of King Edwin of Northumbria.
624	Death of Raedwald – possible burial in ship within mound 1 at Sutton Hoo.
627	Conversion of Northumbria. Destruction of Goodmanham shrine by Coifi.
c. 650–700	Composition of *Beowulf*?
664	Synod of Whitby.
673	Birth of Venerable Bede.
681–735	Bede at Jarrow.
713–49	Reign of King Aelfwald of East Anglia
725	Bede records Anglo-Saxon calendar in his *De Temporum Ratione*.

731/2	Bede finishes his *Ecclesiastical History*.
739	Aethelheard of the West Saxons grants lands to the Bishop of Sherbourne 'from Dodda's ridge to *Grendel's pit*'.
743–51	Reign of Frankish king Childeric III, last of the Merovingians.
793	First Viking raid on Lindisfarne.
869	Martyrdom of St Edmund, last of the Wuffinga kings of East Anglia.
871–99	Reign of Alfred the Great of Wessex: Scef, Scyld and Beow are placed in the Wessex genealogical list.
c. 900	Date of the Rällinge Freyr.
941–6	Reign of Edmund I. During his reign, the monks of Abingdon Abbey perform the strange land-claiming ceremony involving the sheaf and shield.
978–1016	Reign of Aethelred the Unready.
985	Abbo sees the preserved body of 'St Edmund'.
950–1050	Composition of Anglo-Saxon magico-religious manuscripts such as the *Lacnunga*.
991	Battle of Maldon, Essex.
994	Olaf Trygvasson baptized in England. 40,000 people killed by ergot poisoning in Aquitaine.
995	Death of Earl Hakon. Olaf Trygvasson takes throne of Norway.
c. 995–1000	Gunnar Helming imitates the god Freyr in a ritual procession in Sweden.
1000	Death of Olaf Trygvasson at the sea-battle of Swold.
c. 1000	Penning of *Beowulf* manuscript.
1015–30	Reign of St Olaf Haraldson.
1066	Battle of Hastings.
1140	William of Malmesbury writes about 'Sheaf'.

1220	Snorri Sturluson composes his *Edda*.
1536–40	Dissolution of the Monasteries under Henry VIII.
1571–1631	Life of Sir Robert Bruce Cotton who received the *Beowulf* manuscript from Laurence Nowell, dean of Lichfield.
1731	Fire at Ashburnham House in which Beowulf manuscript is nearly destroyed.
1936	Tolkien's lecture on *Beowulf*, 'The Monsters and the Critics'.
1938	Basil Brown begins excavations at Sutton Hoo.
1939	Brown discovers the ship burial of Raedwald (?) in mound 1 at Sutton Hoo.

THE WUFFINGAS

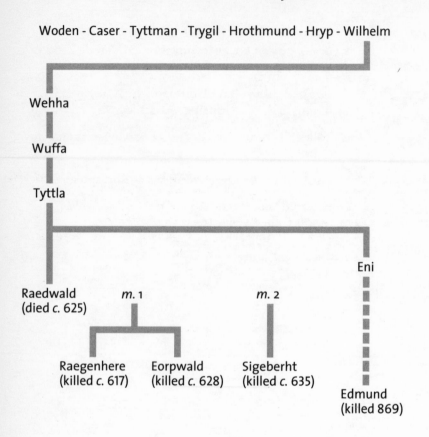

Woden - Caser - Tyttman - Trygil - Hrothmund - Hryp - Wilhelm

Wehha

Wuffa

Tyttla

Raedwald
(died *c.* 625)   *m.* 1   *m.* 2   Eni

Raegenhere   Eorpwald   Sigeberht
(killed *c.* 617)   (killed *c.* 628)   (killed *c.* 635)

Edmund
(killed 869)

THE GEATS

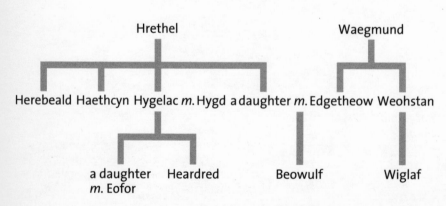

Hrethel   Waegmund

Herebeald Haethcyn Hygelac *m.* Hygd a daughter *m.* Edgetheow Weohstan

a daughter   Heardred   Beowulf   Wiglaf
m. Eofor

232

THE SWEDES (SCYLFINGS)

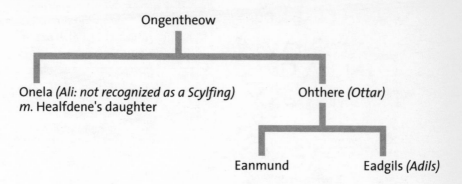

Ongentheow

Onela *(Ali: not recognized as a Scylfing)*
m. Healfdene's daughter

Ohthere *(Ottar)*

Eanmund

Eadgils *(Adils)*

THE DANES (SCYLDINGS)

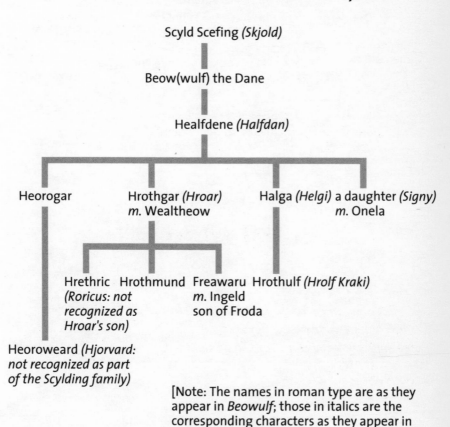

Scyld Scefing *(Skjold)*

Beow(wulf) the Dane

Healfdene *(Halfdan)*

Heorogar

Hrothgar *(Hroar)*
m. Wealtheow

Halga *(Helgi)* a daughter *(Signy)*
m. Onela

Hrethric Hrothmund
*(Roricus: not
recognized as
Hroar's son)*

Freawaru
m. Ingeld
son of Froda

Hrothulf *(Hrolf Kraki)*

Heoroweard *(Hjorvard:
not recognized as part
of the Scylding family)*

[Note: The names in roman type are as they
appear in *Beowulf*; those in italics are the
corresponding characters as they appear in
Scandinavian legend.]

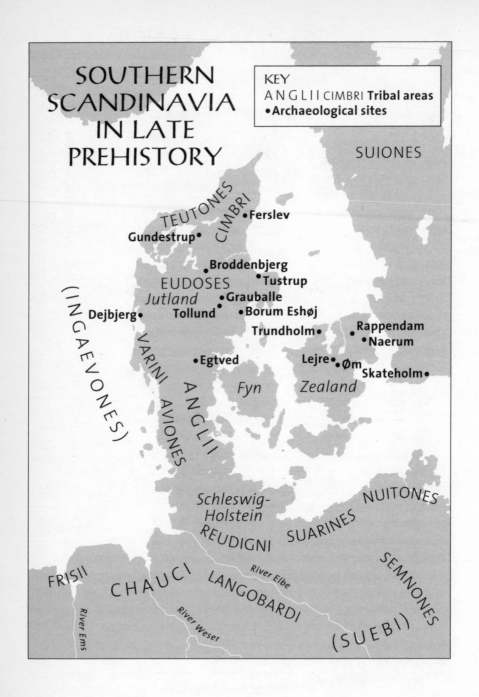

SOUTHERN
SCANDINAVIA
IN LATE
PREHISTORY

KEY
ANGLII CIMBRI **Tribal areas**
•**Archaeological sites**

SUIONES

TEUTONES

CIMBRI

•Ferslev

Gundestrup•

•Broddenbjerg

EUDOSES

•Tustrup

Jutland

•Grauballe

Dejbjerg•

Tollund

•Borum Eshøj

Trundholm•

•Rappendam

•Naerum

(INGAEVONES)

VARINI

Egtved

Lejre•

•Øm

Skateholm•

AVIONES

ANGLII

Fyn

Zealand

NUITONES

*Schleswig-
Holstein*

REUDIGNI

SUARINES

SEMNONES

FRISII

CHAUCI

LANGOBARDI

River Elbe

River Ems

River Weser

(SUEBI)

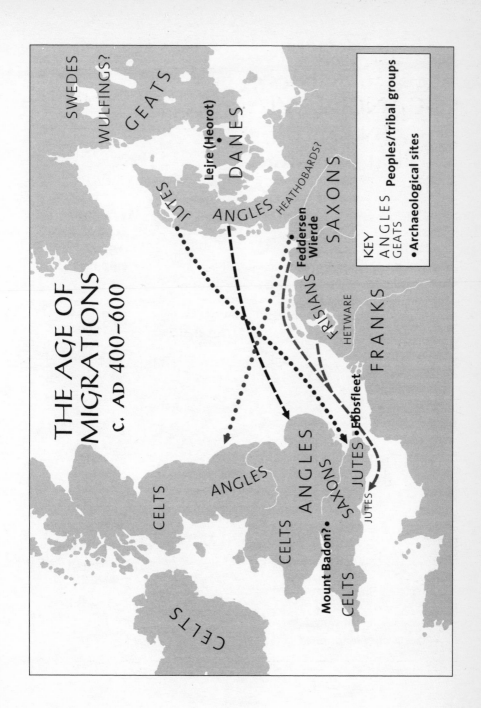

THE AGE OF MIGRATIONS
c. AD 400–600

KEY
ANGLES
GEATS Peoples/tribal groups

• Archaeological sites

SWEDES
WULFINGS?
GEATS
SWEDES
DANES
Lejre (Heorot)
JUTES
ANGLES
HEATHOBARDS?
Feddersen Wierde
SAXONS
FRISIANS
HETWARE
FRANKS
CELTS
ANGLES
ANGLES
CELTS
SAXONS
JUTES
Ebbsfleet
JUTES
Mount Badon?
CELTS
CELTS
CELTS

THE
ANGLO-SAXON
KINGDOMS
c. AD 600–700

Gododdin
BERNICIA
(NORTHUMBRIA)
• Yeavering
• Monkwearmouth
• Jarrow

Rheged

Emhain Macha•

• Catterick

Elmet DEIRA

York •

Goodmanham

River Humber

LINDSEY

Newgrange•

Dun Ailinne•

Gwynedd

MERCIA EAST
ANGLIA

Powys

Dyfed River Thames ESSEX

Abingdon• MIDDLESEX

Canterbury•

WESSEX KENT

SUSSEX

Dumnonia

KEY

MERCIA
ESSEX **Anglo-Saxon
Kingdoms**

Gwynedd **Celtic Kingdoms**

•**Place names mentioned
in the text**

EAST ANGLIA

Bury St.Edmunds

• Snape

Rendlesham•

Sutton Hoo

Maldon

ESSEX

•London

Ebbsfleet
•

INDEX

Abbo of Fleury, 205, 219, 230
Abingdon, 70, 230
Adam of Bremen, 54, 90, 211
Adils, 141, 144, 161
    See also Athils, Eadgils
Adonis, 76, 77, 84, 88, 91, 212
Aecerbot ('*field remedy*'), 43, 96, 206, 213
Aelfsiden, 109, 214
Aesir, 47, 48, 50, 51, 91, 92, 103, 109, 161,
    167, 168, 172, 173, 175, 182, 183, 189,
    192, 193, 194, 206
A__ma, 185
Aethelweard, 64, 212
Agamemnon, 134
Agni, 129, 179, 215
Alaric, 21, 81, 228
Alcibiades, 82, 227
Alcock, Leslie, 1
Alcohol, 32, 176, 178, 179, 184
Aldhelm of Sherbourne, 90, 213
Alfablot, 106, 214
Alfheim, 50, 103
Ambrosius Aurelianus, 38, 228
Ancestral cults, 5, 9, 28, 29, 30, 47, 50, 91,
    100, 105, 111, 183, 199, 201, 206, 214
    and Elves, 104
Aneurin, 184
Angelcyn, 38
Angeln, 24, 37
Angles, 24, 35, 36, 37, 193, 199, 201, 202
Anglii, 24, 25, 34, 38, 53, 56, 65, 185, 203
Anglo-Saxon Chronicle, 24, 37, 41, 93, 204, 210
Anglo-Saxon language and literature, 2, 3,
    12, 23, 24, 32, 35, 37, 38, 43, 50, 51, 64,
    69, 85, 93, 101, 103, 106, 110, 111, 124,
    182, 204, 208, 210, 219, 229
Anglo-Saxons, 1, 4, 14, 37, 38, 40, 41, 43,
    44, 51, 101
Angus, 156 *see also* Macc Oc
Anubis, 114
Apollo, 49
Arthur, King, 1, 2, 72
Asgard, 47, 50, 172, 174, 177, 188
Ashere, 10
Asva Medha, 126, 127, 215
Athils, 14, 209 *see also* Adils, Eadgils
Attis, 76, 77, 83, 84, 86, 87, 90, 100, 118,
    124, 133, 191, 213
Augustus, 21
Aviones, 24

Bachlach, 165, 166
Badb, 152
Balan, 134
Balder, 47, 75, 133, 134, 135, 157, 161, 204
Balderus, 135, 216 *see also* Balder
Balin, 134
Barley, 22, 30, 56, 64, 66, 69, 75, 79, 80,
    82, 84, 85, 88, 92, 97, 111, 116, 117, 125,
    169, 173, 177, 183, 187, 192, 195, 196,
    202, 203, 204, 207, 212
Barley wolf, 192, 195, 202, 207
Barleycorn, John (ballad), 66, 67, 68, 75,
    76, 77, 178, 179, 184
Battle Axe culture, 32
Battle of Maldon, 23, 93, 209, 230
Beaker culture, 32, 226
"Bear's son" folktale, 15, 195
Bede, The Venerable, 38, 41, 42, 43, 45, 46,
    50, 51, 193, 194, 198, 210, 211, 229, 230

Bedivere, Sir, 63
Beli, 89, 134, 157
Bendith y Mamau, 103
Benty Grange boar-helmet, 185 *see also*
    Boar symbolism
Beow, 7, 64, 66, 69, 72, 116, 124, 196, 230
Beowulf (the poem), 2, 3, 4, 5, 6, 12, 13, 15,
    19, 20, 23, 24, 27, 36, 39, 51, 52, 54, 58,
    59, 60, 63, 64, 65, 69, 74, 100, 112, 116,
    117, 131, 137, 138, 144, 145, 146, 147,
    148, 159, 164, 167, 183, 185, 190, 192,
    201, 203, 207, 229, 230
    'bear's son' folktale and, 15
    as Christianized interpretation of
        pagan cosmology, 101, 102, 110
    combining of English and Danish
        traditions in, 73
    as 'family myth' of the Wuffingas, 202
    manuscript of, 3, 13, 183, 190, 218, 231
    parallels with *Hrolf's Saga*, 143
    poet of, 14, 40, 59, 65, 85, 100, 102,
        120, 190
    quoted, 12, 19, 26, 36, 40, 52, 69, 101,
        119, 132, 136, 138, 145, 148, 171,
        185
    Sir Gawain and the Green Knight and,
        163, 166
    translation of, 2
    use of term *Ingwine* in, 98
    vegetal symbolism in, 69, 72, 74, 79
Beowulf (the hero), 2, 14, 52, 59, 119, 132,
    136, 145, 146, 161, 166, 168, 171, 181,
    182, 194, 206 *passim*, 7-12
    as 'Barley-wolf', 192
    as historical figure, 5, 14, 194, 195
    as Odin, 192
    as sun god, 14
Bera, 139, 140, 195
Bernicia, 99, 184, 213, 229 *see also* Angles;
    Deira; Northumbria
Berserkers, 186, 218
Bertilak, 162, 163, 165
Bjorn, 139, 140, 195
Black Annis, 114, 215
Black Dogs, 114, 215
Black Shuck, 114, 190, 218 *see also* Black
    Dogs; Scucca,
Blathnat, 158, 165, 176, 177
Blodeuwedd, 134
Boand, 154

Boar symbolism, 8, 10, 50, 76, 77, 88, 89,
    129, 141, 143, 151, 156, 164, 185, 190,
    199, 213, 218
    Boar's Head Feast, 89
Bodvar Bjarki, 140, 142, 186, 195, 139
Bogs, as ritual sites, 54, 55
Bolverk (Odin), 174, 192
Borremose man, 55
Borum Eshøj, 33
Bous, 135
Bran the Blessed, 134, 153, 156, 157, 158,
    159, 175, 177, 178, 216
Bricriu's Feast, 164, 165, 217
Brimwylf, 10, 183, 189, 218
Brisingamen necklace, 10, 50, 132
Broddenbjerg idol, 45, 95
Bromios, 80 *see also* Dionysos
Bronze Age, 26, 31, 33, 34, 35, 51, 125,
    129, 173, 215, 227
Brother symbolism, 19, 37, 47, 52, 76, 77,
    84, 91, 95, 102, 133, 134, 135, 136, 137,
    140, 142, 143, 145, 146, 147, 148, 149,
    152, 153, 156, 174, 201
Brown, Basil, 4, 198, 231
Brugh na Boinne, 104, 154, 155 *see also*
    Newgrange
Burial mounds, 11, 12, 14, 27, 29, 30, 31,
    34, 44, 95, 104, 105, 111, 112, 163, 198,
    199, 210
Burning, 4, 56, 116, 148, 149, 158, 160,
    188, 189, 218
Byblos, 77
Byggvir, 69, 212
Byrhtnoth, 23, 93

Cadbury, 1
Caesar, Caius Julius, 21, 22, 49, 50, 191,
    227
Cailleach, 115, 117, 215
Cain, 7, 10, 52, 101, 102, 109, 110, 136
Calendar, 41, 42, 43, 50, 59, 69, 196, 210,
    229
Camelot, 1, 162, 163, 165
Carrion symbolism, 112, 114, 115, 117,
    118, 119, 129, 136, 144, 147, 186, 189
Celts, 1, 2, 20, 22, 23, 32, 38, 40, 42, 44,
    48, 49, 51, 53, 65, 90, 103, 104, 132,
    134, 149, 150, 151, 153, 154, 156, 157,
    158, 159, 178, 184, 186, 202, 209, 211,
    214, 216, 226, 227, 229

Ceres, 128
Ceridwen, 116, 117
Cernunnos, 90, 104
Charm 'against a sudden pain', 107, 112,
    182
Chauci, 24, 25, 209
Childeric III, 123, 125, 230
Chochilaicus, 14, 209, 228
Christianity, 26, 32, 38, 40, 41, 43, 48, 76,
    94, 96, 97, 99, 101, 102, 105, 108, 109,
    111, 113, 120, 124, 125, 157, 165, 166,
    171, 190, 193, 198, 203, 204, 205, 206,
    207, 214, 218
Christmas, 106, 154, 162, 165
Cichuil, 151, 152
Cimbri, 20, 35, 186, 209, 227
Cimbric Peninsula, 25, 26, 34, 50
Coifi, 45, 113, 193, 194, 195, 218, 229
    as Odin, 193
Coligny calendar, 42, 210
Conaire Mor, 150, 151, 152, 153, 156, 157,
    158, 161, 178
Constantine III, 37, 228
Copenhagen, 3, 27, 55, 58, 208
Corded Ware culture, 226
Cotton, Sir Robert Bruce, 13, 231
Crete, 1, 26, 35, 80
Cronos, 189
CúChulainn, 132, 158, 165, 186
CúRoí Mac Daírí, 132, 158, 165, 176, 177
Cybele, 76, 84, 86, 87, 100, 118, 133, 213

Da Derga, 150, 151, 152, 156, 157, 216
Dadhyanc, 178, 217
Dagda, 104, 112, 151, 153, 154, 155, 176,
    217
Danes, 8, 9, 10, 25, 32, 35, 36, 40, 63, 66,
    73, 74, 98, 99, 114, 136, 137, 139, 141,
    143, 148, 166, 167, 197, 202, 204, 228
    see also Denmark
Deira, 184, 229 see also Angles; Bernicia,
    Northumbria
Dejbjerg, 57, 114, 228 see also Wagons,
    ritual use of,
Demeter, 75, 79, 80, 81, 117, 118, 119, 133,
    173, 188, 215
    Black Demeter of the Phigalian cave,
        117
    as Erinys, 117, 215
    see also Eleusis

Demophoön, 81, 188
Denmark,
    cult of Freyr in, 97, 99, 110, 124, 125
    Dark Age religious conflict in, 128,
        144, 145, 166, 168, 181, 183194, 195,
        203, 206
    as original homeland of the English, 2,
        20, 26
    pagan sacrifice in, 54, 55, 82, 84, 120,
        135, 136, 215
    in prehistory, 21, 24, 29, 31, 33, 35,
        226, 227
    prehistoric religion of, 45, 50, 51, 56, 57,
        58, 59, 60, 74, 79, 83, 129, 173, 210
    in the sagas, 7, 12, 52, 141, 152, 157
    in Viking age, 93
Deor, 3, 208
Diana, 133, 135
Diarmuid, 156, 159, 216
Dionysos, 79, 80, 81, 83, 84, 86, 88, 89, 90,
    118, 120, 160, 173, 191, 212
Djed column, 78, 83 see also Osiris
Domaldi, 127, 128, 150, 215
Donegal kingship rite, 126, 215
Dragons, 2, 11, 12, 14, 19, 23, 140, 179,
    199, 200
Drowning, ritual, 5, 23, 53, 56, 60, 84, 87,
    115, 133, 135, 159, 178, 179
Dun Ailinne, 158

Eadgils, 11, 14, 200, 209, 228 see also Adils;
    Athils
Ealh, 44, 45
Eanmund, 11
East Anglia, 14, 190, 197, 198, 199, 203,
    204, 218, 229, 230
Easter, 42, 43, 76
Ebbsfleet, 19, 37
Edgtheow, 8
Edmund, king of East Anglia see St
    Edmund
Edmund I, king of England, 70, 230
Edwin, king of Northumbria, 113, 193,
    229
Efnissien, 153
Egtved Girl, 34, 79, 206, 227
Elbe river, 24, 25
Elcmar, 154, 155, 157
Eleusis, 81, 82, 85, 173, 176, 177, 227, 228
    see also Demeter

Elfshot, 106
Elk-Frodi, 140
Elves, 7, 50, 101, 102, 103, 105, 106, 107,
    108, 109, 110, 111, 115, 142, 147, 151,
    213, 214, 215
    offerings to, 31
Emhain Macha, 158
Eostre, 42, 43
Ergi, 191, 218
Ergot, 56, 57, 82, 136, 188, 192
Etain, The Wooing of, 154
Ethelbert, King, 19, 198
Ethelred II, King 93
Eudoses, 24
Evans, Sir Arthur, 1, 5
Eye,
    burning, 9, 114, 180
    loss of, 155, 156, 180
    one-eyed figures, 49, 151, 152, 156, 159,
        161
    symbolism, 68, 156, 190
Farming, 22, 28, 30, 33, 35, 43, 59, 66, 70,
    74, 76, 77, 79, 82, 84, 86, 91, 92, 100,
    105, 111, 173, 174, 181, 206, 217, 226
Feddersen Wierde, 36, 228
Feis, 126
Fenrir, 47, 161
Fer Caille, 151, 152, 153, 161, 166, 216
Fergus Mac Roich, 133, 134, 157, 159
Ferslev, 31, 157, 158
Foederati, 38
Franks, 11, 14, 24, 38, 123, 124, 229, 230
Frau Holda, 114
Frau Perchta, 114
Frazer, Sir J G, 135, 136, 166, 212, 216, 218
    The Golden Bough, 135, 216
Freawaru, 148, 149
Freyja, 50, 51, 58, 84, 85, 86, 87, 88, 91,
    109, 112, 115, 116, 118, 129, 132, 134,
    148, 149, 151, 172, 177, 185, 186, 191,
    213
Freyr,
    and Angus, 156
    and Beli, 89, 157
    cult-animals of, 88, 89, 185, 193
    death of, 91, 161, 180,
    and elves, 103, 104
    as embodied in the person of the king,
        124, 125, 127, 136, 159,
    as fertility god, 84, 89, 90, 91, 120, 206

    123, 131, 148, 151, 164
    and Gerthr, 92, 125, 129, 134
    and Ing, 97, 99, 128
    name related to Freyja, 87
    'peace' of, 124, 155
    and sacrifice, 130, 132
    same god as Njorthr, 88
    as Vanir god, 50, 58, 69, 85, 172
    'wagon-tour' of, 93, 94, 95, 166
Fricco, 90 *see also* Freyr
Frig, 44, 47, 49
Frisians, 11, 24, 38
Froda, 148
Frodo, 124
Frothi, 124, 125, 148, 156, 180, 215
    Danish king, 124, 159
    Frótha-frith, 124
Funnel-necked beakers, 30
Fyolnir, 159, 217

Gabiae, 51 *see* Mothers, The; Gefion
Gaul, 21
Gawain, Sir, 162, 163, 164, 165, 166, 171,
    208, 217
Geat, 171, 192, 218
    the lost tale of Maethild and, 3
Geats, 8, 9, 10, 11, 12, 14, 15, 27, 59, 140,
    142, 143, 167, 168, 171, 185, 199, 200,
    209
Gefion, 51, 58, 59, 60, 88, 99, 100, 132,
    139, 194, 212, 216
    as Geofon, 58
    see also Freyja
Gefn (Freyja), 51
Genii Cucullati, 103
Geoffrey of Monmouth, 2
Gerald of Wales, 126, 215
Germania, 16, 20, 21, 22, 25, 26, 37, 39, 48,
    52, 53, 60, 91, 117, 125, 147, 155, 180,
    191, 209 *see also* Germans
Germania (Tacitus), 21, 24, 26, 85, 125,
    155, 185, 191, 209, 227
Germans, 3, 5, 14, 15, 20, 21, 22, 23, 24,
    26, 32, 36, 38, 39, 40, 41, 44, 48, 49, 51,
    53, 59, 65, 87, 89, 98, 102, 114, 126,
    157, 188, 201, 202, 209, 210, 211, 214,
    227, 228
Gerthr, 91, 92, 104, 125, 129, 134, 156
Getica, 26, 210, 229
Gidig, 108, 120, 189

Gildas, 37, 229
Glob, Peter Vilhelm, 30, 33, 55, 57, 129, 210, 211, 215
  The Bog People, 55
Goddess, 42, 50, 57, 103, 112, 113, 115, 118, 129, 172, 210, 211 *see also individual names*
Gododdin, 229
Goodmanham, 45, 193, 194, 229
Götar, 14 *see also* Geats
Götland, 27
Grauballe Man, 55, 56, 120, 227
Graves, Robert, 182
Green Knight, 161, 162, 163, 164, 165, 166, 177, 205, 208, 217
Gregory of Tours, 14, 44, 46, 113, 193, 209, 215, 229
Grendel,
  and 'brother-killing' motif, 101, 136,
  as 'dark' side of Vanir gods, 102, 110, 116, 120, 181, 183
  as fertility god, 181
  and the Green Knight, 163, 164
  and Irish myth, 151, 152, 153
  and midwinter death of the king, 161, 163, 166
  passim, 2, 5, 7, 13, 14, 15, 40, 123, 201
  place names mentioning, 197
  severed head of, 178, 180, 181, 182, 183
  watery abode linked to sacred lake of Nerthus, 59, 60, 85
  and dog/wolf symbolism, 189, 190, 192
  and 'Yuletide' troll, 142, 143, 144, 147
Grendel's mother,
  and 'brother-killing' motif, 136,
  as 'dark' side of Vanir gods, 109, 110, 182
  and dog/wolf symbolism, 189, 190
  as a fertility goddess, 79, 102, 116, 120
  and Irish myth, 153
  passim 2, 5, 10, 14, 166, 171, 195, 203
  and ritual regicide, 144, 147, 151, 161, 164
  and 'straddling' motif, 119, 131, 132, 136
  watery abode linked to sacred lake of Nerthus, 52, 59, 60, 85, 100
Grindylow, 115, 120
Gronw Pebr, 134

Gudrun lundasol, 125, 129
Gullinbursti, 88 *see also* Boar symbolism
Gullveig, 172, 188, 217
Gundestrup cauldron, 90, 104, 131, 151, 159, 188, 213
Gunnar Helming, 94, 95, 166, 213, 230
Gunnlod, 174, 177
Gweir, 130
Gwion Bach, 116 *see also* Taliesin
Gylfi, 58

Haddingjar, 196, 197, 219
Hades, 81, 112, 114
Hag-riding, 118, 119, 215 *see also* Hags; Nightmare
Hags, 107, 114, 115, 118, 120, 127, 132, 162, 163, 164, 195, 215
Hakon, 93, 94, 125, 129, 215, 230
Halga, 7, 145, 147, 148
Halls, 106, 112, 138, 150, 157, 216
Hallucinogens, 30, 57, 82
Haumavarga, 186, 192
Head, the severed, 10, 12, 33, 47, 56, 58, 64, 66, 67, 69, 79, 113, 117, 129, 140, 152, 153, 156, 158, 159, 162, 163, 164, 165, 171, 172, 175, 178, 179, 180, 181, 183, 185, 186, 190, 199, 204, 205, 206, 213
Healfdane, 7
Heardred, 11
Heid, 172, 188, 217 *see also* Gullveig
Hel, 47, 76, 161, 189
Helgi, 141, 147, 148 *see also* Halga
Henbane, 30
Hengist, 10, 19, 20, 38, 126, 196, 198, 219, 228 *see also* Horsa
Heorogar, 7, 146
Heorot, 7, 8, 9, 54, 123, 136, 137, 138, 139, 144, 145, 148, 149, 153, 159, 161, 166, 171, 181, 217
Heoroweard *see* Hjorvard
Herakles, 111
Hereward the Wake, 1
Herminones, 23
Hjorvard (Heoroweard), 141, 146, 147, 148, 149, 152, 153
Hlafdige, hlaford (lady, lord), 33
Hleidargard, 139, 140, 142 *see also* Lejre
Hodr, 47, 76, 133, 134, 157
Horsa, 19, 20, 37, 38, 126, 196, 219, 228 *see also* Hengist

Horse, 34, 45, 88, 92, 117, 126, 127, 193, 196, 208, 215

Horus, 77, 132, 180

Hotherus, 135 *see also* Hodr

Hott (Hjalti), 140, 141, 142

Hrethel, 8

Hrethric, 145, 146, 201

Hroar, 138, 144, 148 *see also* Hrothgar

Hrolf Kraki, 138 *passim*, 139, 140, 141, 142, 143, 144, 145, 146, 147, 149, 153, 157, 161, 163, 167, 195, 200, 201, 216

Hrothgar, 7 *passim*, 8, 9, 10, 14, 15, 35, 36, 63, 120, 123, 136, 138, 139, 144, 145, 146, 148, 161, 164, 167, 194, 201, 203 *see also* Hroar

Hrothmund, 145, 146, 201, 219

Hrothulf *see* Hrolf Kraki

Hrunting, 10, 11

Hugin, 19, 47

Hungary, 20

Huns, 36, 228

Hvit, Queen, 139, 140

Hygd, 11

Hygelac, 8, 10, 11 *passim*, 14, 20, 132, 140, 144, 148, 209, 228

Idols, 40, 210

Idunn, 134

Iliad, The 5

Inanna, 75

Indo-European languages, 86, 102, 126, 130, 156, 171, 173, 182, 184, 188, 214, 215, 216, 217, 218, 226

Ing, 36, 65, 97, 98, 99, 120, 124, 128, 132, 148, 149, 150, 154, 156, 166, 181, 196, 197, 206, 212, 213, 216 *see also* Ingui

Ingaevones, 23, 24, 26, 36, 40, 53, 59, 79, 80, 83, 97, 98, 100, 124, 128, 148, 149, 167, 181, 196

Ingcel, 152, 156, 157

Ingeld, 145, 148, 149, 152, 153, 157, 216

Ingui, 99, 213 *see also* Ing

Ingvaeones, 98 *see also* Ingaevones

Ingwine, 36, 52, 98 *see also* Ingaevones

Ireland, 93, 103, 104, 106, 113, 115, 126, 152, 155, 157, 226, 227

Iron Age, 21, 22, 35, 54, 55, 79, 86, 104, 147, 167, 195, 209, 227

Iron John, 55, 211

Ishtar, 75

Isis, 75, 77, 81, 83, 84, 86, 91, 132, 134

Istaevones, 23

Jaettestuer (giant's graves), 29

Jordanes, 26, 210, 229

Judith, 13

Jutes, 24, 35, 36, 37, 38, 126, 128

Jutland, 24, 27, 28, 30, 33, 37, 54, 57, 90, 98, 226, 228

Kalevala, 69, 70

Kent, 14, 19, 37, 38, 44, 45, 54, 126, 228, 229 *see also* Jutes

Keres, 110, 111, 112, 114, 115, 118, 127, 143, 189, 214

King of the Wood
  The Golden Bough, 135, 136, 137, 161, 166
  see also Frazer, Sir J G

Kirk, Robert, 119, 131, 215

Knossos, 5

Kvasir, 172, 174, 175, 217

Kykeon, 82

Lacnunga manuscript, 107, 230

Ladon river, 117, 118, 133

Lady Bertilak, 162, 163, 164

Landvaettir, 103

Langobards, 24, 27, 65, 209

Lejre, 54, 58, 139, 143, 157, 159, 160, 210, 217 *see also* Heorot

Letters of Alexander to Aristotle, 13, 190, 208, 209

Leucippe, 118, 215

Lif and Lifthrasir, 161

Liknites, 82 *see also* Winnowing fan, ritual use of

Lindow Man, 55, 211

Litha, 42, 69

Lleu, 134, 157

Loki, 47, 69, 76, 133

LSD, 57

Lucan, 49

Lug, 49, 51

Lugaid, 133, 134, 157

Lyssa, 186

Lytir, 96, 213

Mac Cecht, 152

Macc Oc, 154, 155, 156, 157, 216 *see also* Angus

Maethhild and Geat, 3
Mannus, 23, 206
Marius, Caius, 21, 227
Mars, 43, 49
Matholwch, 153
Mead of inspiration, 159, 174, 176, 179,
    180, 184, 191, 205
Medb of Connacht, 133
Medusa, 182
Megalithic age, 5, 28, 31, 32, 39, 54, 80, 91,
    105, 106, 154, 157, 194, 195, 226
Mellitus, Abbot, 46, 194, 229
Mercia, 14, 197, 204
Mercury, 43, 49, 192, 211
Merovingians, 123, 199
Mesolithic age, 27, 28, 114, 226
Middle Earth, 9, 47, 101
Middle (Near) East, 28, 76, 79, 80, 83, 84,
    85, 86, 88, 91
Midir, 154, 155
Midsummer, 31, 106
Midwinter, 31, 42, 56, 60, 89, 104, 129,
    135, 136, 137, 143, 147, 150, 154, 156,
    157, 158, 160, 161, 162, 163, 165, 166,
    216, 217
Mimir, 156, 172, 178, 180
Minerva, 49
Minotaur, 1, 5
Modranicht, 42, 43, 51, 59, 206
Moon, 42, 49, 77
Morgan le Fay, 112, 163, 164, 166, 171
Mórríghan, 104, 112, 113, 118, 151, 152,
    161, 163
Mothers, the (Matronae), 42, 43, 50, 58,
    59, 103, 206
Mound People, 33, 34, 36, 55, 79
Muein, 177
Munin, 47
Mycenae, 26, 35
Mysteries, 53, 81, 133 see also Eleusis

Nanna, 75, 135
Near East see Middle (Near) East
Neolithic age, 5, 28, 30, 31, 51, 70, 74, 79,
    80, 91, 103, 104, 105, 128, 154, 157,
    158, 182, 210, 226
Nerthus, 53, 54, 57, 58, 59, 74, 79, 80, 82,
    83, 84, 85, 86, 95, 97, 99, 103, 104, 114,
    115, 117, 119, 133, 139, 155, 159, 160,
    181, 182, 183, 195, 213

as a form of Gefion, 58
as a male divinity, 86, 87
related to Njorthr, 58, 86
Newgrange, 104, 154, 155, 156, 158, 216,
    226
Niflheim, 47
Nightmare, 119, 120, 131, 181
Nile river, 77, 84, 132
Njal's Saga, 113
Njorthr, 50, 58, 85, 86, 87, 88, 91, 118,
    120, 129, 213 see also Nerthus
Noatun, 86
Norman Conquest, 2
Norns, 113, 142, 144, 215
Northumbria, 14, 41, 45, 113, 193, 194,
    198, 201, 218, 229 see also Angles;
    Bernicia; Deira
Nowell, Laurence, 13, 231
Nuada, 127, 166, 215
Nuitones, 24

Oder river, 33
Odin,
    attributes of, 19, 46, 47, 48, 112, 186,
        189
    as 'Beowulf'/Barley-wolf, 194, 202
    as a Celtic god in origin, 49
    as 'Coifi', 193
    death of, 117, 161, 181
    establishment of cult, 166, 195, 203
    and 'ergi', 191
    as father of Balder, 75
    as father of Skjold, 58, 66, 73, 183, 194
    and Mimir's head, 156, 178, 180,   as
        one-eyed, 49, 180, 218
    and the theft of the 'mead of
        inspiration', 174, 175, 176, 177, 191,
        192
    and the war with the Vanir, 172, 182
Odysseus, 112
Offa, king of Mercia, 197
Olaf Haraldson (St Olaf), 105
Olaf Tryggvason, 93, 94, 95, 125, 129, 213,
    214, 215, 230
Olaf, Elf of Geirstad, 105
Old English (people) , 2, 6, 19, 41, 42, 43,
    50, 102, 103, 148 see also Angles; Anglii;
    Anglo-Saxons
Old English (language) see Anglo-Saxon
    language and literature

Old English Rune Poem, 98, 213
Olympians, 80, 91, 111, 173
Øm passage grave, 31, 104, 157, 210, 226
Onela, 11, 144, 200, 228
Oral tradition, 2, 13, 65, 160
Orkney, 30
Orpheus, 178, 218
Oseberg ship burial, 58
Osiris, 75, 77, 79, 81, 83, 84, 86, 88, 89, 91, 132, 134, 180, 212

Passage graves, 30, 104 *see also* Øm passage grave
Passion of St Christopher, 13, 190
Paulinus, Bishop, 113
Peg O'Nell, 115
Peg Powler, 115
Pekko, 69, 212
Perseus, 182
Pietroasa neck-ring, 132
Poland, 20, 27
Porridge (ritual meal), 30, 31, 56, 96, 104, 106, 111, 136, 176, 187, 217
Poseidon, 117, 118, 133
Pryderi, 118, 130
Prydwen, 72
Ptolemy of Alexandria, 25

Quffah, 72, 212

Raedwald, 198, 199, 202, 203, 219, 229, 231 *see also* Sutton Hoo
Ragnarok, 47, 89, 117, 157, 160, 177, 189, 217
Rahu, 175, 178, 182
Rällinge, image of Freyr from, 90, 104, 131, 230
Rappendam, 58
Ravens, 19, 47, 49, 112, 114
Reudigni, 24
Rex Nemorensis, 135, 166
Rheda, 43, 211
Rhiannon, 118, 130
Rhine river, 20, 21, 24, 33, 51, 227, 228
Rhineland, 49
Riding symbolism, 10, 119, 131, 132
Ritual deposition, 35, 227
Robin Hood, 1
Roggenwolf, 188, 192, 218
Romans, 20, 21, 22, 36, 37, 38, 43, 48, 49, 51, 53, 87, 98, 100, 209, 210, 211, 227, 228
Rome, 20, 22, 26, 35, 48, 76, 83, 84, 85, 106, 209, 227, 228
Runes, 98, 228

Sabazios, 80 *see also* Dionysos
Samhain, 150, 152, 155, 157, 216
Sämpsä Pellervoinen, 69
Sarama, 176
Saxo Grammaticus, 90, 135, 148, 149, 153, 157, 212, 215, 216
Saxons, 24, 25, 35, 36, 38, 51, 83, 101, 197, 209, 228, 229, 230
Scandinavia, 26, 65, 70, 72, 74, 79, 84, 106, 125, 129, 139, 202, 212, 215, 226
Scandza, 24, 26, 28, 32, 34, 65, 84, 91, 99, 210
Scef, 64, 65, 66, 69, 70, 72, 73, 74, 85, 196, 212, 230
Schleswig-Holstein, 24, 26
Schliemann, Heinrich, 1
Scucca, 190, 218
Scyld Scefing, 7 *passim*, 16, 19, 36, 58, 60, 63, 64, 65, 69, 70, 72, 73, 79, 199, 212, 230
Scyldings, 7, 8, 13, 15, 20, 54, 63, 64, 73, 128, 137, 143, 144, 146, 148, 149, 152, 167, 183, 201, 202
Scylfings, 14, 200
Seithr, 109, 118, 130, 144, 153, 191, 218
Semnones, 45, 108, 209, 227
Seth, 77, 84, 134
Sheaf, 64, 65, 69, 70, 73, 74, 75, 77, 79, 82, 83, 86, 89, 99, 116, 120, 128, 166, 183, 194, 196, 206, 212, 230 *see also* Scef
Shield symbolism, 70, 72, 82, 116, 194, 199, 230
Sídhe, 111 *see also* Tuatha De Danaan
Sigurd, 95, 179, 186
Sin (moon god), 72, 212
Sinfjotli, 186, 187
Sir Gawain and the Green Knight, 164, 208, 217
Skara Brae, 30, 80
Skateholm, 27, 114, 226
Skathi, 118, 129, 215
Skírnir, 92, 125, 134
Skjold, 58, 65, 73, 99, 124, 194, 212 *see also* Scyld
Skjoldungs, 58, 137, 146, 201 *see also* Scyldings

Skuld, 113, 141, 142, 144, 146, 147, 148, 149, 151, 152, 153, 157, 161, 163, 167, 175
Sleipnir, 47
Snorri Sturluson, 42, 48, 51, 58, 72, 85, 86, 88, 89, 91, 92, 124, 127, 158, 172, 186, 191, 192, 211, 213, 215, 217, 218, 231
    Heimskringla, 94
    Prose Edda, 48, 58, 72, 88, 91, 92, 103, 191, 213, 216, 217, 231
    Skáldskaparmál, 85
    Ynglingatal, 95, 127, 129, 158, 159, 172, 217
Soma, 175, 176, 178, 179, 180, 181, 182, 184, 186, 192, 217, 218
Sovereignty, 117, 126, 127, 134, 147, 148, 161, 166, 167, 177, 196
St Augustine, 19, 41, 46, 198, 229
St Christopher, 190
    Passion of St Christopher, 13, 190
St Edmund, 204, 205, 206, 219, 230
St Gregory, 14, 44, 46, 113, 193, 209, 215, 229
St Olaf (Olaf Haraldson), 105, 214
Stonehenge, 30, 158
Strabo, 160, 217
Strangulation, 54, 55, 127, 130, 131, 133, 136, 188, 189 *see also* Neck-ring
Suarines, 24
Sucellos, 49
Suebi, 24, 56, 83, 228
Sun, 14, 30, 34, 35, 42, 43, 50, 71, 77, 88, 96, 99, 104, 117, 125, 154, 156, 157, 158, 161, 166, 196, 199, 209, 227
Surt, 157, 161, 189
Sutton Hoo, 4, 117, 198, 199, 200, 202, 208, 219, 229, 231 *see also* Raedwald
Suttung, 174, 175, 177
Svein Forkbeard, 93
Sweden, 14, 20, 24, 26, 27, 34, 36, 54, 58, 90, 94, 95, 97, 114, 141, 144, 167, 194, 199, 200, 219, 226, 228, 230
Swedes, 11, 14, 58, 94, 95, 97, 119, 127, 128, 129, 142, 144, 200, 202, 203, 209, 228
Syr (Freyja), 116, 129
Tacitus, Cornelius, 21, 22, 23, 24, 25, 26, 27, 35, 40, 44, 45, 48, 49, 51, 53, 54, 56, 57, 59, 83, 84, 85, 86, 87, 118, 128, 133, 167, 185, 191, 209, 213, 214, 227

Tacitus, Cornelius (cont.)
    Germania, 21, 24, 26, 85, 125, 155, 185, 191, 209, 227
Taliesin, 72, 116, 117, 212
    Spoils of the Abyss, 72, 130, 212
Tammuz, 75, 91, 212
Taranis, 49 *see* Sucellos; Thunor
Tegid Voel, 116
Tennyson, Alfred, 63, 212
Teutoburg forest massacre, 21
Teutones, 20, 35, 186, 209, 227
Thietmar of Merseburg, 54, 58, 139, 211
Thokk, 47
Thor, 47, 48, 60, 87, 161
Thorir Hound's Foot, 140
Thunor, 43, 44, 47, 49
Titans, 79, 111, 189, 214
Tiw, 43, 44, 47, 49
Tolkien, J R R., 2, 4, 73, 101, 120, 124, 147, 186, 208, 211, 212, 217, 231
    'Beowulf: The Monsters and the Critics', 4
    The Hobbit, 2
    The Lord of the Rings, 2, 4
Tollund Man, 54, 55, 56, 90, 120, 227
Tragedy, origins of, 80, 90
Trance states, 30, 45, 108, 109, 142
Trolls, 2
    'Yuletide troll', 142
Troy, 1
Trundholm sun chariot, 34, 35, 227
Tuatha De Danaan, 103, 104, 127, 155, 176, 215
Tuisto, 23
Tungri, 21
Tustrup, 30, 106, 210, 226
Tyr, 47, 189
Tyttla, 199, 200, 229

Uffington White Horse, 126, 215
Ulfhednar, 186, 189, 218
Ull, 72
Uppsala, 14, 54, 90, 159, 191, 200
Ursula, 7
Valhalla, 112, 161, 177
Valkyrie, 112, 113, 116, 118, 146, 161, 189, 190, 214
Vanir, 50, 51, 53, 58, 59, 60, 69, 79, 84, 85, 91, 100, 102, 103, 151, 152, 160, 163, 167, 168, 185, 186, 188, 189, 191, 192, 193, 194, 196, 203, 206, 211, 214

Vanir (cont.)
  as Elves, 102, 103,105, 106, 107, 108, 109
  negative side of, 110, 112, 115, 118, 119, 120; 136, 144,
  war with the Aesir, 172, 173, 175, 181, 182, 183,
Vargr, 186, 191, 218
Varini, 24
Varus, Publius Quintilius, 21, 209, 227
Vedbaek, 27, 226
Vegetal symbolism, 43, 69, 75, 88, 91
Vikings, 5, 14, 23, 54, 59, 84, 86, 92, 93, 139, 145, 159, 197, 198, 204, 211, 217, 230
Volva, 109, 118, 124, 127, 130, 160
Vortigern, 37, 38, 228
Votadini, 184 *see also* Gododdin

Wagons, ritual use of, 53, 57, 83, 87, 88, 124, 213
Waldhere, 3, 208
Wanderer, 3
Wantsum Channel, 19, 209
Wealtheow, 8 *passim*, 132, 145, 201
Wehha, 199, 200, 201
Weland, 10, 211
Wergild, 23
Weser, 25, 36
Weser river, 25, 36
Wessex, 13, 14, 37, 64, 65, 73, 90, 197, 200, 230 *see also* Saxons
Widsith, 3, 65, 145, 148, 197, 201, 202, 208, 212, 229

Wiglaf, 11, 12, 23, 200
William of Malmesbury, 64, 212, 230
Windeby Girl, 56
Winnowing fan, ritual use of, 81, 82, 178
Woden, 32, 43, 44, 46, 49, 51, 64, 192, 193, 196, 202, 203 *see also* Odin
Woexstan, 11
Wolves, 5, 10, 47, 66, 112, 114, 117, 143, 152, 159, 161, 169, 185, 186, 187, 188, 189, 190, 192, 195, 196, 200, 202, 204, 205, 206, 207, 218, 219
Wonders of the East, 13, 190
Woodhenge, 158, 217
Wuffa, 199, 200, 202, 229
Wuffingas, 198, 199, 200, 201, 202, 203, 204, 205, 206, 219, 230 *see also* Raedwald
Wulfings, 200, 201, 202
Wyrd, 113

Yeats, W B, 156
Yeavering, 45, 46, 211
Yggdrasil, 47, 161, 177, 192
Ylfig, 108, 120, 189
Ynglings, 97, 119, 127, 128, 129, 167
Yrsa, Queen, 141, 142
Yule, 42, 89, 140, 142, 143, 146, 161, 163, 166, 179

Zagreus, 80 *see also* Dionysos
Zealand, 27, 34, 54, 58, 104, 139, 226
Zeus, 79, 80, 111, 189, 214